Burning Japan

BURNING Japan

Air Force Bombing Strategy Change in the Pacific

DANIEL T. SCHWABE

Potomac Books

An imprint of the University of Nebraska Press

All photographs included in this volume are used courtesy of
the National Museum of the U.S. Air Force.

Library of Congress Cataloging-in-Publication Data
Schwabe, Daniel T., 1980–
Burning Japan: Air Force bombing strategy change in the
Pacific / Daniel T. Schwabe.
pages   cm
Includes bibliographical references and index.
ISBN 978-1-61234-639-7 (cloth: alk. paper)
ISBN 978-1-61234-640-3 (pdf)
1. World War, 1939–1945—Aerial operations, American.
2. World War, 1939–1945—Campaigns—Japan. 3. Incendiary
bombs—History—20th century. 4. Bombing, Aerial—Japan.
I. Title.
D790.S343 2014
940.54′49730952—dc23
2014032683

Set in Minion Pro by Lindsey Auten.

To my father, Tom Schwabe.
You said remember the good times,
and I can't think of any others.

The only point in flying a bomber in this war, and crewing it up and bombing it up and gassing it up and arming it, and spending all the money and all the effort—and all the lives—Only point in proceeding on such an operation was to drop bombs where they would do the most harm to the enemy.

—CURTIS LEMAY, in Kantor and LeMay, *Mission with LeMay*

CONTENTS

ILLUSTRATIONS

PREFACE

THE END OF WORLD WAR II in the Pacific is known for its bloody island battles and the use of two atomic bombs, bombs that marked the end of one era and the dawn of a more modern and colder one. Part of the sweeping away of the old ways in 1945 was the scrapping of the fleets of bombers that tore apart the Axis powers. Fleets of B-17s, B-24s, B-26s, and even B-29s were crushed, smelted, or sold by the airfield as scrap metal. The conventional strategic-bombing doctrine that dominated the 1930s and 1940s was pushed aside and replaced by a nuclear strategy of massive destruction.

The first plane to carry the mantle in this new era of massive destruction was the one that started it all over Hiroshima and Nagasaki, the B-29 Superfortress. Lost in this new paradigm of atomic warfare, however, was the larger role the B-29 played in the last year of the war in the Pacific, one of conventional bombing. The B-29s of the 20th Air Force (AF), like those of its fellow numbered air forces in Europe, carried out a strategic-bombing campaign against the industrial power of Japan. True, the strategic bombers in the Pacific never achieved close to the number of planes the European forces did, or operated in theater for nearly as long as the European units, but they did contribute mightily to the defeat of Japan and the evolution of strategic airpower. The men of the 20th AF bombed specific targets with iron bombs and burned to the ground almost all the major cities of Japan.

This book tackles the question of how the U.S. Air Force, dedicated to precision bombing, moved to area attacks as an avowed tactic. Others have written about what the Pacific air campaign, 20th

AF, and B-29s did (though never close to the amount written about what the B-17s and B-24s did in Europe), but the decision-making process for such a monumental tactical shift has never been fully investigated. I started what became this book while trying to answer this question in graduate school. The initial research took me to the United States Strategic Bombing Survey (USSBS), Pacific, and quickly expanded through the records of the United States Air Force and associated organizations that helped develop policy during World War II. The answers I found developed a picture of a world at war, both overseas and at home, and a race to win the war for the sake of humanity, but also to earn the recognition of having contributed to this most noble victory—all this while managing an endeavor that stretched over millions of square miles and cost billions of dollars.

While the ultimate outcome was successful—Japan was defeated, and the Air Force received the recognition it deserved—the contribution and controversy of the conventional bombing campaign against Japan was pushed aside, forgotten like the many war-weary planes consigned to the scrap pile. The Air Force and strategic-bombing doctrine moved on, never telling the story of how the precision-bombing doctrine, so much a part of the Air Force identity entering the war, found its most significant battle against the flammable cities of Japan, and how the evolution of that doctrine contributed to the end of the war in the Pacific as much as if not more than two atomic bombs. Now that story is told.

ACKNOWLEDGMENTS

THIS WORK STARTED as an idea for a graduate thesis provided by my thesis adviser, Dr. Gordon Bakken. When I told him I wanted to write about bombers, he suggested a topic waiting for a historian to uncover its secrets: why we switched to incendiary bombing against Japan during World War II. To him I am continuously grateful for the idea, the mentorship, and the guidance. Cheers to you! And cheers to Dr. Robert McLain and Dr. Stephen Neufeld, who sat on my thesis committee and gave important feedback that helped make a thesis a book.

Thank you to John Ebbe at Servite High School. When I was a long shot for advanced-placement U.S. history you took a chance on me and ignited my love of history—your class fired my mind like no other. I went down a path of history study because of your inspiration, and what a cool path it has been.

I give my thanks to Mike Runion, who has been my friend for the majority of my life, and to Steve Colletti, Mike Nangano, John Martin, Carl Roza-Pereria, and Mark Bradshaw at war gaming each week. Your friendship, feedback, encyclopedic knowledge, and vast libraries made writing this book bearable. Steve deserves special mention as both a friend and colleague. The long discussions and debates on all manner of things add immeasurably to my efforts as a historian and as a person. Your proofreading abilities, too, were a boon as you discovered a spelling error that would have made this book more of a legal history than a military one.

Credit and thanks for bringing my manuscript to Potomac Books go to Elizabeth Demers, and for guiding me through the editing process to Bridget Barry, Sabrina Ehmke Sergeant, Sabrina Stellrecht, and Jonathan Lawrence. Having navigators in the publishing world is a must, and you are four of the best.

Credit and thanks also go to the people who helped pull the sources together: the interlibrary loan team at Cal State Fullerton, for finding all the volumes published by the USSBS; the folks at the Air Force Historical Research Center, for their patience with my questions and their diligence pulling all the records I needed; and last but not least, Brett Stolle and the archives staff at the U.S. Air Force Museum, for their help and hospitality. There would not be pictures in this book without Brett. And if the reader has never been to Dayton, Ohio, to visit the museum, go there now; it is that cool.

This story would not be possible without the brave men of the 20th Air Force. Writing this as I fly back to Los Angeles, my palms are sweating from the rumble of turbulence and landscape creeping by so small below, I cannot imagine doing it day after day, over the target, a thousand miles from base, braving flak and fighters, especially when it all seemed like it was not working. Your finest hour deserves more credit and serves as an example of the courage, fortitude, and devotion to freedom that America can be.

The final thanks is usually saved for the most important people, and this is no exception. God blessed me with a wonderful and supportive family, so to my sister and mother, who put up with my quirks and historical obsessions I thank you from the bottom of my heart. And to my father, who did not live to see this and to whom this book is dedicated, thank you for being the most important role model in my life.

Introduction

UPON FIRST GLANCE, the list of sixty-seven Japanese cities and the percentage destroyed by fire appears impressive but not shocking. Only when paired with U.S. cities of comparable population does the magnitude of the American incendiary bombing become apparent: Savannah, Georgia (Chiba), 41.0 percent destroyed; Baltimore, Maryland (Kobe), 55.7 percent; Long Beach, California (Okayama), 68.9 percent destroyed; Chattanooga, Tennessee (Toyama), gone completely, 98.6 percent destroyed; Tokyo, a city comparable to New York City, 50.8 percent incinerated, the equivalent of all Manhattan and the Bronx burned to the ground.[1] Starting on the night of March 9–10, 1945, the United States' 20th Air Force (AF) commenced a campaign of firebombing raids against Japanese cities that saw nearly every major Japanese metropolis touched by fire, destroying all industries, homes, and lives in its path. Contrary to Air Force doctrine, the 20th AF switched its primary tactics from high-altitude precision bombing to low-altitude area bombing with incendiaries. This book seeks to show how and why this change came about. In a war that enveloped the peoples of the entire world, replete with rapidly changing technology, and with an eye toward the postwar service structure, what prompted the dramatic change in operational practice by the 20th AF? The answer lies in practical considerations by both the commander in the field, Gen. Curtis LeMay, and the higher Joint Chiefs of Staff in Washington. The switch in tactics occurred because incendiary raids offered the quickest and most efficient way to destroy the war-fighting ability of the Japanese.

Yet the decision came about slowly and deliberately, gaining momentum as alternate tactics failed to meet the needs of the Air Force and the nation as a whole. At a time when airpower's dominance of the battlefield grew from theory to fact, the importance of successful operations that fulfilled the promises of Air Force planners placed inordinate pressures on the units in the field. Fighting on two fronts, the Air Force led the way into battle in Europe, flying over the Continent years before D-Day, pushing forward in the face of adversity the idea that dropping bombs from high altitude, with precision, on specific targets could shorten or even end the war early. Since the end of World War I the members of the Army's aviation arm had looked for a way to distinguish and exhibit the ability of airpower on the battlefield. Following the teachings of Giulio Douhet and Billy Mitchell, these airmen turned to strategic bombardment as their rallying point. Strategic bombardment fulfilled both needs of the airmen: it offered the chance to seriously constrain the enemy's war-making ability, and it was a job only the airmen could do. The specialized mission of strategic bombardment entailed the airplanes flying deep behind enemy lines to destroy the sources of the enemy's war-making ability, places the Army or Navy never neared. For twenty years, the airmen, under their various designations, lobbied to all who listened about the prospects and indispensability of strategic bombardment.[2] World War II finally provided them the opportunity to turn theory to practice.

As the first application of this theory to battle conditions, the 8th and 15th AFs in Europe faced enormous negative pressures both from their allies and the Germans. The British, who dispensed with precision bombing immediately after suffering loss in its pursuit, pushed for the U.S. aircraft to join them at night in area attacks. The Americans demurred, eventually winning the right to carry out their attacks in the daylight while the British kept up the round-the-clock bombing in the dark. Heavy German flak and unrelenting German fighters tore the U.S. formations apart and made the cost for poor bombing accuracy nearly too high to sustain. Despite the losses, commanders and tacticians, like Maj. Gen. Haywood Hansell, sought to measure the effectiveness of the bomber offensive "against the impact upon the German national war machine, not simply in terms of bomber losses."[3] But lack of quantifiable results also dampened the enthusiasm behind the campaign. Despite missions against the most crucial of German targets, deemed successful and accurate, if costly, the Nazis continued on with increased vigor.

Undeterred, the bombers pressed on for two years before the land armies joined the fray. Criticism of the accuracy and effects of the air campaign clouded its achievements, notably the smashing of the Luftwaffe, tying up of resources for local defense, and the destruction and forced dispersal of key industries. The criticism did not all originate externally, as even the proponents of the theory acknowledged its shortcomings. Whereas (major) miscalculations occurred, principally on the invincibility of the bomber and accuracy of bombsights, a large portion of the deficiencies came from above, in the Allied command structure. As part of the larger Allied Expeditionary Force, the bombers ultimately fell under the control of the theater commander, an Army man. In other words, he was not an airman and did not understand the power of the airplane. This caused interruptions to the strategic-bombing campaign that robbed it of its strength and follow-through.

Early in 1944, for instance, the 8th AF, which the airmen argued had finally reached its full fighting size, strength, proficiency, and number of needed fighter escorts, was diverted from strategic objectives to strike transportation targets in France as part of D-Day preparations. Rather than focusing its effort on the individual industrial targets that fed the German war machine, Allied high command diverted the bombers against French transportation hubs, targets both of tactical importance and with high likelihood of civilian casualties. While successful in stalling reinforcements trying to stop the invasion, the Air Force leaders decried the diversion by the theater commander from strategic to tactical targets. The same pressure from high up hit again in 1945 when the 8th AF felt pressure from U.S. leaders to execute Operation Clarion against an array of small targets and pressure from the British to participate in Operation Thunderclap, a switch to U.S. bombers participating in area attacks. Both operations disguised widespread and indiscriminate destruction under the guise of necessity—a necessity to punish the German people, not to eliminate their ability to fight. Lt. Gen. Jimmy Doolittle, then commanding the 8th AF and a convert to the principles of precision bombing, believed that the shift to urban areas would "violate the basic American principle of precision bombing of targets of strictly military significance for which our tactics were developed and our crews trained and indoctrinated."[4] Needless to say, this disturbed the Air Force commanders gravely and threatened to entirely undermine their efforts of the last two years in Europe and fifteen years on the home front.

After the invasion of Europe, two ultimate goals of strategic bombing lay unfulfilled on the side of the road to Berlin. First, and most importantly, the war continued despite the bombing which, in theory, should have brought the Germans to their knees. Second, with troops crawling all over the Continent, the potential for influencing the front-line fighting by destroying production of war goods dissipated. Plants that produced tanks and planes lay too deep in the supply line to allow for a bomb in one to make a difference in a war supposed to end by Christmas. Obviously, the first try at strategic bombing left much to be desired but did not necessarily reveal limits to airpower. If done properly, Air Force leaders believed, strategic airpower could still play a decisive role in the war.

Air Force planners resigned themselves to this situation and looked for another opportunity to make their mark. The Pacific theater was the only logical option. Besides being the only other theater of war, the war against Japan sat as a blank canvas for strategic bombardment. The vast distances of the Pacific Ocean, and Japanese domination of half of it, led to two years of grinding island battles, which by 1944 still placed no bases within bomber range of Japan in U.S. hands. Gen. Henry "Hap" Arnold, commander of the Army Air Force (AAF), knew this would change soon with the capture of base areas in China and the Mariana Islands in the Central Pacific and with the arrival in service of the United States' biggest bomber, the Boeing B-29 Superfortress.

Ever conscious of the Air Force's need to create a separate identity from the Army, and looking at the confused command structure of the Pacific, the restrictions experienced in Europe, and the coming struggle for funding after the war, Arnold saw the B-29 operations as an opportunity for the air arm to operate independently of non-air commanders and thereby prove its worth to a postwar world. To that end, Arnold created the 20th AF, placed it under his personal command, and gained the Joint Chiefs' concurrence with the idea that, outside special circumstances, the 20th AF operated under its own direction. No longer would bombers be diverted to tactical or campaign-specific targets as had happened in Europe. From the start in the Pacific, the strategic-bombing campaign would run uninterrupted, exhibiting the precision and destructive ability of the Air Force. Likewise, a failure in this demonstration promised to relegate airpower to a permanent supporting role, devoid of its own funding or doctrinal innovations. Arnold put his reputation on the line to achieve the ultimate victory, so the commanders he chose needed strong will and the tactics required flawless execution. For him, failure was not an option and would not be accepted.

In many ways, the postwar world looms larger in the story than some of the battles themselves. A wealth of scholarship in the last twenty years has made it evident that once the war appeared within the grasp of victory the Allied leaders recognized that winning the peace mattered as much as winning the war itself. On the international level this evolved into jockeying for zones of occupation and spheres of influence as the Cold War commenced, while on the home front the questions of reduced budgets and deserved recognition echoed in the halls of the Pentagon. For the Air Force this meant the chance to gain its independence from the Army and control of its own funding and missions. Twenty years of rhetoric before the war achieved nothing for the airmen in an Army that had maintained a cavalry arm until shortly before entering World War II. Obviously, the climate for change did not exist before hostilities, but now that the importance of a strong military and the dominance of technology in such matters, especially all forms of airpower, showed itself across the globe, the fruit of independence hung ripe for the picking. Independence meant much more than pride: it came with money, a piece of the defense budget. As long as the Air Force remained part of the Army it received only the small piece of the Army's overall budget that a parsimonious land force decided to relinquish. As its own arm, the Air Force stood to gain a full share of military expenditures, money that would fund advancements in airplanes and spread the gospel of airpower.

By 1944 this plan appeared well on its way to success. The airplane, scoffed at by land-bound soldiers and battleship-bound sailors alike, revealed itself as the most effective weapon on the battlefield. Bombers reached behind enemy lines as they said they would, fighters protected rear areas and devastated ground troops, patrol planes helped reopen the Atlantic to shipping, and everyone found out the hard way the capabilities of a dive-bomber. The only hang-up came from the fact that most of the achievements had nothing to do with the promise of airpower that the airmen had touted in the interwar period. The Air Force built its future on a foundation of strategic bombardment, an idea that sent planes deep into enemy territory to strike key targets to end a war quickly. Despite the press releases and newsreels, the strategic-bombing campaign did none of these things well. There were too few planes to deal a decisive blow to targets, the crews were inexperienced in the tactics needed to place bombs on target, the weather over Europe limited visual precision bombing, and the German defenses took an awful toll on the attacking bombers. Regardless of the overwhelming success of airpower in every other facet of the war, failure, or perceived failure, at the one task specifically outlined for the airplane threatened to give political opponents the ammunition needed to point to the failure of the institution of an air force and to leave the airplane forever under the command of the ground-bound forces. Arnold and the other Air Force leaders rightly understood that the postwar world offered a fresh start for the United States. Gone were the tribulations of the Depression for the common man, and gone too were the subsistence budgets and old-world attitudes of the military. Freedom from the Army's control meant acting now or never.

These internal power struggles played an important but still ancillary role to the real point of air operations in World War II: victory. The intensity of battle and the number of casualties ratcheted up as the war progressed, and the Pacific in particular saw the intensity of the fighting grow as the noose around the homelands tightened. As the war progressed to an endgame, whether that entailed strangulation of the home islands by blockade or the more probable grinding battle of invasion of Japan proper, action needed to come soon to lay the foundation for those operations.

The delay in the ability to commence a strategic-bombing campaign against Japan, then, came as both a blessing and a curse. The blessing was that the U.S. airmen had time to digest and act upon lessons learned in Europe: formation alterations, aiming refinements, the understanding of the need for fighter escorts, and most important of all, the need for a concentrated strategic effort without tactical distractions. The curse was time. By D-Day in Europe bombers had hit German targets for nearly two years, one of those years at full strength. In the Pacific the first B-29 missions were not expected to start until mid-1944, and the real bases for the B-29s, in the Marianas, would not come into U.S. hands until the same time. Between securing the islands and constructing airfields, operations from the Marianas could not begin until the end of 1944. This meant that, assuming the invasion of Japan occurred in late 1945 or early 1946, the 20th AF had only a year to cripple Japanese industry and pave the route to victory, if not end the war entirely. European experience showed that the two years of attacking did not succeed in this goal, so prospects for Japan seemed grim. True, Japanese industry lagged behind that of Germany in both size and sophistication, but knowledge of it and its weaknesses did not yet exist in any quantity and quality.

This made the bombing of Japan a crucial crossroads for the Air Force, both for its contribution to victory and its future independence. Success counted on many levels and to many people. The measure of failure came in postwar politics, and most importantly in lives. Airpower promised to end wars and make the world a safer place. Europe was a dress rehearsal; the Pacific was where the theory either became reality or bled to death on the shores of the Kanto Plain. Arnold, whether he wanted to or not, placed all his remaining eggs in the basket of the B-29, the longest-range and most technologically advanced bomber of the time.

So how then does a story of purely precision bombardment result in the burning of nearly every major city in Japan? The answer evolved over time. Starting with an idea, one of a myriad of ways to strike back at Japan after Pearl Harbor, the concept of burning Japan's cities survived the evolving fortunes of war. The cities of Japan presented targets unlike those of any Western city. Because these cities were composed almost entirely of wooden structures in densities far exceeding those of Europe or the United States, a fire in a Japanese metropolitan area threatened to burn the entire city down. A vulnerability like this defied a blind eye by either attacker or defender. The Japanese, who had experienced the dangers of fire in these cities many times, most recently after the 1923 Tokyo earthquake, began to take steps to abate the threat before the war with the United States ever began.

At least early on for the Americans, the potential for destruction to the enemy outweighed the potential moral issues of wanton destruction or alteration of avowed strategy. While in the early planning stages of an air offensive against Japan, all options deserved consideration. But as options for Japan fell off the table and time grew short, the interest in testing incendiary attack as a serious strategic option grew. The planners viewed firebombing as a broad stroke to sweep away the industry of Japan's major cities in one swift maneuver. Planners kept up target folders and information pertaining to the destruction of *urban industrial* areas through incendiary attack from the beginning of the Joint Target Group's development of files on individual Japanese targets. Once tried for effect by Curtis LeMay on March 9–10, 1945, the potential was realized and moves were made to implement the destruction across Japan. Contrary to popular belief, the shift was by no means as total or as dramatic as it sounds.

1

The Origins of Destruction

THE STORY OF JAPAN'S incineration began twenty years before the first embers flickered as air forces in Europe and the United States struggled to find their place in the aftermath of World War I. In the United States, the small cadre of officers left in the Army Air Corps found themselves beholden to the Army for funding and tasking. Seeking to carve out a niche beyond reconnaissance duties and find a mission that would shorten (or even prevent) wars, the Air Corps leadership looked to strategic bombardment. Strategic bombardment focused on striking behind an enemy's lines to destroy targets that supported the long-term military objective. In its most basic sense, this entailed the destruction of the war-making industries that directly supported troops on the front lines. In contrast to tactical bombing missions, which directly affected the Army in the field, strategic bombardment gave the Air Corps a job that possessed the potential to end a war early through supply deprivation of the enemy; it was also a job exclusive to the Air Corps' capabilities.

The Air Corps leaders found spiritual guidance on both sides of the Atlantic, from Giulio Douhet in Italy and Brig. Gen. William "Billy" Mitchell in the United States. Douhet led the philosophical push in his books *The Command of the Air* and *The War of 19—*, where he described a new paradigm for war. Historian Ronald Schaffer summarizes Douhet's thesis as follows: "In this total war the primary object of military action would no longer be the enemy's armed forces, as in Clausewitz's time, but the vitals of the nation itself, the source of enemy military power, now exposed by technology to attack from the air." Douhet tried to rationalize the collapse of the moral bar-

rier between killing combatants and killing civilians. He cited the
evolution of strategic air warfare (and technical evolution), which
made the barrier obsolete.[1] In Douhet's worldview, society's rapid
mechanization and the superiority of airpower opened the realm of
enemy combatant to any member of the enemy's population. Front-
line troops no longer represented the strength of a nation; instead,
the industry and people supplying and supporting them mattered as
much, if not more. The extent of Douhet's influence on the doctrine
that developed in the United States remains a matter of debate, but
one thing remains unequivocal: the Air Corps dedicated itself to a
strategic doctrine and tied its destiny to such.

On the other side of the Atlantic, the more outspoken Mitchell
forced the practical side of the argument, advocating strategic bombardment, demonstrating the ability of the airplane to bomb and
destroy large targets, and presenting a rallying point for young Air
Corps officers. He spoke out loudly in support of the Air Corps and
the abilities of the airplane, even going so far as defying Navy beliefs
in the impotence of the airplane and sinking the former German
battleship *Ostfriesland* with air-dropped bombs during a demonstration. Whereas Douhet spoke in theory of war's future, Mitchell
showed the officers of the Air Corps the physical potential the airplane possessed and where their future lay.

This is not to say that Mitchell shied away from talk of tactics.
Living in a more open society than Douhet, Mitchell felt free to
paint a frightening picture of air war. He left his readers with the
impression of the "fragility" of civilian will as well as a belief that
"all industrial powers were alike"; all resembled the United States.
One could neither escape the tremendous precision airpower offered
nor ignore the threat of total destruction that Mitchell promised airpower could provide. With the horrors of prolonged ground warfare in World War I fresh on their minds, any reasonable remedy
to trench warfare warranted consideration. To this end, "the dom-
inant theme emerging . . . was not the desire to attack civilians
directly but desire to sever the populace from the sources of production." Civilian deaths were inevitable, but they were a way to
end the horrors of ground warfare. Mitchell, the most prominent
airpower proponent of his time, taught a generation of Air Corps

officers that the airplane offered possibilities in war, from the swift to the catastrophic.[2]

To create a cohesive train of thought on tactics and shaping of doctrine, the Air Corps established the Air Service Field Officer's School in 1920, an institution that evolved into the Air Corps Tactical School in 1926. The Tactical School believed the air arm would take the lead in battle, first against enemy air, then political infrastructure, and finally industrial centers. Early school writings leaned toward the striking of the enemy's population as both an economic and a psychological target. As early as 1926 the text of the course *Employment of Combined Air Force* gave the air arm the aim of "destruction of the enemy's morale and will to resist, preferably by means of attack on the interior." For historian of air doctrine Thomas Greer, "there seems little doubt that such notions gained momentum during the '30s and were expressed with greater emphasis and detail." The *History of the Air Corps Tactical School* confirms that "by 1930 the concept of the primacy of bombardment was firmly established at the Tactical School." Initially, "the idea of limited area bombing, accomplished by night missions," was being taught at the School. "Within a few years this notion was dropped," and the new idea of High Altitude Precision Daylight Bombing (HAPDB) against key nodes of the enemy infrastructure, began to take form. Focus shifted to daylight precision strikes of economic targets in lieu of area bombing or night attacks. The greater emphasis on detail manifested itself in a transformation of the concept of striking the "will to resist," evolving into the more palatable destruction of the "ability to resist."[3]

As the 1930s progressed the school instigated its own refinement of strategic bombing theory and explicitly endorsed the concept of daylight bombardment during the 1932–33 session. A 1932–33 lecturer summarized the rejection of night bombing as a viable tactic and advocated daylight operations: "We want to transport our mass to the objective. If we can, it is that much simpler when we arrive at our objective, the better the visibility, the better our chance of accomplishing our desired destruction." Implicit in the desire to strike in the daylight came the desire to see and destroy specific targets forming the source of the industrial strength. The belief in technology as the foundation of future tactics stemmed from precision bombardment's having taken over the curriculum of the school, giving "purpose and direction to the body of ideas on the employment of airpower."[4] Instructors looked to the creation of a "systems doctrine" that identified and attacked the vulnerabilities of an enemy's economy, the specific bottleneck industries that fed or enabled all other production. By destroying these bottlenecks in the precise mechanism called industry, the enemy's wartime economy would grind to a halt. The increasing capabilities of planes and aiming equipment enabled this belief, giving promise to the idea that pinpoint targets easily lay within the grasp of the mighty American airman. Questions of morality never needed to surface if only legitimate military-industrial targets were struck, especially if the war ended before bloodshed occurred on the battlefield.

The text of a course from 1934 labels national morale and industry as more crucial objectives than the enemy army, but blindly executing on that plan simply did not sit well with the instructors and policy makers of the Corps. As an instructor at the school, the eminent World War II planner Brig. (later full) Gen. Muir S. Fairchild pressed for use of airpower "in a manner which would make the maximum contribution to victory." Fairchild stressed the flexibility of airpower, the selectability in its targeting on the basis of factors distinct to each situation. He stressed viewing an enemy through the lenses of national security considerations, one's strategic stance, the nature of the enemy's military power, and whether the enemy's national structure was vulnerable and within range. While Fairchild did not fasten himself inseparably to the doctrine of purely precision bombardment, he did reject bombing and gassing of civilians on both humanitarian and moral grounds. "For all these reasons," he stated in the 1939 Air Corps Tactical School lecture "National Economic Structure," "the School advocates an entirely different method of attack. This method is the attack of the National Economic Structure." Rejected were the Draconian and apocalyptic tactics of mass destruction from the air, and in their place the Air Force planners placed their faith in technology and the superiority of the American airman, both in skill and in morality.[5]

To push this agenda, the leaders of the school and Air Corps, a young and vibrant group of hardcore airmen, developed the "system of systems" doctrine and its implicit belief in an industrialized economy consisting of interrelated and dependent industries. Their system pointed to the perceived similarity of all industrialized nations, and their requirements to sustain a population and conduct war.

It should also not be forgotten that this destruction of the will to resist would be accomplished by precision bombing, not indiscriminate terror bombing. Air Force historian Lt. Col. Peter Faber references Maj. Gen. Haywood Hansell, a graduate of the school in 1935 and teacher there from 1935 to 1938, and his description of the theory of HAPDB as one that "would destroy an opponent's will to resist only if it focused on destroying or paralyzing 'national *organic systems* on which many factories and numerous people depended.'"[6] This meant attacking things like electrical power, transportation, fuels, and food distribution, but not through area attacks. This was the natural extension of the bottleneck theory, in which industrial economies, regardless of their location, relied on specific entities to function. By hitting those specific points, the attacker could cripple industry and bring the economy as a whole to a halt. Hansell elaborated after the war that in the belief of the Tactical School, "Loss of any of these systems would be a crippling blow. Loss of several or all of them would bring national paralysis."[7] He summed up the doctrine established at the school as consisting of five fundamental aphorisms:

1. Modern great powers rely on major industrial and economic systems. . . . Disruption or paralysis of these systems undermines both the enemy's *capability* and *will* to fight.

2. Such major systems contain critical points whose destruction will break down these systems, and bombs can be delivered with adequate accuracy to do this.

3. Massed air strike forces can penetrate air defenses without unacceptable losses and destroy selected targets.

4. Proper selection of vital targets in the industrial/economic/social structure of a modern industrialized nation, and their subsequent destruction by air attack, can lead to fatal weakening of an industrialized enemy nation and to victory through air power.

5. If enemy resistance still persists after successful paralysis of selected target systems, it may be necessary as a last resort to apply direct force upon the sources of enemy national will by attacking cities. In this event, it is preferable to render the cities untenable rather than indiscriminately to destroy structures and people.[8]

Only if the first four failed would the fifth be invoked. It acted as insurance, if only by chance, for the inability to strike precisely. The doctrine demanded precision to avoid the "killing [of] thousands of men, women, and children [which] was basically repugnant to American mores," while reserving the right to escalate hostilities as necessity demanded.[9]

The overlooked shortcoming in this aspect of the theory stemmed from the theorists' reliance on the belief that all economies mimicked one another, and especially that they mimicked the U.S. economy. This revealed itself prominently in the implementation of the theory before World War II. Planners, encumbered by an official policy of not planning wars against other nations, planned a bombing campaign against U.S. industry with the assumption that the conclusions and target list would translate to any other nation. Only later, once an in-depth investigation of Japanese targets was made, would the drastic differences between industrialized nations become apparent and the utility of strategic-bombing theory come under question.

Against the theory, coupled with the believed invulnerability of the bomber and dedicated target selection and analysis, the enemy stood no chance. As Faber writes regarding the history of Air Force thought and planning, "They relied on deductive reasoning, analogies, and metaphors to develop their working propositions into a pseudoscientific theory of strategic bombardment." While attacking cities might prove necessary if enemy resistance persisted, the preferable method of destruction would "render the cities untenable rather than indiscriminately to destroy structures and people."[10] The near verbatim use of Mitchell's ideas is not surprising, for Mitchell stood out among top Air Corp officers at the time as a leading tactician and man who truly held the service's best interests in hand.

Working in conjunction with the procurement efforts of the Air Corps at large, the school's doctrine dismissed the inefficiency of night bombing, preferring to concentrate on building bombers whose speed, armament, and accuracy would protect them in daylight from pursuit planes and ensure the bombs struck the target. The belief in the invincibility of the bomber—an idea that remained pervasive for decades, much to the detriment of thousands of airmen over occupied Europe—stemmed from the roughly equal capabilities of fighter and bomber aircraft produced at the time. After World War I, aircraft technology and performance numbers rose on a steep curve, the performance improvements affecting both the large bombers and smaller pursuit planes.

A comparison of fighters and bombers of the time illustrates how the bomber's performance surpassed its contemporary fighter counterparts and made it the master of the skies. Just after World War I, the best American fighter available came from the Curtiss Company, the P-1. Known as the Hawk, it flew at a top speed of 198 miles per hour, possessed a range of 300 miles, and could reach an altitude of 22,000 feet. The comparable bomber of the time, the Keystone Series of planes (the B-2 through B-6), flew noticeably slower and lower, 121 miles per hour and 14,000 feet, but achieved greater range than the smaller fighters, flying 430 miles on a tank of fuel. By the 1930s performance stabilized between the types, and the Martin YB-10 bomber flew as fast as the period's pursuit plane, the P-26 Peashooter, at 230 miles per hour. The Peashooter held a slight altitude advantage, but only by 3,800 feet: 24,200 for the YB-10 and 28,000 for the P-26. The maximum-range competition still had the bomber flying farther than the fighter, 700 miles versus 635 miles. Over the course of ten years, the performance gap between what a one-man fighter aircraft could do and what a bomb-laden and multi-engine strategic bomber could do narrowed substantially. No longer could the fighter rely on its speed to chase down a bomber, and now the fighter needed to fly to near its maximum altitude to intercept the attacking plane. On paper the advantage shifted to the bomber.

The late 1930s saw the culmination of the bomber's perceived superior abilities. The Boeing B-17 Flying Fortress promised performance better than any previous fighter, and superior to any entering service. The B-17's maximum speed of 287 miles per hour and range of 1,100 miles made it formidable, but its operating altitude above 25,000 feet made it invulnerable. The best fighter in America at the time came, again, from Curtis, in the form of the P-40. Faster than the B-17 at 357 miles per hour and with a range just short of three-quarters of the B-17's, the fighter stretched its capability to reach 30,000 feet, much less fight there. While all these numbers are specification and best-case-scenario figures, not real-life combat experience, in peacetime they represented the basis for arguments made about planning and procuring of the Air Corps' meager assets. While the range difference between fighter and bomber represents little—after all, the fighters presumably wait for the bombers and intercept them close to their target—the speed and altitude figures make the bombers appear as war winners. Against front-line fighters the B-17 would be noticeably slower, but against any of the previous generation of fighters, such as the P-26, which did see a short and unremarkable combat experience in World War II, the B-17 would pull away at almost 50 miles per hour. The most telling statistic, though, is altitude. An old playground adage says that what cannot be caught cannot be hurt, and flying 5,000 feet above any fighter of its day made the B-17 uncatchable.

This is not to say that the B-17's performance alone made it invincible; the plane gained its moniker "Flying Fortress" for a reason. Designers included machine-gun positions around the plane that covered all approaches. Nine to thirteen .50-caliber guns adorned the B-17, whereas its heavy-bomber counterpart, the B-24 Liberator, carried at least ten. Whether alone or in numbers, the bombers possessed the ability to fend off all fighter attacks, or so the Air Corps planners believed. What planners did not have was practical experience on which to base their claims.

With the start of 8th AF operations in Europe in 1942 the theorists quickly learned how wrong they had been. But entering into World War II the Air Corps planners and officers firmly believed in the near dogma of high-altitude daylight precision bombardment. The moral question over bombing civilians and technical questions over the Air Corps' place in the future found their answer in planes designed for and flown at maximum altitude while destroying the individual targets decisive to victory.

One of the leading proponents of the precision-bombing concept came again in the form of Haywood Hansell. Hansell describes the strategic air warfare doctrines and principles as involving defeat of the enemy by

1. destroying industrial and civic systems which support the enemy state,

2. destroying industrial systems which support the enemy armed forces, and by these means,

3. undermining the nation's will and capability to resist.[11]

The doctrine ingrained in the Air Force officer was one of hitting the enemy where it would hurt most and quickest, thereby destroying the enemy's ability to carry on and ending the war as quickly as possible. A crucial developer and proponent of the systems doctrine, Hansell was destined to play a major role in the execution of the bombing theories in Europe and over Japan.

The systematic approach came through in 1941 in *Air War Plans Division Report One* (AWPD-1), which Hansell coauthored with fellow career airmen, staff officers, generals, and Tactical School students/instructors Lt. Col. Harold L. George, Maj. Kenneth Walker, and Maj. Laurence Kuter. The plan defined the physical requirements for the defeat of the Axis powers, with a major focus on Germany. The advocates of precision bombing used this opportunity to achieve what "'Billy' Mitchell and the believers in his philosophy had been struggling" for: the opportunity to draft "the specifications around which to create American air power." Hansell and his fellow planners took the opportunity to formalize on paper and in procurement plans an American air force dedicated to striking the enemy's industry and war-making ability. AWPD-1 outlined a world where strategic bombardment would be waging continuous combat against the war-supporting structures of Germany, principally electrical power, transportation, and the petroleum industry.[12] While these target groups offered the greatest disruption of the German war machine in the fewest targets, they would also assuredly affect the civilian population relying on electricity to light their homes or on trains to travel. AWPD-1 considered these effects on civilians but found them to be ancillary as opposed to a direct attack on the people. As Schaffer makes clear, American theorists believed that "civilians and armed forces were inseparably linked in national war machines" and that "one way to break those machines was to smash civilian will." To that end, planners considered direct attacks on the populace as a last resort. Timing was crucial, for attacking the people too early in the war would harden resistance, as it did in England. The planners thus deferred strikes to destroy German morale until "widespread defeatism had been engendered by heavy air attacks against the systems which supported the means to fight and the means to live."[13] Attacks on the three industries selected by the planners promised to cripple the German war machine and demonstrate to the German people the effectiveness of strategic airpower. While German people would feel the pain as accomplices in the war started by their government, the American planners could rest easy that they had not resorted to the widespread and random destruction that came from Douhet's worst prophecies.

The decisions recommended in AWPD-1 fed directly into the conduct of future operations in the Far East. The experience and lessons learned in Europe promised to guide the actions against Japan in later years, establishing a precedent to achieving accuracy and minimal collateral damage that further raised the U.S. war effort on the moral high ground. Attacks on Japan would be an expansion of the attacks on Europe, continuing the aim of breaking the war machine while sparing the populace direct harm.

While implementing a strategic-bombing plan in the European theater posed no great difficulty, as the unsinkable aircraft carrier of Great Britain placed the B-17 and B-24 bombers well within range of any vital German target, the Pacific offered the opposite scenario. At the start of the war the closest American bombers came to Japan proper was the Philippines, and they neither provided the range for bombers of the day, nor did they last long enough to give any benefit to the Air Force when they came under Japanese invasion in December 1941. After that, the next closest territory firmly in Allied hands was in Australia or China, both long out of range of any bomber available. A strategic-bombing campaign of any type would require both closer bases and a plane of longer range.[14]

The necessary plane already existed on the drawing board: the Boeing B-29 Superfortress. Designed as both the next generation of bombers, the very heavy bomber, and a plane capable of attacking mainland Europe from bases in Ireland, the B-29 featured twice the range and double the payload of the B-17 while incorporating a host of technological advancements. Although the B-17 could carry 10,000 pounds of bombs 1,100 miles at 20,000 feet going 200 miles per hour, the B-29 could carry 20,000 pounds of bombs 3,200 miles at 30,000 feet going 300 miles per hour. The B-29 presented the next step in the development of an invincible bomber, its altitude and speed advancements enabling it to fly above flak and fighters to strike targets more precisely than the B-17 ever could. This new graceful giant of a plane would open the way to destroying Japan's industrial strength, if only it flew.[15]

From its beginning in August 1940 the B-29 pushed the boundaries of aeronautical engineering. Almost every modern feature found its way into the design. At 99 feet long and more than 141 feet wide it dwarfed both the B-17 and the B-24. Operating at the planned altitudes required a pressurization system to provide oxygen and maintain a shirtsleeves environment for the crew, a feature not found on passenger planes of the time, much less bombers. Instead of manned guns for defense, the B-29 incorporated remote-control turrets operated from safely inside the pressurized confines of the beast. A cross-strapping system allowed the several gunner positions to accurately control, aim, and fire any of the turrets, adding a further level of complexity. The bombs were aimed not simply by the trusty optical Norden bombsight of old but with the AN/APQ-13 bombing radar, ostensibly allowing for precision strikes regardless of weather over the target. Despite operational development of radar bombing in Europe, the primitive state of radar at the time and the lack of well-trained radar operators limited the advantages the equipment provided.

As if all these features did not provide enough complexity, the plane relied on the propulsion of a new breed of radial engines, the Wright R3350. No component of the B-29 caused more trouble than the R3350. So intricate were the four engines on each plane that they necessitated a dedicated flight engineer's console designed into the aircraft to provide continuous monitoring of the power plants. Regardless, overheating problems plagued the engine, leading to repeated fires and losses of planes. An air-cooled engine, the

R3350 used eighteen cylinders in two successive rows, boosted by two turbo-superchargers and lubricated with an astounding eighty-five gallons of oil per engine. With only as much facial area, fifty-five inches around, as the single-row nine-cylinder engine used on the B-17, the R3350 suffered from a drastic lack of air over its rear cylinders. When he arrived in India to lead the B-29 effort out of China, Gen. Curtis LeMay found the engines to have a nasty habit of swallowing valves, which led to the cylinder head coming off, the cylinder being chewed apart, the entire engine breaking down, and the greatest danger of all, fire. In the first half of 1944, as the B-29 entered into service, seven out of ten times when a plane had an engine failure in flight it started a fire.[16] Complicating this troublesome situation was the inability to control the fires or their spread. Insufficient fire extinguishers proved unable to suppress a raging oil fire, which easily burned through the wing, igniting fuel tanks and shearing the entire wing off. This very issue led to the loss of the prototype XB-29 on February 18, 1943, at the hands of Boeing's most experienced test pilot, Eddie Allen. An engine fire in the number one engine raged out of control, engulfing the wing and bringing the plane and its crew to their demise in a Seattle, Washington, meatpacking plant.

Mitigation of these problems remained elusive as new cowl designs and added cooling fillets on the cylinders, to increase the surface area over which cool outside air traveled, competed with operational considerations. Yet the strain the fully loaded plane put them under continued to complicate the engine problems. When Boeing first delivered the plane to the Air Force, it was rated for a maximum takeoff weight of 120,000 pounds. Through "urging and pleading" the 20th Bomber Command (BC) persuaded the Air Force technical staff at Wright Field to increase the takeoff weight to 132,000 pounds, only to go to combat deployment and daily push the planes off the runway loaded to 140,000 pounds with fuel and bombs. B-29 pilot Col. Charles L. Phillips Jr. tells of his experiences coaxing the Superfortress off the ground, trying to keep the engines from overheating: "After takeoff the B-29 would be held in level flight with reduced power, at about 50 or 100 feet off the ground, often for 50 miles," only "when the flight engineer reported that the cylinder head temperatures had stabilized on all four engines, our climb could begin." The subsequent climb to a bombing altitude of 30,000 feet while fully loaded continued to strain the engines, keeping the window for engine failure open well into the long flight to Japan. In January 1945, six months into the operational use of the plane, the 21st BC still experienced a 16.8 percent grounding rate for its planes due to engine issues alone. On top of that, 2.5 percent of all losses during sorties were due to mechanical failure. A significant portion of the B-29 striking force fell victim to itself long before encountering the Japanese.[17]

All told, the B-29 program cost nearly $4 billion, more than it cost to develop the atomic bomb. Though the plane was initially kept a secret, when it appeared in public it became the face of a modern Air Force that would take the fight to the Japanese home islands and, through bombing alone, drive the nation to surrender. To take the B-29 into combat, General Arnold created the 20th AF, an independent unit responsible only to him, and not the whims of theater commanders. The 20th AF reported directly to Arnold as commanding officer and carried with it a level of independence from outside influence granted by the Joint Chiefs of Staff themselves. As much an experiment in the viability of an independent air arm as a fighting unit, the 20th AF represented the validity of the theories and doctrines developed over the previous twenty years by the airmen.

By the time the kinks were worked out of the B-29 adequately to turn it loose in combat, only one place in Allied hands lay within the B-29's 1,600-mile combat radius to Japan: an airfield being built by hand labor in Chengtu, China, and designated as the home of the 20th BC and the 20th AF. Distance from logistics lines and proximity to Japanese lines, though, required the B-29s to stage at the base only immediately before and after missions. The planes, crews, and ground personnel all resided 1,500 miles away in Kharagpur, India. The lack of logistics train also forced the B-29s to assume responsibility for carrying supplies to Chengtu. Virtually every gallon of fuel, bomb, and spare part that arrived at Chengtu came in the B-29s that then took it to Japan. On average it took eight trips "over the hump" of the Himalayas to supply one plane for one mission to Japan. The time spent flying these supply missions, plane losses incurred in flying them, and concurrent loss of training and operational experience resulted in an average of only three missions a month flying from China during 1944, often with pitifully poor results. An additional detriment of Chinese-based operations appeared on their target list, where the limited number available for attack in Japan proper obviated the stationing of bombers on the mainland. Only the southernmost main Japanese island, Kyushu, was within B-29 range from Chengtu; the industrial and political heart of Japan on the main island of Honshu remained out of reach to American strategic bombers.

The future lay in the Marianas, but until then China-based bombers had to take the lead in taking the war to the Japanese. Concurrent naval operations in the Marianas promised to secure the needed islands in range of Tokyo for the B-29s, and in anticipation of this opportunity the 20th AF slowly began focusing its efforts away from the 20th BC and toward the assembling 21st BC. Under the leadership of the capable planner Haywood Hansell, the 21st BC would finally take the fight in the Pacific to the enemy.

2

The Makings of a Mission

WITH THE PIECES IN PLACE to strike Honshu, the need to overcome the basic challenges of bombing remained. Flak, weather, bombing accuracy, and fighters plagued a bomber in different ways, and the skies over Japan came as no exception. Experience in Europe taught several harsh lessons to the strategic-bombing adherents. Flak's accuracy and volume proved a real danger to the bombers, and the accuracy of visual bombing in combat conditions failed to meet the theoretical and controlled test numbers determined before the war. Worst of all, fighter technology had not only caught up with bomber development but left it well behind. The ferocity of the fighting and the losses experienced over occupied Europe left American bomber commanders shaken. The men destined to lead the B-29 into combat over Japan all experienced the tribulations of the European campaign firsthand. Haywood Hansell commanded the 1st Bomb Wing (BW) and served as deputy commander in chief of the Allied Expeditionary Air Force. Curtis LeMay took the 305th Bomb Group (BG) to England and personally led them on the mission against the Messerschmitt aircraft factory in Regensburg, Germany, during the infamous Schweinfurt-Regensburg missions of August 17, 1943. Brig. Gen. (later full Gen.) Lauris Norstad, before taking his position as Hap Arnold's righthand man, distinguished himself as chief of staff for operations of the 12th AF in Italy. The challenges lurking over Japan offered no surprises to these men, men who knew the potentially frightful cost strategic bombing could incur over enemy territory.

The challenges were the same but unique over Japan. Halfway around the world from Europe, the Japanese had the same basic tools as the Germans, but in different quantities and different qualities. A few geographical surprises added to the challenge.

The omnipresent threat to bombers rose to meet them in the form of antiaircraft fire, solid or exploding projectiles at low altitude and exploding shells from larger-caliber guns at high altitudes. Attacking fighters came and left, but flak hounded the attacking force, with one unlucky hit sending a plane plunging to its doom. The Germans made antiaircraft fire an institution, coining the name *flak* as a shortened version of *Fliegerabwehrkanone*, meaning aircraft-defense cannon. Daily over occupied Europe, planes flew through flak said to be thick enough to walk on, creating a deadly reputation for the weapon. According to Curtis LeMay, though, this reputation was based more on perception than reality. A veteran of the European bomber war, LeMay had no respect for flak. In various interviews and his autobiography he relates how he sat up one night shortly after arriving in England with his B-17 group to calculate how likely the infamous German flak was to shoot down a bomber flying straight and level. Using his old field artillery manual for guidance, he accounted for rate of fire, altitude of the bombers, intelligence estimate of the number of guns, and typical artillery dispersion and came up with 372 rounds as the number needed to hit a bomber. "They've got to lift a lot of rounds upstairs to get a hit on a target our size," he concluded. "We could take this."[1] Take it they could, and take it they did.

What the Germans had in spades with flak weapons the Japanese simply did not have at all. As bomber war historian Kenneth Werrell points out, the Japanese "received only limited assistance from the Germans and also failed to fully mobilize their civilian scientists."[2] This limited their production and development of antiaircraft weapons and left their cities vulnerable.

Like the Germans, the Japanese possessed flak for varying altitudes. Lower altitudes were covered by 20- or 25-millimeter guns with effective ranges out to 8,000 feet. With high rates of fire but minimal range, these guns protected against small fighter/bomber aircraft but provided no value against high-altitude strategic bombers. To hit altitudes above 20,000 feet, large-caliber guns with time-fused exploding shells were required. In this category the Japanese possessed guns ranging from 75 to 150 millimeters, but they relied almost exclusively on the Type 88 75-millimeter cannon. Adopted for service in 1928, the Type 88 fired a 14.5-pound time-fused shell designed to explode at the altitude of the bombers. At a firing rate of ten to fifteen rounds per minute, the Type 88 could be a formidable weapon, but its limitation was its nominal range, only 23,500 feet. Any B-29 at its normal cruising altitude would fly above the flak with 6,500 feet to spare. Larger guns existed in Japan, just not in quantity. An 88-millimeter gun based on the legendary German Type 36/37 88-millimeter found use by the Japanese, but in very small numbers. Even larger guns like the 120 or 150 millimeter, with its supposed range of 45,900 feet, saw production, but never in numbers large enough to protect the country. One hundred fifty-four of the 120-millimeter guns were produced, and a whole two of the 150-millimeter guns rolled off the assembly line.[3]

One type of flak the Japanese did not field in great numbers covered the middle-altitude gap. Medium-flak guns caused problems for all militaries in World War II, owing to the difficulty of finding the proper slew rate and a compromise between rate of fire, volume of fire, and speed at which the gun can be trained on a target. Smaller guns possess high rates of fire and swift moving mounts, but they lack range, while large guns exhibit great range but have low rates of fire and difficulty traversing or elevating quickly. Smaller guns attack a target by leading it with a stream of fire, seeking to strike the plane directly with bullets. At high altitudes, heavier guns aim to anticipate the seemingly slower-moving aircraft by firing a barrage into the general area the enemy aircraft flies, hoping time-fused or proximity-fused (late-war) flak will splatter the plane with shrapnel as it flies by. A medium gun must have the slew rate of the smaller gun to hit the plane moving perceptibly faster at medium altitudes and the range of the larger gun to reach the plane. With the exception of the American 5-inch .38-caliber gun, which technically did not qualify as a medium gun, no one in World War II achieved this holy grail of antiaircraft fire, least of all the Japanese.

The lack of quantity of guns could be made up with accuracy. Like the Germans, the Japanese concentrated their guns into batteries (about six guns each) and grouped batteries together under unified fire control. Unlike the Germans, the Japanese possessed little gun-laying radar. Flak, then, needed to be fired by visual means in bar-rages against the invading force. At night, when visibility equaled nil, a time when radar's effectiveness showed its greatest value, the Japanese used large numbers of searchlights to frame their targets for antiaircraft punishment. These lights focused fire on single tar-gets and did more to blind the pilots than to direct accurate fire. If radar was present it was used to direct the searchlights rather than the guns, and if radar was lacking entirely the Japanese fell back on their copious number of sound detectors to direct fire.

This lack of quantity represented the real limitation on Japanese antiaircraft defenses. One rationale for the initial B-29 strikes on Japan occurring at or above 30,000 feet—one of the selling points of the B-29 as a bomber—was its immunity to flak at those altitudes. Experience in Europe had not only eviscerated belief in the invinci-bility of the bomber but had illustrated the effects of concentrated, intense, flak on bombers. Even discounting the accuracy LeMay had personally discredited, the sheer quantity of fire wreaked havoc on the bomber formations over Europe. The prospect of similar con-centrations over Japan ensured that the higher service ceilings of the B-29 would be used.

Initial missions played this fear out. The main target over the first two dozen missions flown by the 21st BC, the Nakajima Musashino aircraft engine plant, just outside Tokyo, forced the bombers to fly through heavy antiaircraft fire. During two months of operations the 21st BC struck Musashino five times, losing eleven planes to flak. Unapparent at the time, the 21st BC chose to fly into the concentra-tion of Japanese flak guns. A postwar accounting showed that the Japanese home defenses only had two thousand guns total in the home islands, more than a quarter of which were positioned to pro-tect Tokyo. Even a "Preliminary Report on the Japanese Air Defense System," written after the 20th BC began its strikes on Kyushu, noted that "the Japanese have evidently not been completely prepared for attacks directed against Japan." In an unnoticed harbinger of things to come, the report noted that Nagasaki housed only six heavy anti-aircraft guns, while the main target in range of operations in China, the Yawata steel mills, only sat under the cover of an estimated 23 heavy and 108 other antiaircraft guns.[4]

Reading further into the daily intelligence summaries, as the targets moved away from Tokyo the reported intensity of flak decreased dramatically. Despite initial impressions, Japan proved to be nowhere near the flak trap of Europe; this partly negated the need for the increased altitude capability of the B-29, a conclusion not readily evident to the crews flying the first strikes against Japan.

What the "Preliminary Report" touched on without realizing it was that the Japanese had failed to anticipate the level of effort required. Before the war started, the Japanese had designated the aircraft as the primary means of defense, deemphasizing production or improvement of antiaircraft defenses. Japanese authorities complicated matters by failing to create central fire-control locations or targeting-data distribution networks. These decisions hurt more when the rivalry between the Japanese army and navy prevented coordination of the meager air-defense assets. Using the limited range of their limited number of search radars, the largely decentralized Japanese air-defense establishment could prepare defenses but not coordinate them. The intensity of flak experienced by American crews on the early missions indicated the obvious nature of the target far more than it provided a true reflection of Japanese defenses. As the targets expanded beyond Tokyo the air defenses needed to be moved to other probable targets, and then they were hard pressed to fire (accurately much less at all) without coordination with radar. Time would show that Japanese air defenses only existed as a thin shell with nothing behind it.[5]

Flak's persistence created continuous fear, but enemy fighters charging in presented the real possibility of a bomber plunging down in flames. Experience in Europe against the Luftwaffe shattered the mystique of the invincible bomber. Bomber formations without fighter escort, no matter how many machine guns the planes carried, stood little chance against skilled and determined enemy fighters. Only when dedicated fighter escorts accompanied the bombers did the benefits of daylight precision bombing outweigh the costs. With this knowledge in hand, the B-29's prospects over Japan appeared grim. The bases nearest Japan coming into Allied control barely met the range needs of the B-29, let alone a fighter aircraft with half the endurance. So, in a throwback to the prewar invincibility of the bomber, the B-29 would be required to fly at its planned 30,000 feet, above the capability of enemy fighters, and at over 300 miles per hour, faster than a pursuing aircraft at that altitude could go. To top off the defenses, the Air Force and Boeing conspired to replace the man in the loop as much as possible, opting for a system of remote-control gun turrets in place of the manned weapons of earlier bomber designs.

The B-29 ended up with a revolutionary analog computer system that allowed strategically placed gunners throughout the aircraft to fire one of four gun turrets accurately at enemy aircraft. The tail gunner, who acted as the sole user of the tail turret, continued to sit at the rear of the plane, to fire the fifth turret facing behind the aircraft. Instead of placing gunners immediately behind the guns with the weapons in their hands, as done on previous bombers, the B-29 placed gunners in positions around the plane that provided the best visibility around the bomber. This meant that the defensive crew comprised a central fire-control gunner in a bubble at the top of the plane, two gunners in side blisters behind the wings, and the bombardier. The gun turrets sat two in the front, two in the rear, one on top of the plane, and one below at each end. Using the central control system, each turret could be operated by at least two gunners. The obvious problem of accuracy was handled by the analog computers tied into each turret. The computer received not only immediate inputs from each gunner during the attack, through adjustments to the gun sight, but also data from the navigator, incorporating all these factors into its equations. The gun computer factored in target speed, range, and direction received from the gun sight with altitude, speed, and outside temperature from the navigator, in addition to ballistics of the bullet, parallax between gunner and turret, and deflection angles to aim the guns appropriately and increase the likelihood of hits. The system did as much as possible to remove the human error from defensive fire while maximizing the effectiveness of the available weapons.

Despite problems in development and initial operational use, which almost led to its cancellation, the system worked amazingly well. Claimed enemy kills numbered 267 by the end of February 1945, compared with only 39 B-29s lost to enemy air action.[6] More importantly, reliability of the turrets proved good, with no call for their removal by operational crews. A report of the 20th BC Operation Analysis Section in February 1945 found the B-29's armament "satisfactory from the point of view of serviceability as indicated by the small number of malfunctions which occurred during combat and by the fact that the system was maintained without excessive effort." On the more important subject of combat effectiveness, the B-29's remote system scored high. The tail turret gained the most praise (which is only fitting, as it was the simplest of the positions), with the system as a whole establishing an exemplary combat record in a short period. Using that record as a basis, the report proclaimed the B-29's gunnery system "one of the most, if not the most effective airborne gunnery system[s] developed to date."[7] This was high praise for a system that sought to usher in an automated age still years away.

The Achilles' heel of any mechanical system, its reliability, was detailed in an appendix to the report. After discounting the initial missions of the command as statistical outliers, the Operation Analysis Section found that only 4.23 percent of guns flown on the missions in question had gone out of commission for any reason. Of those failures, 29 percent were attributable to the central fire-control system. The majority of failures fell into the category of "machine gun malfunctions," a situation not correctable in flight on the B-29 because the turrets were isolated from the pressurized cabin. In all, the reliability of the complex collection of gears and electrical switches surpassed all expectations.

The other side of the air-defense equation, the Japanese response, came with less force than expected, and much less than the Germans delivered in defense of their homeland. The once formidable Japanese army and naval air arms, long eroded by fighting in the Pacific, lacked the numbers and quality to engage the B-29s. The mainstays of the Japanese air capability, the naval Mitsubishi A6M Zero and army Nakajima Ki-43 Oscar fighters, utterly lacked the speed and altitude capability to engage a bomber at high altitudes. To their detriment, the Japanese military establishment rested on their laurels and did not develop in any quantity any quality fighters to follow up on the Zero's early war success. While the Americans shed their bulky and slow F4F Wildcats and P-40 Warhawks for fast and rugged F6F Hellcats and P-51 Mustangs, the Japanese continued producing the same plane that attacked Pearl Harbor so many years earlier. For once, the ideals of the U.S. air planners appeared to be coming true. The Japanese could not catch a B-29 to shoot it down.

Slowly, the Japanese army started production on several follow-on fighters to the Zero, long delayed by what has been referred to as an "early and sustained belief by the General Staff in the invincibility of the Zeke," a belief "adhered to religiously."[8] Full production was expected to begin late in 1944, and these planes incorporated Western design features of ruggedness, horsepower, and lethal amounts of firepower. The Tony ranked first among these. Similar in design to the German Bf-109, the Ki-61 Tony combined a top speed of 370 miles per hour with a decent climb rate and ceiling of 36,000 feet. It also was produced in large numbers and a proven combat plane, having first seen action in New Guinea in early 1943. The N1K1 George and later models of the Ki-43 Oscar both could reach 360 miles per hour and 38,000 feet, making them good candidates for B-29 interception. Despite eventually carrying a devastating 4 x 20-millimeter blast from the wings, the George, with its unreliable engine, barely entered production by the time the 20th AF appeared, looking to destroy its factories. The severely undergunned and overproduced Oscar did worse, disintegrating under the .50-caliber firepower preferred on American aircraft.

The twin-engine fighters relied more on tactics than performance to make their mark. Large and cumbersome, the Ki-45 Nick and Ki-46 Dinah often focused on night fighting, a situation complicated by their lack of radar. Their advantage came with guns firing at an angle from the top of the fuselage. Using a tactic pioneered by the Luftwaffe, the Nick climbed under the targeted bomber, raking its underside with the twin 12.7-millimeter guns as it flew by, before succumbing to the thin air and plunging downward. The Dinah, the only Japanese fighter that could truly operate at B-29 altitudes, sneaked up underneath a B-29 illuminated by searchlights, and hammered it with the 37-millimeter cannon poking from its roof. When it worked the B-29 suffered catastrophic damage, but to be in that position the Dinah flew square in line with the B-29's bottom turrets.

The one truly formidable Japanese fighter did not see production in numbers enough to make a difference in the war. The Ki-44 Tojo, considered by some as the equivalent of Allied planes, sported four 12.7-millimeter guns and an enviable climb rate of 3,950 feet per minute (compared with 3,475 feet per minute for the P-51 Mustang). Like most Japanese fighters, though, it could not maintain extreme altitude, where it seemed to "literally only 'float' in the sky, and instantly dropped hundreds of metres if a turn was made."[9]

All these planes lacked the key ingredient for a piston engine at high altitudes: a turbocharger. American fighters all came with the system that compressed and forced the rarefied air into the engine, allowing smooth engine performance at altitude. The Japanese experienced trouble installing the smaller and simpler supercharger, which ran its air intake off a belt turned by the aircraft's engine. They never found a way to make the more complicated turbocharger, which was powered by the engine exhaust, operational. This deprived the Japanese of an extra 2,000 meters (6,560 feet) of altitude versus a plane with a supercharger, and 4,000 meters (13,120 feet) against a normally aspirated aircraft. In practical terms this meant a Zero could effectively fly at 20,000 feet, while a super-turbocharged Mustang or B-29 operated at 32,000 feet.[10]

All of the planes sent against the B-29 suffered from severe undergunning until late in the war. Most used only a pair of 12.7-millimeter guns, equivalent in size to the American .50 caliber. In a volume on *Japanese Air Weapons and Tactics*, the United States Strategic Bombing Survey (USSBS) discusses the subject, noting that Japanese ground tests found that "a gun of at least 30 millimeters was required for an effective percentage of heavy bomber kills." These results came out early in the war and found validation in the field by 1943, but Japanese pilots protested change to their armament scheme. Even with larger guns available, pilots preferred to not carry guns in the wings of their planes—the only reliable place to carry the larger weapons—in an effort to retain the performance advantages in climb speed and maneuverability that their lighter fighters exhibited.[11] Not until B-29s actually appeared in the skies over Japan did up-gunning occur on Japanese fighters, an abortive effort that paid few dividends.

Organized into *sentai* (squadrons), these dedicated air-defense units covered specific areas of Japan, normally tied to districts and commanders designated for ground defense, rarely leaving their

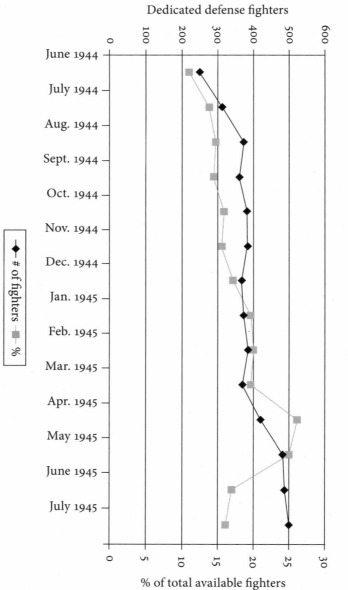

Dedicated defense fighters

% of total available fighters

Fig. 1. Japanese defense fighters

assigned areas to concentrate against an attack. Confusing the issue more, the army held responsibility for homeland defense, except over naval installations, the exclusive domain of naval fighters. The fiercely guarded division between branches of service in Japan extended all the way back to its homeland and its defense.

When the 20th BC first appeared over Kyushu in June 1944, the Japanese assigned only 260 planes to the defense of the home islands, a figure that equates to roughly 11 percent of all Japanese fighters available. As seen in figure 1, this ratio stayed constant through the end of the war, with the only drastic increases in fighters allocated, and thus percentage of allocation, coming in April 1945 when the loss of Iwo Jima and Okinawa conspired to give the Japanese nowhere else to send their meager production of aircraft.[12]

What the Japanese lacked in overall numbers of available planes they made up for with preparedness and courage. Thanks to coastal early warning radar, picket boats, and until its capture, Iwo Jima, the fighters had up to seven hours to take off and climb to intercept altitudes. Yet, poor-quality radar and ground control coupled with a lack of identification, friend or foe (IFF) equipment gave the pilots little information about bomber headings and altitude, leaving them in the perceived area of engagement but not properly vectored for attack. With the cream of the Japanese air service dead on the waters and islands of the South Pacific, especially the Philippines, many of the defense pilots came from China or had been employed as instructor pilots in Japan and thus avoided the fate experienced by most other Japanese combat pilots. To that extent they entered the battle well seasoned as pilots but with little combat experience, most notably against large, well-defended bombers. This lack of battle testing made them more reliant on ground control to execute their mission, substituting technology for hard-earned experience.

The speed and extreme altitude of the B-29s pushed the Japanese aircraft to their physical limits and curtailed the number of effective passes a fighter could make. Study data based on the first twenty-five missions by B-29s found that almost half of Japanese attacks pressed to fewer than 250 yards, with some pulling as close as 25 yards. The defensive armament on the bombers violently discouraged rear attacks and made beam approaches costly. The same study saw 41 percent of attacks made against the front of the bombers, with the rest evenly distributed around the plane, though favoring the right side a bit more than the other angles.[13] The Japanese discovered the same things their German allies did: American bomber weakness was in the front, so attack head-on. A charging assault at closure speeds of over 500 miles per hour perfectly suited the warrior spirit of the Japanese pilot, a flier determined to take down the giant aggressor even if it meant mutual destruction in a collision. To combat this, the forward top turret of the B-29 received two additional .50-caliber machine guns, with marginal results. At the same time, the Japanese pilots and tactics evolved to include a larger number of coordinated attacks, designed to overwhelm the bomber's defenses.

As the number of B-29s appearing over Japan increased, the urgency of pushing them back increased. One response that played well to the Japanese *bushido* (code valuing honor above life) sensibility culminated in ramming a fighter into an American bomber, destroying one or both. Ramming attacks tore a B-29 apart, destroying the airplane and crew and terrorizing the other bomber crews. The first incident occurred spontaneously on August 20, 1944, two month before kamikazes made their first appearance at the Battle of Leyte Gulf. While defending against a 20th BC attack on the Yawata steel mills, 1st Lt. Isamu Kashiide drove his Nick's right wing through the B-29 *Gertrude C*'s left wing, tearing it off just past the number one engine. The fireball and debris caught another B-29, sending both plummeting to the ground with all hands save one.[14]

By the time the 21st BC entered the fray in late 1944, suicide attacks held a firm place in the tactical doctrine of Japanese defense forces. The 10th Fighter Division established dedicated ramming sections in each of its groups. While not entirely committed to self-destruction, the ramming pilots courted death openly when trying to make contact with a bomber. Their goal was to down the bomber at direct risk to their life and plane, though not specifically through their own death. One advantage of the dedicated ramming aircraft came from the removal of armament and armor from the plane. Lighter than a conventional fighter, the dedicated ramming planes potentially gained 500–1,000 meters (1,625–3,250 feet) in altitude capability. This sat well with unskilled pilots who experienced difficulty performing interceptions of high-altitude bombers. In the words of the last commander of the 53rd Sentai, Maj. Masato Kodama, "Unskilled pilots would try to improve . . . performance by decreasing equipment and trying to ram their targets."[15]

Ramming offered a near sure kill of the B-29 and a way to die for the honor of the emperor. While ramming attacks were rare (one source lists only twenty-four B-29 missions during which such attacks were undertaken), ramming gained a sense of fame on both sides for its sacrifice and spectacular results. Summarizing the effectiveness of the attacks after the war, the USSBS attributed the loss of only four B-29s to ramming attacks, but it conceded the value of the tactic: "It is evident that even these haphazard attacks, which at first glance seem highly inefficient, were in reality very efficient." Taking into account the crews lost and targets left untouched, the report saw a high value in ramming and was thankful that the Japanese did not organize the effort better both in numbers and concentration.[16]

The United States' capture of Iwo Jima in February 1945 not only removed the Japanese threat from the B-29 path to Japan but also placed an American air base just in range of the home islands from which to operate fighter escorts. Having been found to be so necessary in Europe, thus far the B-29s had done without "little friends" and held their own, but starting on April 7, 1945, fighter escorts became the norm. Using the extremely long-range P-51D and P-47N fighters, Air Force pilots eagerly engaged the Japanese interceptors, clearing the skies around their "big friends." Lacking the navigation equipment to make a journey that far across the open ocean, the fighters relied on the B-29s to guide them to the target and back to Iwo Jima. Breakdowns in this system left the bombers vulnerable and resulted in the ditching of numerous fighters in the expanses of the Pacific, but when it worked, the intercepting Japanese pilots faced a real threat to compound their difficulty shooting down bombers.

Initial intense air opposition gave way slowly in early 1945 until the futility of the effort and an emphasis on kamikaze tactics took over the Japanese mind-set. The invasion of Okinawa lent new intensity to the belief in the kamikaze as the saving grace of the empire, and from April onward aircraft were held in reserve for the invasion. In his magnificent work on the planning for invasion of Japan at the end of the war, *Hell to Pay*, D. M. Giangreco confirms that "after some initial sparring with carrier aircraft and Far East Air Force elements flying out of Okinawa, the Japanese essentially glued their aircraft to the ground in order to preserve them for use during the invasions." Not only did a desire to preserve these vital mechanical resources hold the planes on the ground, but even those units insistent on fulfilling their duty found their way blocked by a lack of fuel. Giangreco, who illustrates the ample reserves in fuel Japan still possessed despite years of blockade, notes that conventional air units in Japan "had no access to strategic fuel supplies." In the eyes of the Japanese, as well as Giangreco, "The massive Japanese response would occur only when they could confirm U.S. landing operations had commenced." The Japanese consciously chose to curtail airborne interception. At the end of the war they possessed 1 million barrels of fuel, more than enough for ten thousand suicide sorties of five hours each. With the noose tightening daily, the invasion loomed sooner rather than later, forcing the Japanese people to endure the B-29 attacks, whatever their form, without the luxury of massive airborne response. As far as Japanese leadership were concerned, B-29s did not present as grave a threat to the survival of the home islands as invasion, or at least were a threat they could not counter.[17]

The main industrial areas of Japan, the central plains of Honshu and points south, lay under a blanket of clouds for extended periods throughout the year. A typical month offered only five days of visual bombing weather.[18] Japan lay between a cold "polar front" of Siberian air and the warm air mass of the South Pacific. These winds follow two currents, the cold Oyashio Current, which comes down from the Arctic to flow down Hokkaido and Honshu's east coast, where it meets the warm Kuroshio (Japan) Current. As often happens, this interaction of hot and cold moisture causes persistent clouds.

The geography of Honshu amplified the clash of warm and cool air through orographic effect on its mountainous backbone, resulting in a solid wall of clouds from one thousand to three thousand feet. In clouds this intense, no altitude offered a decent chance for visual bombing. As these fronts moved south, the low clouds dissipated and left a thick overcast of middle and high clouds between fifteen and twenty thousand feet. This overcast did eventually burn off, giving strike planners the challenge of guessing when to send planes to bomb a target visually, hoping to see through a hole in the clouds.[19]

This gave prediction of weather an immediate importance for the 20th AF leaders. Despite reports from China, reports from patrol aircraft poking around the ever-shrinking Japanese sphere of influence, rare submarine reports, daily single-plane weather-strike missions by the 21st BC, and even the occasional decrypted Russian weather report (they did not share willingly), no one but the Japanese ever had a clear picture of the real-time weather over Japan. The delay in, or pure lack of, weather data inhibited planning missions and limited the effective follow-up of previous attacks by often forcing formations reaching an obscured target to bomb blindly or switch to a secondary target. During the 21st BC's second attack on the Musashino plant, the number one target on the 21st's list, of eighty-one planes airborne none hit the primary target, forty-nine attacked the secondary, and thirteen dropped on no target, all due to obscuring weather. Both alternatives to bombing the primary target cut deeply into the effectiveness of the much-vaunted B-29, leaving primary targets barely touched and secondary targets struck haphazardly by the now-disorganized formation.

Even the assigning of dedicated planes and crews to fly the weather missions could not fill the crucial void of knowing the weather conditions of Japan at a given point of time. Previously, planes performed weather reconnaissance as a secondary task on flights otherwise focused on more mundane daily tasks like training or radarscope photography. Only in June 1945 did a separate squadron with specially modified planes and trained crews undertake missions focused solely on tracking and gathering weather data over Japan.

Another weather-related impediment to bombing accuracy came as a scientific discovery in its own right. The jet stream, the fluctuating high-speed winds that form where the polar front meets warm tropical air, can achieve four hundred miles per hour. Flowing west to east, the jet stream placed a headwind in front of planes bombing westward that nearly froze them in their tracks, or put a tailwind on planes heading east that pushed them well past the not-to-exceed speed of 300 miles per hour posted in the pilot's console. Experienced velocities at altitudes above 25,000 feet from December 1944 through February 1945 showed that 46 percent of the time planes encountered winds above 149 miles per hour. The higher a plane flew the greater the winds, topping out at 276 miles per hour observed by one crew at 31,000 feet. Over the course of the three months the average winds experienced reached 154 miles per hour, and they progressively grew stronger as winter deepened.[20]

Lt. Col. (later Gen.) Jack Catton, the head of the 73rd BW during the early missions of the 21st BC, recalled never having seen a drift rate (the difference between the longitudinal axis of the plane and its actual motion over the ground) like the one he experienced over Honshu. After making a twenty-degree correction to align himself with the initial point of the bomb run, Catton found out just how disadvantageous the jet stream made acquiring and bombing a target. Fellow B-29 pilot Maj. (later Gen.) David Burchinal found that a plane could end up doing five hundred or more knots of airspeed, a point reinforced by LeMay: "If you went upwind . . . you sat there forever. . . . If you came downwind then the bombardier had a hard time getting synchronized." And "If you bombed crosswind the bombsight wouldn't take the drift that you needed."[21] These speeds not only stressed the airframes but played havoc on the Norden bombsight. Designed for lower altitudes and slower speeds, the venerable instrument could not handle the extreme environment in which the B-29 flew.

The key word in the term *precision bombardment* is *precision*, without which the rest of the effort expended by bombing appears pointless. The unequivocally best bombsight of the time was the Norden Mark XV M-series (known as an M-7 or M-9 to the U.S. Army). A gyroscopically stabilized optical sight integrated with the plane's autopilot system, the Norden promised the mythical accuracy of placing the bombs in a pickle barrel. Stephen McFarland masterfully explains the inherent difficulty of dropping a bomb from altitude in the appendix of his book *America's Pursuit of Precision Bombing*, but in short it comprises a complex calculation of air speed, deflection, drift angle, range, trail, altitude, sighting angle, and the ballistic characteristics of the bomb, with constant variation as the plane's acceleration altered on any axis. The Norden bombsight contained an analog computer that turned the inputs of the bombardier and autopilot into a precise time to release the bomb load. As with any machine, though, the calculations only rendered a result as accurate as the inputs, so any variations or sudden changes created the chance of throwing the sight off and bombs missing the target. Outside the mechanical capability to calculate the effects of these variables, two crucial factors played into the Norden's ability to work: stability of the plane dropping the bomb, and visual acquisition of the target.

Stability of the plane aiming and dropping the bomb had a marked effect on the accuracy of the strike. A variation of two miles per hour and twenty-five feet of altitude changed the bomb's range from the target by 115 feet. In addition to normal oscillation of the aircraft, the changes in flight stemmed from fear, a desire to avoid enemy fire. Dropping bombs accurately required an extended and steady run to the target. Invariably, the enemy concentrated their antiaircraft fire near the target area, intensifying the flak at the time the plane needed to be flown straight and level. A natural reaction of pilots was to try to move to avoid the flak bursts, or throw off the aim of the gunners. This was activity strictly forbidden both tactically and practically speaking; no matter how bad the flak was, the formation and each plane needed to drive straight through it from the initial point of the bomb run to the actual drop. To help with bombing accuracy, both from a mechanical and physical standpoint, the Norden bombsight was integrated with the Sperry autopilot system. Ordinarily, the integrated autopilot dampened the effects of the plane's natural movement, but when integrated with the bombsight control the plane was automatically steered to the drop point on the basis of the targeting inputs of the bombardier. This improved accuracy and enabled a hands-off approach by the pilot on the bomb run, eliminating human error. Coupled with mandated early initial points, the start of the straight and level approach to the target, and thus a longer and straighter bomb run, it put the true ability of the Norden bombsight on display. Under ideal circumstances the Mark xv could achieve a circular error probable (CEP) of 164 feet from 15,000 feet up, and even better the lower the altitude.[22]

Without visually acquiring the target, an optical bombsight offers no value. To that end the greatest enemy of bombing in World War II was not fighters or flak, but clouds. The B-29 attempted to meet these challenges with incorporation of a radar bombsight. Using technology implemented on a limited scale operationally in Europe, the B-29 crew trained primarily in the use of the AN/APQ-13. Like its European antecedent, the AN/APQ-13's visual acuity amounted to patches of light and dark on the screen; this was good for picking out targets on shorelines where the radar returns from the water differed significantly from those of the land, but it was pretty useless over vast uninterrupted expanses of land looking for specific buildings. Worse for the operators, the sets required a great amount of skill to operate and read the radar returns under even the best conditions. LeMay, for instance, sent a radar expert from MIT out with "about a dozen of the stupidest radar operators he could find and see if they could fly over this spit of land sticking out of the northern part of Saipan. A seemingly easy task, to find a distinct topographical feature with aid of the radar contrast between land and water." The expert came back "shaking his head; he just could not understand how poorly trained the operators were."[23] Even the easy tasks caused fits for the green bombing crews, especially the radar operators grappling with new technology.

Despite its obvious drawbacks, radar's redeeming trait—its ability to see through the clouds—made it the bombing system of choice for the B-29. While the Superfortress carried a Norden bombsight, the primary means of dropping bombs on a target was designated as the radar. The visual bombsight almost came as a piece of standard equipment for bombers, and the team developing the B-29 had little intention that it would be used. Haywood Hansell would repeatedly mention in the years after the war that the crews were trained for radar bombing, not for visual bombing. In the limited amount of flight time each crew received—by Hansell's estimation fewer than one hundred total hours in a B-29 before reaching combat—radar bombing had not been practiced nearly enough to impart proficiency on the radar/bombardier. And while the bombardier would have experience from bombardier school with the operation of the Norden sight, he had not trained in an integrated manner with the plane and crew to drop bombs efficiently visually.[24] When the first missions showed the inadequacy of the radar to find specific targets, factories in particular, the fallback posi-

3

Planning Japan's Demise

THE PLANNING FOR INCENDIARY attacks on Japan started soon after Pearl Harbor. In the years before the war, General Mitchell touted the cities of Japan as "congested" and built from "paper and wood." Maj. Gen. Claire Chennault, the leading Air Corp expert on the Far East, concurred, and pressed President Franklin Roosevelt to fire-bomb the Japanese cities. Jimmy Doolittle, on his token raid of Tokyo in 1942, accepted the prevailing wisdom of Japan's susceptibility to fire and loaded his planes with four 500-pound conventional bombs and one incendiary. Doolittle told his men to aim for military targets only, though, and to "Definitely not!" attack residential areas because there was "absolutely nothing to be gained" by such actions. Burning Tokyo down appeared as an option, and some would argue that in ordering the attack Roosevelt was "setting expectations for the nature of that offensive: destruction of Japanese cities," but it presented an option not yet accepted by America. In 1942 the United States still stood on the moral high ground, the victim in the Pacific bent on vengeance, but also on maintaining the fair play of wars long gone.[1]

The United States developed a number of different types of incendiary bombs, anticipating needs in both the European and Pacific theaters. Nothing should be read into the anticipation of using firebombs in Europe, or the Pacific for that matter. As a matter of prudence, and in light of existing British experience, the arsenal of democracy warranted the inclusion of incendiaries. As the United States entered the war the only real-world experience with strategic bombing came from England, where daylight precision gave way to night area raids almost immediately and incendiaries took center stage.

Table 1. American incendiary weapons

Weapon	Weight (lb.)	Size	Fill	Delivery method	Notes
AN-M47A2 (aka M-47)	100	4 ft. L, 8 in. D	Rubber, lye, gas, coconut oil	M12 or M13 cluster	
AN-M50 / AN-M52	4	2 ft. L, 3 in. D	Powdered AL, Iron oxide	M17 500 lb. aimable cluster	Modified British Mk II
AN-M69 (aka M-69)	6.2	20 in. L, 3 in. D	Gasoline gel	M13, M18, M19, or M23 500 lb. cluster	
M74	8.4 (10)	19.15 in. L 2.87 in. D	Magnesium gasoline paste	E48 cluster, 500 lb. aimable cluster	
AN-M76	500	59.16 in. L 14.2 in. D	Gasoline gel and magnesium mixture	individually	General-purpose bomb filled with flammable liquid

The Americans developed five primary incendiary types. Table 1 lists the types of weapons and key features of each. Each bomb was developed with a specific goal in mind, most importantly, finding the balance between a weapon small enough to allow broad dispersion yet large and heavy enough to penetrate a building. Initially, American incendiary development borrowed heavily from British designs, designs tested and proved over a year and a half of retaliatory raids against German cities. The primary British unit evaluated by the Americans was the AN-M50 family of 4-pound bombs. Small and light, they burned from one and a half to six minutes depending on their filling and exhibited good penetrating characteristics. More importantly, they could be bundled into 500-pound clusters for more efficient loading in bomb bays. Although the Air Force ended housed in low, compact structures. Contrast this to modern-day New York, which, even with its tremendous vertical growth, only averages 26,557 people per square mile.[9] To prevent fires from growing or spreading, the locals needed to bring them under control, because the professional firefighters would find it difficult to efficiently respond. Even if a pumper truck arrived, the water system gave no guarantee of constant pressure, making the local groups' static storage basins the first line of defense. Periods of high demand created the greatest problem, sometimes completely crippling the system. Bombing compounded it further with bombs, even the incendiary bombs, breaking the underground pipes and severing the city's water supply.[10]

This critical flammability problem and the possibility of overwhelming the firefighting services did not escape the eyes of the men in Washington. Even as early as 1943 a list of cities and their weakness existed, with twenty cities analyzed in the Far East Target Section's report based on their importance to the war effort and vulnerability to incendiary attack. All cities of a population over 250,000 made the target list, with the exception of the cultural center of Kyoto, this while smaller cities, less susceptible to large fires because of their size, generally did not make the list, because "their small number of military objectives did not justify large-scale incendiary attack." By reviewing the list they compiled of major fires in Japan over the previous forty years, the authors determined that the period between December and May was the most advantageous for creating a conflagration of the type desired.[11]

The real value of the report comes from its analysis of the effects large-scale fires offered to defeating the Japanese war effort. It identified three direct and six indirect effects, pressing on the war economy from the top down and bottom up. The direct effects came from the destruction of industrial plants and military objectives, principally production facilities, military establishments, and storage facilities. The indirect effects came through disruption of the workers and economy in general through destruction of homes and consumer goods, necessitating migration and dislocation of the populace along with its associated reduction in morale, damage to transportation and public utilities, absorption of resources for reconstruction, and finally the actual killing of workers. While the packed residential areas most susceptible to fire did lay separate from the main industrial plants, they were adjacent to these targets and had small industries and storage facilities interwoven into them. This allowed the report to assert, "It seems reasonable to assume that the great majority of plants which are located in Zones I and II [the heavily industrial zones] are likely to be destroyed by conflagrations in these zones."[12] All told, incendiary attacks on the major Japanese cities conservatively meant a 30 percent production loss for the Japanese, one whose effects extended out four to six months. The churning of the Japanese economy at all levels and stages of production in some thirty-three missions equaled that possible through dozens more precision attacks. The added benefit of destroying homes and civilian goods and forcing the populace on the road to find replacements for these lost items raised the potential for revolution and overturning of the Japanese war government. Make no mistake, the true target remained war industries, particularly the smaller plants supplying parts to the larger industries, making the idea of torching a city palatable by the rationale of industrial destruction. The key discriminator in Europe between the British and U.S. bombing campaigns spilled over in the planning for the Pacific campaign; the United States would direct its might on the enemy's targets, not its people.

A year later, in February 1944, Eglin Field in Florida conducted tests similar to those at Dugway under direct orders from General Arnold. Arnold, who "seemed completely unaware of the Dugway tests," requested Eglin to "test out the various effects of various types of incendiaries with long and short delay fuses to determine the proper type of bombs to drop on Japanese urban objectives." The Eglin team informed Arnold of the previous tests at Dugway and proceeded with their own as ordered. Eighteen buildings of no particular resemblance to those in Japan lay under the onslaught of aimable clusters of M-69s. Again the results showed promise, starting intense fires on structures hit. The one important difference at Eglin versus Dugway came in the construction of different types of roofs, simulating those found on industrial buildings. The questions centered on the penetrating effects of the 6-pound M-69 against wood, concrete tile, and reinforced concrete. In results difficult to replicate in combat conditions, reputedly the incendiaries penetrated over 90 percent of the roofs they were likely to encounter in Japan. Actual field experience, however, showed concrete roofs particularly difficult for the small incendiary to puncture, even from altitude. The postwar survey of targets by the USSBS found that the 4-pound AN-M50 failed to penetrate more than five inches of concrete, averaging only one and a half inches per strike. Each of these impacts occurred on roofs of at least six inches, thus never breaking through into the flammable contents beneath. Even the 10-pound M74 showed no signs of penetrating a four-inch concrete roof. The favorite incendiary, the M-69, only made indentions on four-inch reinforced concrete and never got close to penetration.[13]

The attack on Pearl Harbor, catching the Americans unaware and thousands of miles away from the nearest Japanese, produced one good outcome—it bought time to plan. With the weapons needed to push the Japanese empire back transferring from the drawing board to the assembly line, the brightest minds in the country converged on Washington to lay out plans and decide which target systems warranted destruction and in what order. The group responsible for recommending strategic targets to hit was the Committee of Operations Analysts (COA). On the committee fell the responsibility to prioritize targets for destruction using the input of a variety of experts, including civilian industry leaders and service members from across the branches. It represented the best the United States had to offer in terms of ability and the first time the country made the "assimilation of industrial intelligence from all sources and analysis of that information for target selection."[14]

A natural preoccupation with German targets delayed work by the COA regarding Japan until mid-1943, when General Arnold sent a directive specifically requesting input on Japan. The request, received on March 23, 1943, directed the COA to survey the Japanese economy to determine targets that would undermine the war economy and ability to fight. The committee faced an uphill battle in terms of data collection. Unlike Germany, which remained open to foreign travel and trade until just before the outbreak of hostilities, Japan closed itself off as early as 1931, with strict censorship laws coming into force in 1937. This forced the committee to rely on tangential sources in their classification of Japanese industry. They looked to

Japanese-language publications, radio intercepts, and eyewitness accounts of those who had traveled and worked in Japan to paint a picture of industrial organization and importance. They also received support from Army A-2 (Intelligence), the Office of Economic Warfare, the Office of Strategic Services (oss), the Navy, the British government, and "other government departments and leaders in the field of industry."[15]

One other source of intelligence on the Japanese economy came in its known reliance on imports. Whether food or industrial raw materials, the Japanese made up for their sparse natural resources through overseas trade. Close to 20 percent of Japan's food supply came from other countries, including almost all the sugar and half the salt consumed by its people. The industrial materials presented a bleaker picture. For years before the war, and after hostilities began, Japan imported a third of its needed raw materials and all of its rubber, bauxite, and cotton. As one of the nations that traded with the Japanese, the United States knew the importance of shipping and of the potential for choking off the industry of the island nation.[16]

The initial report delivered to General Arnold on November 11, 1943, which he forwarded to the Joint Chiefs of Staff, gave as a primary objective for destruction not an industry, or even a land target, but shipping. Japan relied on imports to support its industries and feed its people; sinking the ships carrying those goods from the Dutch East Indies, South East Asia, and the Chinese mainland would cut off said industries and eliminate Japan's ability to make war. The report, to the chagrin of strategic-bombing proponents, discounted harbor installations and ship construction facilities as "not good economic targets." In the committee's opinion, concentrating efforts on the ships themselves offered the best way to slow the Japanese economy. Though not an industry, shipping was the bottleneck that strategic bombardment needed.[17]

How much of this conclusion came from war experience to date and how much stemmed from a pragmatic understanding of the United States' inability to bomb Japan anytime soon is hard to tell. Prescient, however, remains the immediate emphasis on Japan's weakness laying not in the factories or the raw materials plants but in its overseas sources. Without mentioning an air-dropped sea mining campaign that large bombers could support to aid the effort to blockade Japan, the report gives the first glimpse into the uniqueness of the Japanese war economy in relation to that of the United States, Germany, or the Air Corps Tactical School textbooks. Unlike Western economies, Japan lacked the natural resources and size to be self-sufficient. The process of importing goods, not the products they produced, constituted the choke point in Japan.

The most important target system the report identified was the steel industry, more specifically the coke ovens. The basis for ship-building, tanks, trucks, and a host of other needs, the steel industry enabled the Japanese war machine to produce the weapons faced on the myriad of islands throughout the Pacific. Their steel industry presented a "uniquely vulnerable" target due to the concentration of its coke ovens. Coke, the remnants of coal after being cooked in an oven where heat removes the gas and leaves only the carbon, is the key ingredient of steel manufacture, where it is used to transform iron ore into pig iron before further refining makes the iron into steel. Japan's largest coking capacity, providing 73 percent of the supply, fell into five plants—three on Kyushu, one in Manchuria, and one in Korea—all accessible to B-29s launched from China. Destruction of these plants would "deprive Japan of 66 per cent of her total steel production," a catastrophe that would "arrest the expansion of Japanese industry . . . [and] drastically curtail the present rate of war production."[18]

Listed third on the summary of target groups, with implied importance, came urban industrial areas. The committee's report focused its argument away from the unpalatable ideas of attacks on an urban populace outright or strictly against morale, choosing instead to concentrate on the broad industrial base found in the Japanese cites. Promulgating the pervasive belief in the importance of Japanese home-based industries, the report describes Japanese war production as "peculiarly vulnerable to incendiary attack of urban areas because of the widespread practice of subcontracting to small handicraft and domestic establishments." In the opinion of the COA, "many small houses in Japan are not merely places of residence, but workshops contributing to the production of war materials." In words that reach back to the tests done at Dugway and forward to future planning done in theater, the report presses that to do "maximum industrial disruption" ordnance must be dropped in a "magnitude sufficient to overwhelm the fire fighting resources of the area in question."[19] Burning individual targets fails to suffice; a conflagration is needed to eliminate all industry in a city, regardless of where it hides.

The importance of end products was not lost on the COA, though. Aircraft ranked fourth on the list. Air supremacy, especially in naval confrontations, made the air industry an end item that could not wait for destruction. The concentration of the industry also helped its ranking, as the destruction of thirteen plants would cause an esti-mated 70 percent drop in engine production, a 60 percent drop in operational-type aircraft production, and a 50 percent reduction in propeller production.[20] The war in both the Pacific and European theaters demonstrated the power of the airplane and made elimi-nation of the enemy's airpower, both on the battlefield and in pro-duction, a key to final victory.

The committee deemed the remaining specific industries too small, too spread out, or too saturated with excess capacity to warrant priority in their destruction. Attacking antifriction bearing plants offered an "early and pervasive effect throughout the Japanese war effort," but there were only six locations to hit. The steel production industry, not to be confused with crucial coke plants feeding it, was too dispersed and required too intense an effort to destroy. Besides, elimination of periphery industries like the coke ovens and shipping would eliminate its vitality. Aluminum, the true basis of aircraft production, was seen as underutilized and could not be influenced for several years. Industries otherwise crucial to an industrial war machine—petroleum installations, automobile factories, and rail-way transport—all ranked so low they only gained secondary impor-tance as targets.[21]

The COA's admitted crippling problem stemmed from a lack of current intelligence. Making a list of targets ostensibly important to all industrialized nations is easy, but determining actual impor-tance, size, and location requires data. The report emphasized the urgent need for photographic coverage of targets in view of the rapid changes in many parts of the Japanese industrial plant and the defects in currently accepted information.[22] This request fell on impotent ears though, since no planes operated over Japan at the time. Only once the B-29 started its flights did photography of Japanese cities become practicable.

The initial COA report makes one reference to tactics, an admonition that will play an important role in the way the 20th AF struck its targets. The report identified two principles needed to ensure the force of attacks achieved maximum results. The first was concentration on a target system to destroy it completely. It was paramount to choose a target system and focus all effort on it alone. This eliminates the working industry and the excess capacity available to fill that gap. Contrary to the beliefs of the planners, the Japanese did not use their entire industrial capacity in most industries, so any attacks needed to fully smash an industry to prevent recovery, exactly the methodology suggested by the COA.

The planners even believed, on the basis of prewar experience, that the Japanese heavy industry continued to expand, rapidly. The expansion added to the industry's ability to recover and added to any cushion already available. This pushed an emphasis on targets that checked further expansion, such as coke ovens and shipping. Eliminating the supply would render the plants empty and unproductive, a situation as good as bombed. To this same end, burning out the cities, with their small feeder industries and workers' homes, would also leave the main plants empty and unable to produce.

The second tactical principle followed the same idea as the first: speed and follow-up. Once a target came under the bomb bays of the Air Force the attack must be "pressed home." A delay in destroying a target system gave the Japanese time to rebuild or disperse remaining equipment. This point reveals a limitation of the COA's understanding of Japan as an industrialized nation. Experience would show the Japanese penchant for dispersal of industries, but recovery seemed absent from their vocabulary. Assuming that one industrialized nation acted like others, and seeing the incredible expansion of the U.S. economy or the resilience of the British populace to the Blitz, the COA expected the Japanese to put bombed targets back into production. What they did not know at the time was that "at no time during the war did Japan embark upon a large-scale bomb-damage repair program." Thanks to a lack of raw materials and building materials, as soon as the threat of heavy bombardment developed, the government moved to disperse the remaining industry rather than rebuild the damaged portions. But when viewed in terms of Japan as an industrial nation, it only seems natural to expect them to attempt to put damaged facilities back together and back online.[23]

The report closes with a statement that summarizes the entire strategic air war against Japan: "The timing of the war against Japan justifies attack upon industries lying relatively deep in the structure of war production. . . . [T]he most serious long-term damage can be inflicted by disrupting the production of basic materials like steel, which are essential to the manufacture of all military and naval equipment." The late start to the bombing campaign in relation to the beginning of the war meant going to the sources of supply and killing them off, the long way around to destroying an industry. The report could not provide a quantitative effect urban attacks would have, but referred to it as "very severe." The more detailed explanation of potential urban-area attack effects came on a map that listed urban industrial areas and the number of total and key targets on each. Beneath these numbers came an estimate of the tons of incendiaries required to destroy the city. Destruction of the city by fire would eliminate multiple named targets in one mission, greatly accelerating the efforts of the Air Force.[24]

The section listed twenty cities, their population and size, and the tons of incendiaries required to destroy them. The report couched the destruction in terms of disruption of the economy but found no way around pointing out the personal cost to the people living there. The same factors that would "inevitably disrupt the enemy effort at points so numerous as to constitute a major disaster" did so through destruction of public utilities and essential services, "absorption of man hours in repair and relief, dislocation of labor by casualty, homelessness and forced migration . . . [and] destruction of food and clothing supplies."[25]

Food especially presented a weakness of Japan, where "even prior to Pearl Harbor supplies of food in the Japanese islands were sufficiently low to produce sub-marginal nutrition of the populace." Attacking shipping, nitrogen fixation plants, and even the coke ovens that produced nitrogen by-products for fertilizer offered a chance to make an immediate effect on Japan's food supply and rationing. With an eye toward the ultimate, if unrealized at the time, goal of the 20th AF, the report concludes its section on food by referring to invasion: "The Japanese are undernourished. These factors give unusual importance to attacks upon food supply if an effective method of attack can be discovered."[26] In a lightly mechanized military like that of Japan the real fuel of defense was food, not oil, both for the military and eventually for the people who would bear the burden of personally defending their homeland. Incendiary bombing provided an immediate opportunity to clamp down on the Japanese food supply and begin the erosion of both the Japanese physical plant and the human ability to produce. Widespread fires would destroy the existing food stocks in an urban area, tying up labor and transportation to replace them and preoccupying the weakening survivors.

Arnold accepted the report, and its conclusions regarding incendiary attacks started to permeate his discussions of the forthcoming Japanese bombing campaign. He forwarded the report to the Joint Chiefs of Staff, who issued their own report two months later which paralleled the COA's findings. Of note, no reaction came from the civilian members of the government, either supporting or decrying the option. Not even President Roosevelt, whom Arnold briefed personally, voiced a recorded opinion. In a summary of the strategic air assault on Japan, Arnold spoke of the potential and ease of conducting a campaign of fire against Japanese cities, creating "uncontrollable conflagrations in each of them." He did preserve the morality of the campaign, though, noting that the "urban areas are profitable targets, not only because they are greatly congested, but because they contain numerous war industries."[27]

After submittal of their report the COA continued to research and meet to discuss new findings and plans. Informed that the Air Force planned to stage bombers for strikes against Japan first from Chengtu, China, and eventually Saipan in the Mariana Islands, the committee members focused their efforts two ways, looking at goals achievable from both bases. A memo of February 6, 1944, for the Assistant Chief of Air Staff, Plans, from one of the leaders of the COA, Col. Guido Perera, lists "Urban areas" as a primary target relegated after shipping, coke, and steel but before aircraft. The rationale placed a decided focus on the industrial potential of the areas through the destruction of their "essential public utilities and thousands of small plants, as well as a number of large plants."[28] Urban-area attacks meant a broad stroke of destruction for Japanese industry with the effects on the people in the firestorm no more noteworthy than those struck by stray high-explosive bombs. A COA targeting report of the same day summarized in detail the potential of fire-bombing Japanese cities, placing it in terms of a similar potential for German cities. Whereas German cities ranged in roof density coverage from 25 to 60 percent, Japanese cities averaged 50 to 80 percent. To this end, the report points out, "Tests have been conducted to determine the incendiary vulnerability of Japanese structures." This shows a clear link between the tests at Dugway and the COA planners in Washington. The COA knew that the conjecture and theory on flimsy Japanese cities had practical expression in the development and testing of the weapons required to do the job. Without noting the potential human cost, the report shows the ability to create "uncomfortable" conflagrations in twenty Japanese cities, fires that would undoubtedly wipe away homes and people just as easily as industry. The report defends this plan with the same emphasis on the profitability of the target areas due to their great congestion and "numerous war industries, large and small, particularly vulnerable to fire" which the primary COA report made.[29]

The report also provides a hint at potential tactics that could achieve the overall goals of the bombing of Japan, an interjection into the world normally left to the men in uniform. Daylight visual, night visual, and radar bombing are listed as potential tactics, with radar bombing the favored method thanks to improved radar on the B-29 and the coastal placement of Japanese cities and targets. No mention is made of low-altitude tactics or, more importantly, area bombing. All three methodologies listed incorporate a precision element, an aiming of the ordnance at a target. This leads to a belief that, as in Europe, even in an incendiary or area attack, a specific target would be chosen for destruction, with the surrounding area falling victim to the obvious overkill.

Throughout the winter of 1943–44, the first elements of what would become the 20th BC began assembling and training. Under the direction of the experienced procurement officer Maj. (later Lt.) Gen. Kenneth Wolfe, the B-29 had finished its development phase and was now entering service. Chronic problems and constant technical change orders slowed the training regimen, however, and led to an effort by the ground crews to update the planes and ready them for deployment which came to be known as the Battle of Kansas. By May 1944 that battle had ended, and planning of the implementation for an air war against Japan reached a fever pitch, with B-29's under General Wolfe assembling in India as a staging point for their impending move to Chinese bases. In Washington, the COA's efforts started to coalesce into specific operations in place of general plans. Working on plans for initial B-29 operations, Perera sent a memo on targets to Haywood Hansell, then chief of staff of the 20th AF. The first priority for the operations should be coke plants, with aircraft and radio-radar production as second priority. Third, starting in March 1945, when wind and weather conditions would be right, the "general attack on Japanese urban industrial areas should be initiated."[30] This memo is surprising and informative for two reasons. First, Perera describes the attacks LeMay made almost a year later. He uses the precepts of the COA report—attacking with maximum effort in a short period to fully eliminate the target—while giving an initial narrowing of the twenty urban-area targets down to nine. Already his list notes Yawata, Tobata, Wakamatsu, and Nagasaki as scheduled for test raids from China.

The second noteworthy element is its receipt by Hansell. As an author of precision-bombing doctrine, Hansell must have found the slow drift to area attack disturbing. Third on the list of targets appeared an industrial target, but one that explicitly came with the expectation of no precision element. While his command of the 21st BC lay in the future, Hansell knew the nature of the campaign well. After the war he acknowledged that he knew of planning for incendiary bombing. "Night incendiary attacks against Japanese urban industrial areas in 1945 were provisionally considered in the original plans for the employment of the XXIst," Hansell wrote thirty-five years later, "but such operations were to be undertaken only as a last resort, and only if precision bombing of selected targets proved infeasible or failed to bring about satisfactory results."[31] He persisted in wearing the blinders that kept him from seeing the fluidity of the situation and the distinct possibility that plans made in peace often retained little value once hostilities started. Perera offered a way out of the confines of limited target options with a plan based on the availability of a strike force ten months in the future and the results of test raids to validate operationally the vulnerability of Japanese structures found in proving-ground experiments.

While Hansell attended to the business of a growing air force, a conference convened at the Pentagon to determine incendiary bomb tonnages for attacks of Japanese cities. Their interest going beyond academics, they looked to find the incendiary tonnage needed to destroy a Japanese city, a number that translated to plane and mission requirements. Their initial perspective consisted of a desire to ignite a sufficient number of appliance fires to overwhelm the local authorities while also growing a fire into a full-scale conflagration, an uncontrollable living and breathing monster. To that extent, variables such as wind, precipitation, humidity, firefighting capability, existing fire breaks, accuracy of incendiary weapons, and possible supporting effects of high-explosive bombs all found inclusion in the discussion. The seriousness of planning for a campaign of urban-area attacks became evident as each of the existing twenty target cities and proposed density of bombs was evaluated and compared to supply a list of requirements with which to plan strikes.

On May 15, 1944, the AC/AS Intelligence Analysis Division submitted its "Estimation of Force Required to Neutralize a Selected List of Japanese Targets," which focused on the lynchpin industries of aircraft, antifriction bearings, synthetic oil, and others. While the estimation left urban areas off the list of specified targets evaluated, the basic assumptions used are informative regarding the mindset of Air Force planners of the time. Most important, bombing would be done from roughly 30,000 feet by planes flying in combat box formation. The uniform figure used for a bomb load of five tons reveals an understanding of the inefficiency of B-29s bombing from China or the Marianas. Five tons is half the B-29's full load, so the "Estimation" presumes that half the planes' striking power will be left on the ground at the start of the mission. The direct correlation between altitude and its fuel consumption versus practicable bomb load does not manifest itself in the estimates provided, all of which could be bettered if a lower altitude were chosen for the missions.

The "Estimation" also assumes that only high-explosive bombs will be used: "It is assumed that the commander in the field will prefer to determine the degree in which incendiary bombs may be substituted for or added to the estimated H.E. [high explosive] requirement."[32] Incendiaries remained on the table as an option, but not one in accordance with the prevailing doctrine, so not accounted for in the report. The bombing faction of the Air Force stuck close to its well-laid plan, precision.

The summer of 1944 saw the 20th BC of the 20th AF establish itself in India and begin staging for imminent attacks on Japan. In Washington, the pace of planning quickened accordingly. Colonel Perera outlined plans for phased attacks on Japanese targets in a memo to Col. (later Lt. Gen.) Richard Lindsay, the Air Force representative on the Joint War Plans Committee. Perera's plan envisioned a three-phase strategy that began in China but gained its true strength with the establishment of bases in the Marianas capable of reaching Honshu. In his list of target systems, which included urban industrial areas, the only priority given pertained to aircraft factories and the coke ovens. Destruction of the aircraft industry offered "the most effective means of reducing Japan's immediate frontline strength," a factor important to the Air Force's general goal of smoothing the road to Tokyo.[33] The long-term goal of destroying the Japanese war economy pivoted on the coke ovens, which would cripple the steel industry and by consequence every other major war industry.

The phases outlined corresponded to chronological periods and reflected the physical ability of the force to execute them. Phase I lasted from June 1944 to February 1, 1945, and focused on the priority targets of airplanes and coke plants already mentioned. Phase II, from February 1945 to May 1, 1945, kept the pressure on aircraft and coke, preventing recovery, and opened the list to the target systems of radio and radar equipment, antifriction bearings, petroleum products, and urban industrial areas. Phase III, from May 1, 1945, onward, continued against aircraft, coke, and petroleum under the belief that these industries would still be viable and crucial enough to warrant attack while the rest of the systems would be destroyed or dispersed beyond further effectiveness as targets.

The great miscalculation made by Perera hinged on the weather's role in these operations. Basing his beliefs on average conditions over the previous ten years, he thought that for Phases I and II "weather will not be a limiting factor in the accomplishment of the program outlined."[34] For a program dependent on high-altitude precision strikes, reality interjected strikingly on the bombers in the form of clouds and high winds. The inability to see the targets frustrated Perera's plans, making them wishful thinking.

The expectation of incendiary raids on urban industrial areas in Phase II boiled down to two factors. First, the weather in March would be "somewhat more favorable for operations of this nature," justifying the allocation of the whole month's worth of sorties to the endeavor. Second, this satisfied the COA's tactic maxim number two, a concentration of force over time on the system to smash it fully. Perera felt that incendiary attacks could not be completed successfully without a sufficient number of planes and incendiaries to overwhelm a target and its civil services. Only starting in March were enough planes expected to be in the Marianas to carry out such a plan.

His advocacy of burning down the urban industrial areas did not yet possess quantitative justification, though, as he admits, "precise economic effects of the destruction of the listed urban areas cannot be stated." In fact, European experience points to minimal possible effects, not a compelling argument considering the scientific exactness of the Air Force precision-bombing doctrine. The large "but" in this argument turns on the persistent belief that there were "thousands of small home enterprises furnishing semi-finished and finished parts" to the larger industry. All these would disappear in the flames, with an added bonus of housing and public services experiencing upheaval. While the effects defied quantification, the quality of destruction and chaos showed a value all its own, validating its existence as an industrial target.[35]

As mentioned before, the OSS provided inputs to the COA that helped guide their thought and decision making. One document that helped reinforce the belief in focusing on home-based industries came in June 1944 from the Research and Analysis Branch titled "Japanese Small-Scale Factories in Relation to Air Bombardment." The summary, based on available statistics, divided Japanese industrial establishments into two categories: handicraft enterprises with fewer than five workers, and factories employing more than five workers. By the oss's estimate, roughly half of all Japanese workers fell in the first category, working in small local establishments. More important, the oss believed that of the remaining 50 percent of workers, half worked in factories employing between five and thirty workers. This meant that only 25 percent of Japanese industrial workers went to the large factories that the Air Force planners expected to form the lynchpins of the industrial society. With most of the production done in small buildings interspersed throughout the city, a new, broad strategy would be required to destroy the war-making ability of the Japanese.

The oss summary pointed out a noteworthy distinction between Japanese industry and the archetype used by the prewar strategists of airpower, America. Japanese industry, even in situations normally seen as large-scale operations like metals, machinery, and chemicals, seemed "heavily weighted with small-scale factories." Plants with fewer than five workers comprised 75 percent of the metal industry, 60 percent of the machinery and tools manufacture, and an overwhelming 84 percent of the lumber industry. With plants this small, the size of the B-29, or any other heavy bomber, made it overkill to send a fleet after one of these targets, and the number of sorties required to destroy each would run long past a potential invasion date. Also, this all assumed that these factories could be identified in the crowded confines of the city, a task impossible without target photos that did not yet exist.

An important distinction the oss did make concerned the concentration of these small industries as it related to the overall size of the city. It believed large cities such as Tokyo, Nagoya, and Osaka housed small industries as 70 percent of their total industrial base. Yokosuka, Kure, and Fukuoka used it as 80 percent of their base, but even then it was "considerably less important in the large urban centers." This sharp distinction was made because the big cities also contained the massive aircraft and engine plants that did the final assembly and production. The oss believed that in Tokyo and Nagoya, for instance, 15 to 20 percent of all manufacturing workers worked in "establishments so small in size that they can hardly be distinguished from dwelling units." The randomness of their location made striking them precisely nearly impossible, but "fire would probably account for many [of them]."[36]

This also meant that smaller cities relied on home-sized industries for more than 80 percent of their productive output, so any given small city essentially formed a giant urban industrial target making no distinction between the living and working spaces of its population. More damning, according to the oss's estimation, these "small-scale units very often serve as feeder plants and parts-manufacturers to large factories," including aircraft, machinery, and ordnance producers. Destruction of these sources for the large factories could be just as crucial to stopping the Japanese as bombing the main factories themselves. One attack stopped future production, while the other destroyed stock in production on the ground and prevented dispersal and reorganization. At the very least, the summary concluded, destruction of the home industries "might well cause economic dislocation out of proportion to their absolute role in production."[37] Even if striking the urban areas did not hurt the war effort on the battlefield, the chaos and damage to morale might make the costs worthwhile.

On June 5, 1944, the Chinese campaign began with a practice attack launched from the home bases in Kharagur, India, against rail yards near Bangkok, Thailand. Seventeen of the ninety-eight aircraft that took off aborted with mechanical difficulties before reaching the target, while weather and inexperience conspired to allow little destruction of the target. The next mission, the first by the Air Force against the home islands of Japan since Jimmy Doolittle flew more than two years prior, ran on June 15 against the Yawata coke ovens, the prime target in Japan both for the 20th BC and the steel industry as a whole. Destruction of the ovens, an extraordinarily weak link in the steel industry as a whole given their limited number and long rebuilding time, looked to validate the efforts of the COA. Instead, the mission produced few hits on the target area, had many mechanical troubles, and highlighted a persistent inability of the crews to maintain formation over the target: a total failure. For an Air Force with two years' experience in strategic bombing, the most advanced planes on the planet, and finally under its own command, the mission was a disaster, the exact opposite of what it was supposed to be.

Half a month later, on July 7, eighteen planes struck the Sasebo/Omura/Tobata area spreading bombs over the dockyards/arsenal, aircraft factory, and steelworks. A relatively successful strike against the coke ovens in Anshan, Manchuria, followed at the end of the month. Seventy-two planes left Chengtu, with sixty bombing the coke ovens in formation from 25,000 feet. In a sad commentary on the early operations of the B-29, each plane carried only eight 500-pound bombs, 20 percent of the plane's designed load. The range to target and fuel considerations forced the reduction in ordnance, highlighting the issues with crew training and fuel conservation that had limited the plane's capability since introduction. Twelve days later the 20th BC split its forces and went after two targets. Fifty-four headed for the oil refineries of Palembang, Sumatra, while twenty-nine raided the urban areas of Nagasaki. Twenty-four planes dropped fifty-three tons of incendiaries on a city recently dusted by a drizzling rain. The wet conditions and the prearranged plans rigidly followed by both police and the citizenry functioned well, and no conflagration started. According to the USSBS after the war, the "damage, direct or indirect, to industrial production may be assessed as nil," a condition readily evident from post-strike photography showing no smoking hole in the city.[38] In its first test, firebombing Japan failed.

The next two missions, on August 20 and September 8, both returned to steel, hitting the coke ovens at Yawata and Anshan, respectively, again. The Anshan attack went well, with ninety planes (83 percent of those airborne) bombing against minimal resistance, with light losses, and doing considerable damage. The return to Yawata did not fare as well. Seventy-one planes (80 percent of those airborne) struck the coke ovens in two waves. Intense flak and heavy losses offered as a poor return on investment two hits and no serious damage to the ovens or the Japanese steel-making ability.

The pace of operations (two missions a month) and the limited accuracy the 20th BC gave little hope to the 20th AF commanders in Washington. To kick-start the operation, Arnold ordered a change of command for the 20th BC, replacing the logistician Wolfe with a hard-driving navigator named Gen. Curtis LeMay. LeMay carried a reputation to China. A trusted navigator before the war responsible for guiding Air Corps planes on various publicity missions, he gained a tough-as-nails reputation in the bombing campaign over Europe. A stern taskmaster, LeMay looked past the fear and long odds to refine tactics and press his men toward accuracy and survival. He initiated such tactical advancements as longer and straighter bomb runs to better allow the bombardier to aim at the target, and the combat box formation, which gave each plane in a flight mutual protection from fighters. In Europe, LeMay's planes hit targets and brought their crews home, achievements that gained respect from those below and above him in the chain of command. He took command of the 20th BC on August 29 and immediately found "a pretty desperate situation."[39] The logistics, maintenance, and crew issues all combined to convince him of the futility of the operation, but he soldiered on, implementing fixes in lead crew training and maintenance that later paid dividends in the Marianas. In hindsight, his presence in China appears more as a warmup and familiarization with B-29 operations than a truly sincere effort of making Chinese operations viable. If anyone could accomplish the task, LeMay could, but no amount of effort or skill could counter the physical reality that China was the wrong place for B-29s.

• • •

At the beginning of August, Colonel Perera wrote to Colonel Lindsay regarding charts shown to him about employment of the B-29. One of his suggestions for modifying the employment plans stands out as peculiar. He refers to the plans briefed as including China-based bombers attacking urban areas as early as August 1944, with a period of downtime before continuing in strength again in February. His objections to this plan were twofold. First, using European experience as a basis, he did not see the economic consequences justifying the effort. Worse, he indicated, the attacks were directed more for "psychological effects" than a specific economic consequence. His second objection centered on a matter of priority and economy of force. Using the limited bombers in hand, he argued, to destroy precision targets systems gave the force time to build up for a concentrated attack. Remember, earlier in the summer Perera supported incendiary attacks in March 1945. Here he provides additional rationale for that time frame. In accord with the previous admonitions of the COA, success necessitated a concentration of force on a particular target system. Not until the March time frame would enough planes be available to saturate in fire not only one city but a series of the most important cities.

On August 29, Fowler Hamilton, founding COA member and representative of the Board of Economic Warfare, updated Colonel Perera on the work of the incendiary staff. The staff worked for the Joint Incendiary Committee (aka the Incendiary Subcommittee of the COA), tasked with determining the vulnerability of Japanese cities to fire, scoping the forces needed, ordnance requirements, and time schedule for burning down the six major cities of the country. Hamilton introduced the assessment of a 15–20 percent loss in Japanese industry with the destruction by fire of the six largest cities in Japan. Recoverability played the crucial role; if the Japanese acted with the resiliency of the British and Germans the damage estimates hovered at 15 percent, but if the damage overwhelmed the Japanese there was a "possibility that social disintegration and terror may produce a national catastrophe." Any effects, though, came only if the destruction occurred in short order to prevent recovery and dispersal efforts. Hamilton estimated, uselessly he admits, a need for twenty-five hundred sorties to achieve the destruction. For six cities this called for more than four hundred planes hitting each municipality, a number far beyond the 20th BC's capability or any planned capability in the near term for the forming 21st BC.[40]

The same day, Perera wrote a longer note to Colonel Lindsay to give him status on the studies of incendiary attacks. Using only preliminary data from the subcommittee dedicated to urban areas, Perera felt confident in stating that burning down the six major (unnamed) cities of Japan offered the chance to harm 30 percent of Japan's overall industry, 32 percent of its workers, and 48 percent of the priority industries. He used Hamilton's number of 15 percent loss of production for one year as the ultimate result. This estimation included the absenteeism losses the industries faced after the social disruption of the conflagrations. For the cost of thirty-five hundred tons of incendiaries, Perera argued, the Air Force could make up for the three years of immunity experienced by the Japanese. Urban industrial areas did "warrant inclusion in the present strategic bombardment program" assuming the estimates held up in combat experience. Success did not come without a price, though, as one of the first Japanese casualty estimates emerged in Perera's memo. Estimates pointed to successful attacks destroying 70 percent of the houses in the six major cities and killing 560,000 people.[41] For the first time, the magnitude of the destruction possible possessed a number and a face. To stop 15 percent of the Japanese economy in a couple of weeks' worth of attacks, was it appropriate to kill a half a million people? This was a question that needed to be answered by people higher than Lindsay or Perera before the first plane left the ground.

By September the list of cities worth firebombing had been further refined and codified: Tokyo, Kawasaki, Yokohama, Osaka, Kobe, and Nagoya. In addition to narrowing the focus of incendiary attacks, the COA report "Economic Effects of Successful Area Attacks on Six Japanese Cities" fulfilled a more important task that had eluded previous talk of incendiary attacks: it finally officially quantified the destruction and effect these raids would produce. By attacking these six cities, the report asserts, 15 percent of a year's manufacturing output in Japan would be lost, 20 percent if one only refers to major war industries. Finally, those weighing the options on how to strike Japan possessed a real assessment of the capability of urban industrial raids.

This destruction equated to man-months of labor lost, more than that lost to an equivalent tonnage of high-explosive bombs placed on precision targets. More important, it was believed that area attacks would augment the precision strikes by making the recovery more difficult. The expected "substantial damage" to the machine tool industry would not only hurt that industry but "impose . . . an enormous replacement burden" on other industries. The plants struck by precision bombs might rebuild their physical plant, but replacing the equipment and tooling inside would be a futile effort after the tool industry in the urban areas went up in smoke.

The unfortunate shortcoming identified in this plan pertained to the end item effects, the material shortages that would influence the

Japanese forces already engaged in combat. The tardiness of bombing industries in the war and the "apparent existence of considerable stocks of aircraft components and of excess manufacturing capacity in tanks and trucks would probably prevent substantial reduction in final output."[42] Even the blunt instrument of area bombing offered no effects on the battles occurring throughout the Far East. Strategic bombing offered a long-term solution to an increasingly short-term problem in the Pacific that promised to end on the shores of the Japanese home islands.

The COA continued to meet to discuss findings, address issues, and refine strategy. Gen. Lauris Norstad, the recent replacement of Hansell as chief of staff of the 20th AF after the latter took command of the 21st BC headed to the Marianas, attended the COA meeting on September 10. Only an issue of the greatest importance would draw the de facto head of the 20th AF to cross over the line and personally engage the civilian planning advisers. After eight missions (four of which had gone to Japan) by the 20th BC, Norstad wanted a change. The accuracy of the missions carried out at altitude against the coke ovens with bombing by visual means warranted only one description: miserable. He spoke up quickly, "I am not happy about the present target systems." Referring to trying a different system, he continued, "I would rather make a mistake on this one mission than to go blindly and stubbornly along this one target system."[43] The raid on the Yawata Steel Works' coke ovens on June 15 especially galled him and turned him away from coke as a viable target system. Sixty-eight B-29s took off from Chengtu, with only forty-seven striking the ovens, scoring zero hits. For the amount of effort expended to bring the B-29 and 20th AF into being, failure at any point was not an option. Massive failure risked everyone's future. Loyal to Arnold, Norstad realized the implications of failing to destroy Japanese targets and the failure to exert the capabilities of an independent Air Force.

Norstad offered aircraft factories as an alternative, but he left the decision to the committee. Before leaving the meeting he made an observation based on lessons learned in Europe: "The reason we ask that this committee be reconstituted is that there was about a month or six weeks in which we might have changed our targets in Europe and I think the effect would have been tremendous if we had shifted at that time." The right targets mattered more in Japan for two reasons. One was the obvious issue of time. The European bombing campaign went on for almost two years before the first Allied boot hit the dirt of France, and in Japan the planned invasion, Operation Downfall, was scheduled for a year away. If the Air Force strategic-bombing arm would have any effect on the war, it needed to act decisively now. Second, Norstad knew the ambitions of General Arnold and the Air Force to gain its independence from the Army after the war. The cornerstone of the Air Force's uniqueness rested on strategic bombing, and the 20th AF offered the first chance for an independent Air Force to demonstrate the decisive result it promised. Norstad continued by admitting the myriad of factors, political and economic, that limited the European campaign, but insisting that "it is more important here that we are on the right track than it ever was in the UK or in the Mediterranean."[44] General Arnold and the future of the Air Force required success by the 20th AF out of the box. Any delay threatened to end the operational test and turn control of the B-29 over to theater commanders.

Stunned by the turn of events, the members continued the meeting looking at one another for ideas. The first suggestion made, the first thing that came to mind in terms of decisive target systems, came from the OSS member, Edward Mason: "Another system we have always talked about and never come to any firm conclusions on is the urban industrial areas business. What is the status of that?"[45] Colonel Perera then recounted the work of a Lieutenant Hitch from the Navy, who did the economic analysis, and Dr. Ewell, who compiled the force requirements. Echoing the facts contained in the memos he circulated in the preceding month, Perera referred to the 20 percent of industrial production believed removed by incendiary attacks, referring to it as "an important target system" because 20 percent of an economy is "something." The effects would not diminish the front-line strength of the military, but it would cut out the middle of the economy, destroying the productive capacity in the long term. Perera made clear the same proviso still applied of maximization of force, and to answer speculation on the plan there should be an experimental raid to confirm the assessments made by the planners.[46]

The meeting then reviewed the other target systems for their suitability for promotion, but found all wanting. Alumina (aluminum oxide), a component of aluminum refining, lacked the shipping to supply the industry, leaving it with too much excess capacity. Ordnance suffered from a lack of intelligence to show its vulnerability. Shipping, coal, and antifriction bearings all fell by the way too. Only coke (still), aircraft, urban areas, synthetic oil, and (despite its disadvantages) alumina survived the discussion. The disappointing truth behind this list was that only coke sat in range of planes from China; the rest of the targets needed to wait until the 21st BC began operations from the Central Pacific.

The committee reconvened three days later to discuss more options. Members noted additional disadvantages to the two most popular targets, coke and aircraft. Col. John F. Turner from Air Force A-2 gave hope in his assessment that the bulk of the aircraft targets were concentrated in the Osaka-Nagoya-Tokyo area, but a stark lack of intelligence made the data hollow. Eminent committee member Fowler Hamilton admitted fault in the estimates and importance of the coke industry. He dourly summarized the situation by stating that it was "apparent that little damage can be done by bombing of coke ovens in Japan because there is clearly an excess capacity even greater than the large excess for the Empire as a whole."[47]

The bad news continued regarding the other systems. Further consideration revealed alumina's increasingly limited utility thanks to the Japanese accessing their indigenous shale deposits to offset shipping losses. The mistaken assumption that synthetic oil played as crucial a role in Japan as it did in Germany allowed Perera to assert that one-fifth of Japan's oil came from the industry. Not only did this prove completely false (the Japanese never developed a synthetic oil industry worth a damn), but the refineries tended to be on the east side of Honshu, well out of range of current bases. If oil emerged as the new target of choice, the oil fields and refining capacity in the Dutch East Indies appeared more desirable than any target in Japan.

Lieutenant Hitch then gave a presentation on his findings regarding the potential effects of attacking urban industrial areas. He emphasized the timetable involved in urban-area attacks, noting that "no attacks that could be made on cities within range would be more than a pinprick into the Japanese economy."[48] To this end, an experiment took precedence to confirm the effectiveness of the incendiaries available on Japanese cities. Continued tests in the United States showed promise, but no one knew for sure how an actual city would fare against the onslaught. The group agreed on only a single test, though, not wanting to tip off the Japanese to the potential change in tactics.

Hitch confirmed the assessment that these attacks could cause 15 percent total manufacturing loss for a year, an amount he termed "a lot." The aircraft industry stood to lose 20 percent of a year's output owing to the many feeder industries located in the urban areas that would fall victim to the flames. Again, the cushion in the industry, this time in terms of a believed stockpile of excess parts, prompted to him to caution the effects on the aircraft industry as "less important than it appears."[49]

The real issue before the planners of the offensive against Japan, then, was what kind of war did they wanted to conduct. In Hitch's opinion, the urban-area attacks did not offer the chance to remove front-line strength in a timely manner. If invasion topped the list of endgames for the war in the Pacific, burning down cities might not offer the best-value option. On the other hand, if attrition was the order of the day, incendiary raids represented the ultimate in siege weapons. The Bureau of Naval Ordnance representative with the committee, Cdr. Francis Bitter, spoke up to assuage these concerns. While nobody in the room revealed himself privy to the overall plan for ending the war in Japan, invasion did not rest far from their minds. Calling the 15–20 percent estimate "conservative," Bitter saw the potential positive effects area raids offered to invading armies, "the confusion resulting from burning these cities . . . might be decisive at that point."[50] Hitch agreed. The September 13 meeting was a turning point in the high-level planning of the campaign. Not only did the previous target choices start to fall by the wayside, especially coke, but urban-area attacks took on a new level of importance. The COA began to see the practical value of widespread destruction in the cities of Japan, a concept not given much credence up to this point.

The committee reconvened the next day, September 14, to continue their discussion on potential alternative targets. Narrowing their focus to the next two strikes by the 20th BC, Elihu Root Jr., lawyer and son of the former secretary of state Elihu Root, found it difficult to make a firm suggestion, settling on steel or urban areas. One problem facing the committee at this point was the limited range of the B-29s based in China. Viable target systems came up in discussion, but they often fell out of range of the 20th BC planes, which could only reach Kyushu.

Before making a recommendation, the members wished to know the type of war they were fighting. What did the military see as the endgame? Whether the United States planned on invading Japan to force its surrender or blockade Japan to capitulation made a difference in which industries warranted destruction. Ground operations on the home islands did not offer a strong possibility anytime soon, but airpower could single-handedly win the war, as theorists believed, and urban attacks offered a quick way to push the Japanese economy and society over the edge. As of September 14 the COA believed the war against Japan would stretch into 1946 and consist of additional ground campaigns, not necessarily in Japan itself. Regardless, the fifteen-plus months left in the war allowed plenty of time to destroy specific industries, like aircraft, with precision. First the most powerful cards needed to be played, the ones that could push Japan as a nation over the edge.

With this in mind, Mason seconded Root's suggestion of urban raids. He attributed to urban raids the ability to "reduce substantially overall industrial output, distributed over a whole range of items and tremendous property destruction, loss of life and disorganization of the economy and society." This disorganization piqued the interest of Colonel McCormack, who believed that "there is considerable unrest in Japan and the government has insecure tenure."[51] This erroneous assumption, based on viewing the world through glasses that only ever saw the American way of life, gave a big boost to urban-area attacks. The disorganization and privation the raids created would push the teetering Japanese over the edge to revolution, regime change, and suing for peace. Little did McCormack or any of the others realize that the Japanese people held none of the power and influenced none of the decisions regarding their country's involvement in the war.

The group settled on requesting one test raid to gauge the destructive power of urban incendiary attacks. The timing for the test created additional discussion owing to the immediate need for data to analyze and use as a basis for tactical alterations, against a contention for the limited resources of the China-based bombers. Believing that the 21st BC planned on operational readiness from the Marianas by the end of the year, having the test data now provided just enough time to be ready for their availability to enter combat and spread the campaign to the whole of Japan.

Nearly two weeks later, on September 27, the COA met again and continued their debate over priority and viability of target systems. Again, systems fell by the wayside for one reason or another. Intelligence based on the newer maker's plates on downed aircraft engines pointed to the production cushion in the industry shrinking, yet again, a lack of photo intelligence made the believed numbers of plants and production only rough estimates, not enough on which to base a strategy. They saw electronic components as highly concentrated, especially the tungsten filament production, but with their limited use of already poor radar, what difference would its destruction make?

Attacking food production, a questionable choice in humanitarian terms, took too long to take effect. Elimination of the nitrogen plants generating fertilizer would take up to two years to be felt at the consumer level enough to affect productivity. Japan was a heavily agrarian nation, so its food production, processing, and storage largely occurred in the rural areas, making for poor bombing targets. Destruction of shipping helped deny chemicals for fertilizer, reducing the effectiveness of the agriculture and obviating the need for direct attack on food production, but would take several growing seasons before curtailing food production.

In the same vein, attacks on the chemical industry in general took a long time to flow through the economy and affect the people. The real weaknesses of the chemical industry came from two sources. The obvious one started with supplies of raw materials. A dwindling amount of shipping especially affected the coal and salt imports from the Asian mainland, vital inputs to the chemical industry. Pressure on shipping not only destroyed supplies as they arrived in Japan but transferred the pain to the railroad industry, which needed to carry the tonnage that coastal shipping could no longer safely handle.

The second weakness resulted from the wearing out of equipment at the chemical plants. Again, the lack of raw materials did not allow maintenance of the equipment that deteriorated from the effects of chemical exposure. This proved deadly to an industry already teetering on the edge of insignificance compared with the U.S. chemical output. Outdated processes, its small size, and a lack of expansion as the war progressed stymied the Japanese chemical industry. The USSBS, which reviewed each chemical used by the Japanese in the war, picked ammonium sulfate as a perfect example of the limitation of the industry. Used as a fertilizer, early in the war the Japanese produced 1.5 times the amount the United States produced. By the end of the war the Japanese only managed to generate 7 percent of their prewar level because of the divergence of the ammonia to the production of nitric acid for explosives. The best example of the inefficiency and small size of the Japanese chemical industry came in the manufacture of explosives. To make a batch of Tetryl explosive took the American process 2.25 hours, or 67 man-hours per ton produced; in Japan the same process took 32 hours, or 1,178 man-hours per ton produced. In a more shocking example, "The efforts of about 3,000 men for two years in the Fukaya area resulted in the production of smokeless powder equivalent only to that from *one* United States production line for *twelve days*, or of *one* of our large plants for *two* days." The Japanese chemical industry practically took itself out of the war.[52]

Even though the bulk of the Japanese chemical industry was concentrated in a 105-mile radius on the seacoasts of western Honshu, northern Kyushu, and Shikoku, it lay amid the urban areas or part of industrial complexes. Thus it offered a perfect example of the associated industries in urban areas that would fall victim to a large fire, and did not warrant specific attack despite its geographic concentration.

Electrical power, the literal and figurative source of energy for an industrialized economy and favorite of early strategic-bombing theorists, made a terrible target in Japan. The country operated primarily on hydroelectric power from more than thirteen hundred dams far from the cities, dams that converted the melting runoff to power. In times of peak use or low water levels, steam plants supplemented the power grid. The committee realized the futility of this task quickly. The dams sat all over the country in unknown locations, and the steam plants required precise hits to destroy their generators. This only warranted action if the margin between capability and need were close in the industry, and the committee had no way to know. Their belief in an expanding Japanese economy suggested little margin, but how to actually identify and hit the primary source of the power, the dams? After the war the USSBS summarized the futility of this plan: "Had a successful attack been made on the 50 largest generating stations, 16 of which are steam-electric stations . . . would have reduced the electric energy supply only 30 percent."[53] This reinforces a rather shocking fact: Japan's power came from far outside the cities, eschewing the Western dependence on generating plants. To curtail the industry only 30 percent, the B-29s needed to blow thirty-four dams. A quick survey of RAF Bomber Command would show dam busting as a tricky art.

Ground transportation, principally trains and the Shimonoseki Tunnel connecting Honshu to Kyushu, gained the same priority it did in Europe: low. Bombing the transportation network was more of a tactical necessity than a strategic requirement and thus was saved for just before an invasion to disrupt the movement of troops to the front rather than goods to and from factories. Trucks remained unattractive, and precision measuring instruments and abrasives remained a mystery. The fact remained, Japan did not possess real industrial targets of importance, which made strategic bombing extremely difficult.

The conversation swung to urban areas again. Armed with more information, Lieutenant Hitch reiterated his belief that attacks on six key cities would reduce the manufactured output 15 percent across the board. He added a more practical statistic, saying that in an incomplete study of the target areas, his people located 320 "important plants." In Tokyo, two-thirds of the two thousand plant names provided by military intelligence fell within the target area. (Apparently, not all these plants warranted the moniker "important," so this number does not relate back directly to his earlier assertion.) Out of the one hundred most important plants, forty-two sat in the fire zones.[54] Not allowing his case to seem too strong, Hitch cautioned that not all the plants may be vulnerable to fire, so the total losses may dip to as low as 11 percent. More important in light of future events, he asserted that according to employment statistics, only the six cities offered a good return on investment in urban-area attacks. The concentration of Japanese industry and the industrial base within these major cities made the rest of the country a collection of intermittent towns rather than an industrialized nation.

Evidence suggested to Hitch and his team that general-purpose machine tools would bear the brunt of the damage from area raids, suffering from eight months to a year's worth of losses if the attacks occurred successfully. Here he makes an important observation: "The evidence is the Japanese engineering industry as a whole is working on a one-shift basis." This confirms the suspicion of an underutilized Japanese economy. By only working one shift, the Japanese left one-half to two-thirds of their productive ability idle on the floor at night. Loss of one plant could be compensated for by starting a second shift at a standing factory producing the same product. Unknown to the planners, though, the Japanese never experimented seriously with two-shift labor until 1944, and at that point they started to abandon it because of reasons other than a lack of personnel. As the USSBS report on utilization of manpower points out, the allusion to labor shortage was frequently used to cover up the failure to skillfully use available labor or as a substitute for "shortage of skilled labor." The draft sucked up eligible males, regardless of their importance to the war economy, and deprived the industries the much needed skilled workers. Food and housing shortages and even difficulty concealing illumination at night also contributed to their inability to implement a multishift system, the system that proved so crucial to the American industrial might. Knowing of the single-shift plan used by the Japanese, the planners in Washington easily fell under the belief in a cushion in the Japanese economy, but this impression did not reveal the overall weakness in the structure that prevented the Japanese from utilizing their excess capacity.[55]

The presentation on urban-area attacks wrapped up with speculation regarding the social issues created by mass incendiary raids. In the blunt phrasing of Colonel Burgess, "Would bedlam be created?"

A concentration of attacks over a short period raised the possibility of overwhelming the administrative functions of Japan, not an immaterial issue for the paperwork-minded Japanese, and undermine the control of the leadership. Commander McGovern stepped into the conversation at this point. "If we lose records, our factories can go on," he told the meeting. "Once you lose your records in Japan, factories will be in pandemonium, they are so accustomed to taking written orders with serial numbers."[56] This meant that even though the factory producing a weapon escaped destruction, its production suffered if records related to its work burned in the fire. Mass confusion on an administrative/industrial level achieved the same goal as the bombs themselves: stopping production.

McGovern advocated "going all out" because of the psychological factors involved and the Japanese propensity for panic. He explained how while the Japanese in uniform showed no fear in the face of enemy fire, the Japanese as a whole were prone to panic and pandemonium in a crisis. Fire especially frightened them from childhood, and confronting a conflagration like the one the committee proposed created the potential for it to "explode in their psychological center, [where] you will be able to get mass panic in and out of your cities."[57] This placed McGovern squarely in the camp of waiting until a concentration of force existed before attacking the six cities in quick succession. As the resident expert on Japanese morale, he pushed the element of panic, even going as far to suggest warning Tokyo of a raid and following through hard to exult it over the Japanese people.

The belief, expressed by Commander McGovern, of the primacy of Tokyo in the Japanese mind-set also played into the value of attacking Tokyo in a devastating and memorable manner. "Knock out Tokyo and the Japanese throughout the country would say, we have been hit," he told them. Referring to the people's opinion of their government, he said that "after two or three panics in the Tokyo area, you would get the attitude among the people: turn this group out."[58] The Japanese appeared as dominos waiting to fall on themselves if bombing in the appropriate place occurred.

The next day's meeting proceeded along the same lines. Numerous possibilities for targets were raised with no definitive decisions arising. Colonel Turner finally spoke the words no Air Force personnel wanted to hear, but did not deny: "I can see no more profitable employment of the B-29 from Chengtu then [sic] in tactical operations."[59] No greater blow to the hopes of the 20th AF was possible. The whole point of independence in the short term meant keeping the very heavy bombers out of the tactical arena and proving the utility of uninterrupted strategic bombing. Failure in China struck a blow at that theory, though not a fatal one. From the start, basing bombers in China came more from political and chronological necessity than expected results. Colonel Turner's comment read the writing that had been on the wall for a while. The real future lay in the Marianas, so now the real pressure rested on the COA and Air Force to plan these missions properly and make strategic bombing work.

After dropping the bomb regarding the utility of China-based bombers, Turner went on to say what others feared to admit: "We all feel a little sadistic about it but I would look forward to a great deal of pressure seeing a great deal of effort of incendiary attacks of the six Japanese cities." The grasping at other target systems had taken its toll on the group. Regardless of which other industry they mentioned—electronics to affect radar and antiaircraft fire, aircraft plants out of range of Chinese bases, or steel and the coke ovens they failed to hit accurately—all suffered from a dearth of (photographic) intelligence or concentration. So with some hemming and hawing even Dr. Edward Earle, a historian from the Princeton Institute for Advanced Study and one of the most distinguished members of the COA, admitted he placed "disaster attacks higher than anybody in the room."[60] Options ran short, and the one option that kept emerging and carried with it a reasonable possibility of success involved massive incendiary bombing.

One of the last meetings of the COA regarding operations in Japan took place on October 2. The target list came full circle as again shipping took center stage. This time a real solution emerged: mining the seas. Mining destroyed ships, cut off raw materials to industries, and supported Allied operations in real time by curtailing outgoing reinforcements. The limited amount of Japanese technology inhibited their ability to defend against mines, giving the underwater weapons a high probability for success. The low risk to planes and ease of aiming mines made this an ideal mission for the B-29s. The only draw-back was that this was not the mission the Air Force intended for the B-29, as it did not involve bombing anything specifically. Choosing mining missions over precision strikes or even area attacks relegated the B-29 to a job normally left to the Navy. Like the Japanese merchant fleet, the future of an independent Air Force was at risk of being sunk by mines.

It was the COA meeting of September 28 that had gone a long way in narrowing the problem of strategic bombing of Japan. With planes in the field and another year of analysis under their belts, the COA team focused on a series of conclusions that drew the blueprint and forecast the ultimate end of the Japanese war. In his survey of the development of the American air arm, *The Rise of American Air Power*, Michael Sherry assigns to the civilian advisers and experts the credit for "refining the means of waging war by settling straightforward problems." That is to say, they looked past the political considerations and saw the "air war less as a strategic process aiming at victory and more as a technical process in which the assembly and refinement of means becomes paramount."[61] If Sherry is correct in his assertion that by September 1944 the Air Staff committed itself to an incendiary campaign the following spring, the calculating validation of the civilian advisers was necessary to assuage any doubts. While the Air Force's commitment at the time to a particular strategy seems doubtful, Sherry is correct in believing in the value of the COA and its supporting organizations. In a branch of the service so wedded to a theoretical doctrine, and practicing it unflinchingly in Europe, outside options needed an independent voice to affirm their viability and applicability; the COA provided that voice. Up until the final COA report, the idea of burning down Japanese cities rested on a foundation of vengeance; now it rested on a foundation of science.

Finally, on October 10, 1944, the revised report of the COA arrived on General Arnold's desk. The report broke operations into two contingencies: one based on blockade alone, the other based on blockade and invasion. Both plans started with the destruction of the aircraft industry; after that, either shipping (via mining) and then urban industrial areas if no invasion was planned, or the inverse if invasion was planned. Other industries fell off the list owing to a lack of information, but review was warranted if more data became available. Despite their positions as second and third on the list, mining and urban-area attacks held more importance than realized. The report held open the opportunity to downgrade the aircraft industry "in case fighter defense is ineffective." The aircraft industry took precedence only because of its danger to the bombers itself, not in consideration of campaigns outside Japan or a future invasion. The planners truly saw the strategic campaign as a war unto itself, one in which victory in the skies over Japan automatically translated to victory in the war overall. The ghosts of Douhet and Mitchell slept happy the night of October 10, their dream about to come true.[62]

The executive summary memo to General Arnold, sent with the report, sheds additional light on the conclusions and the rationale behind them. Assuming no invasion, urban attacks not only offered significant economic effects but weakened the enemy's "will to resist." The memo considered urban areas as part of the strategic target program, revealing the continued understanding that burning these areas down represented not an indiscriminate attack on the populace but a broad-based method of destroying a lot of industry at once. In the COA's eyes, the urban-area attacks did not constitute the epitome of attacks on will, though they did serve that purpose, as all strategic bombing should. If after exhausting the six cities chosen Arnold wanted a reevaluation done, they suggested that he consider other ways of weakening this "will to resist." The alternative method given involved a "comprehensive attack designed to reduce food supplies," a far more barbaric enterprise that steps into the realm of worst-case scenarios for true adherents to the strategic-bombing doctrine. The people could run from fire, losing only their possessions, but starving them made every single Japanese citizen a soldier.[63] Escalating the war to this level of civilian involvement was a step not to be taken lightly, and came only as a last result resort for students of strategic bombing.

In the event of an invasion concluding the war in the Pacific, the committee put forth the aircraft industry and urban areas as the main targets. Under this assumption, the forces in China no longer sat in range of any "strategic targets of great importance." The memo explained the obsolescence of the 20th BC by referring back to their original estimates of November 1943. At the time, "the Japanese economy had been expanding rapidly and attacks on steel through coke and on shipping were considered by the Committee as the best means of checking that expansion. The coke attack was possible from Chengtu and from Chengtu alone. Since then, the attack on shipping has checked the expansion of the Japanese economy and rendered the attack on steel through coke much less important." Thus the Chinese experiment must end in failure.[64]

This placed the focus on the 21st BC in the Marianas. The aircraft industry, with a special focus on five key plants, including the Nakajima Musashino aircraft engine plant, became the main target recommendation of the COA. After that, and when sufficient forces became available, the six cities should be burned down in short order. The memo confirmed that all the industries considered in the previous report received consideration again, but "none appear to offer primary target systems for attack at this time."[65] Because the COA was writing to an audience privy to the successes and failures of the European bombing campaign, the differences between German and Japanese industries needed to be addressed. The targets so important to the highly industrialized German economy, ball bearings and petroleum, did not provide nearly as much value to the Japanese or the war in the Pacific. This underscored the fundamental differences between the theaters. The continent-wide battles between mechanized armies in Europe showed little relation to the tiny islands covered in bunkers and caves in the Pacific. Japanese industry and military lacked the dependence on machines and fuel expected of an industrialized nation, because they did not need them where they fought. Defeating Japan by air, then, would be much harder than stifling the German war machine.

An attachment to the letter devoted to urban areas presented the quantitative estimates of production loss, corroborating the 15 percent of total industry referred to in the committee meetings, as well as selling some of the larger benefits of widespread destruction. While no single industry save machine tools risked substantial damage, the flames might "significantly increase and prolong losses effected by precision attacks on war industries."[66] Area attacks compensated for a lack of specific industrial targets, offering the bombers targets in the absence of the big factories producing tanks, trucks, or artillery shells. In the place of increased precision came an emphasis on maximizing the effects of the precision attacks already made, so area targets qualified as strategic since they supported the larger industry. The direct damage to housing fell under the same guise as the small parts producer next door, both destroyed as supporters of the larger industry, one as a parts producer and one as a source of the labor that ran the machines.

With the submittal of the revised COA report, the responsibility for target selection shifted to the Joint Target Group (JTG). The JTG, composed of members of the Office of Air Staff, Intelligence Branch, represented a military viewpoint of target selection: a switch from planning to execution. With the official mission of integrating and coordinating pre- and post-attack analysis of air targets in the war against Japan, the JTG collected intelligence and strike reports, creating and updating air target system folders. These packages of analyses, maps, and data on individual targets listed essential details and weapons recommendations and guided commanders in the field in their mission planning and target selection.

One historian of the rise of American airpower asserts that "after September 1944, no one outside the air force carefully examined its methods of bombing. Whether it chose to blast factories, mine sea-lanes, or level cities was largely for Arnold and his subordinates to decide."[67] Largely true, this statement ignores the luxury of civilian oversight up to that point and the fact that the switch to the JTG only put the responsibility of target selection and analysis into military hands, hands that continued to receive inputs from the same organizations as the COA.

The JTG put the ideas on bombing Japan into stark military terms, assembling target information sheets on each factory, building, or urban industrial area of note. As intelligence increased, especially photographic augmentation, the sheets and target folders were updated. From these sources a field commander could develop specific strike plans for each mission. The JTG used specific guidelines and principles for target selection, striving for the maximum efficiency and effect of bombing operations. These principles echoed the maxims of the Air Corps Tactical School in their emphasis on attack in "great quantity upon great objectives."[68]

The JTG also took over the process of studying target options and different ways of hurting the Japanese war machine. A big component of this research went toward optimization of targeting to achieve the most damage in a limited amount of time. In December 1944 one such effort culminated in "JTG Estimate No. 1: Strategic Air Employment Suitable to the Current Strategy of Japanese War." This initial estimate took the position, months before it became official U.S. military policy, that the end of the war in the Pacific rested on an invasion of the home islands, and to that end airpower's role until then entailed "preventing an increase and limiting replacements in certain weapons and materials of war essential to the defense of the Japanese homeland."[69] Unlike earlier COA documents and estimates, the JTG's work went beyond the academic musings of civilians and stood as an actionable plan for operations. The JTG's efforts translated directly into field use.

"Estimate No. 1" believed in invasion as the final act of the war in the Pacific, and that translated into priorities of targets, by system. Atop that list, as usual, sat aircraft engines. The JTG underestimated the recuperability of the industry after attack, believing that difficulties in replacement of machine tools and dispersal made it less likely to recover after attack, but nevertheless it found the industry essential to future victory. Second on the list came urban industrial areas. Not only did these areas contain their own resident industries, but the JTG believed they held some of the larger industries already dispersed, a belief the USSBS confirmed after the war when it surveyed Japanese industries and discovered they did disperse their operations throughout the big cities to buildings normally used for other industries. Attacking the urban areas, then, both achieved the main goal of crippling the industry in the area and also pursued the other Japanese industries to their demise as they tried to disappear in the urban morass.

Arsenals jumped to third on the priority list, owing to the ease with which munitions spread out in Japan. Attacking the production of munitions before the defending army hid them away enabled their destruction. The JTG saw no benefit in attacking transportation targets to stifle ammunition movements once invasion occurred, as by that time the stocks surely would sit in prearranged staging areas for a protracted campaign. After that, the list closes with mining of the waters around Japan, electronics plants for their utility in defense, and finally electrical power on Kyushu, a continuation of the Western belief in the importance of modern industry in the survival of a society.

Once additional air assets arrived in theater and the invasion drew imminent, the target priorities necessitated a shift toward those that straddled the line between strategic and tactical necessity. In this second phase, urban industrial areas fell to sixth on the priority list behind targets more pertinent to daily battle, such as aircraft repair facilities, combat airfields, and arsenals. The JTG understood that returning to the urban areas only made sense if the previous attacks on a city had failed to cause significant destruction. "Recuperation of these urban industrial areas if attacked effectively will be parasitic," making them a continued drain on the Japanese long after their destruction.[70] The value of large fires went beyond the damage to war industries; restoring the basic functions of everyday life after such a disaster took time, manpower, and the physical resources that were otherwise allocated to defense. The bleeding from the area attack wounds sapped the overall strength of the nation, making it a valuable tactic for defeating the Japanese even during an invasion.

So according to its first official estimate, the JTG saw the value of striking the dispersed industries in urban areas, but only to the point of their immediate destruction. After they received a going over by the B-29 forces, and as the noose tightened around the home islands, the utility in attacking urban areas decreased dramatically. Thus the JTG only foresaw urban areas as a target group like any other, worthy of destruction and then moving on to the next group; outside the elimination of identified concentrations of urban industry, no prolonged campaign of firebombing was planned.

The JTG inherited and retained the main target concern of the COA: the Japanese aircraft industry. In a stunning reversal of prewar disdain for the power of the airplane over the battlefield, by December 8, 1941, everyone realized the dominating power of the air arm.

The planes of the Japanese led this revolution, and the course of the war continued to reinforce their deadly reputation, a reputation the emergence of kamikazes only made greater. An early JTG "Japanese Aircraft Industry General Analysis," dated January 6, 1945, contained the staggering estimate of industry producing twenty-one hundred combat aircraft per month. At best this meant a continuous Japanese air threat over American operations closing in on Japan; at worst this meant twenty-one hundred guided missiles a month coming out of the factory and aimed at American ships and invasion beaches. This also threatened the very nature of the bombing operations, as 60 percent of those planes produced were fighters. So eliminating this industry paid dividends to all and stood as a requirement for the defeat of the Japanese empire as a whole.[71]

Although Japan would come under increasing pressures in imports, supplies, and direct attack, the JTG saw the possibility of recuperability and even expansion in the aircraft industry. With the understanding that engine availability drove the viability of the aircraft industry, the apocryphal belief that "unless Japanese production is reduced by an attack the end of 1945 will see at least 1000 more combat engines produced per month, and probably 1500" forced emphasis on sending the B-29s to the main engine plants, principally the four major plants that accounted for 90 percent of the country's engine output.[72] This placed an emphasis on precision bombing, a welcome relief to Hansell.

The JTG advocated three crucial understandings regarding the Japanese aircraft industry in its "Japanese Aircraft Industry General Analysis." First, the industry continued to produce at or near capacity. Second, new fighters like the Frank were taking the place of older models like the Zero, and that is what the target plants produced. While still converting over to the new designs, as 1945 progressed the thousand-plus planes a month rolling off the assembly lines would consist of aircraft nearly comparable to current American designs. Gone were the days of absolute American superiority over Japanese plane types. Third, new or previously unknown plants almost surely existed and remained unknown to planners at the current time. Keeping in mind that photo reconnaissance of Honshu only started when the 21st BC arrived in the Marianas in November, there was a real possibility that the aircraft industry target list would expand exponentially.

This unknown factor, combined with another ambiguous intelligence matter, unwittingly played into the hands of urban industrial attacks. Based on European experience and a general assumption about the reaction of an industry under attack, all understood that some level of dispersion of Japanese industry would occur as late as the first bombs striking its plants. This dispersion could occur anywhere, especially within the cities themselves, owing to the need for skilled workers and a supply of parts with which to build engines and airframes. This made urban industrial areas, and even urban areas in general if one stepped out on a limb, important targets for eradicating the aircraft industry. Likewise, the component and tool manufactures known to be in the urban industrial areas came into greater focus as important targets. Despite the "cushion" believed to exist in the available supply of these parts, they still formed a crucial part of aircraft production. If the final assembly plants moved they still needed parts and tools to complete their work, making attacks on the areas these small shops existed in vital to the overall war effort.

Regarding urban-area attacks, the JTG continued the tempered enthusiasm expressed by the COA. They made explicitly clear that area incendiary raids should only be directed at industrial areas. The "General Analysis of Japanese Urban Areas" plainly stated that "the concept of areas as target objectives is interpreted as an attack directed, in general, against a geographic concentration of diversified industrial facilities and/or housing." Attacking homes and workers obviously fell under this directive, but at least the intent of striking an industrial target remained the primary objective. In line with this maxim, the selection of target areas was predicated first on the area's economic importance in the war effort and second on its flammability. While this sounds like an open-ended directive viable against nearly any city of Japan, the definition of "industrial cluster" placed strict parameters on selection. Each area measured a "4,000 foot radius with a concentration of diversified industrial facilities." The selection placed an emphasis on concentration of buildings of combustible materials as well as fire- and earthquake-resistant materials. Also important was the radar image the target area created, allowing the planes to attack at night and in adverse weather. A distinct area of return made finding the target easier for new and inexperienced crews, giving them the full offensive power of the B-29. A final consideration regarded the potential for accidentally creating firebreaks, a sign that urban industrial attacks never intended to utterly destroy an entire city. The existence of these barren patches in an otherwise intact city precluded follow-up missions from starting fires anew. The current attacks meant to hit specific areas, but that could change. The urban industrial areas were the only target right now, and broad destruction did not fit in the JTG intentions, yet they held the concern that striking these objectives might prohibit further escalation if and when the need arose.[73]

The goal of destroying these cities went much further than simply eliminating the established factories; the household shops generated the same level of consternation for the JTG as the main plants. The JTG saw these small shops as "suitable area targets" that supplied a "relatively large amount of industrial production." Citing prewar statistics, the JTG believed that fifteen thousand of these shops existed in Tokyo and Osaka and five thousand in Nagoya, accounting for "a large proportion of [the] total gainfully employed." While they understood that the conversion to a war footing probably consolidated some of these shops out of business and into larger subcontracting firms, their place in the machine tool industry, production of components and subassemblies, and vulnerability to fire made them significant targets.[74]

The industries in the urban target areas comprised a variety of types and vulnerabilities. The aircraft industry, heavily concentrated in Tokyo and Nagoya, lay outside the city, so hurting them came "through absenteeism and interference with subcontracting and components supply lines from the city itself." In contrast, the munitions industry sat adjacent to urban areas, making 80 percent of heavy gun ammunition and 50 percent of general arms ammunition vulnerable. In addition, 90 percent of antifriction bearings sat at risk in the urban areas, and the shipbuilding industry stood to suffer from absenteeism, but the biggest effect waited for machine tools. As an integral part of all industrial work, machine tools affected both production and recoverability after attack. Too small and dispersed for precision attack, they appeared spread throughout the urban areas. Burning out an industrial cluster and wiping out the small tool shops hurt the aircraft industry, the ordnance industry, and the tool industry itself. The JTG came to the same conclusion as the COA: destroying the tool manufactures in area attacks complemented well the loss of tools themselves in precision- and area-bombed industrial sites. It destroyed the all-important tools and the ability to replace them, capping both ends of the bottleneck. When combined with precision attacks on the aircraft engine plants, urban attacks promised a crippling of the ability of the industry to rebuild or even disperse.[75]

The anticipated overall benefits of the area attacks ranged from direct production loss, to the burden of repair and replacement, to the loss of flow of materials or components from supporting industries. Production loss came both from elimination of plants themselves and damage to the infrastructure supporting those plants. By cutting off power or road and rail access through widespread devastation, even plants not hit would suffer after the attack.

The report seemed less enthusiastic on the effects against repair and recovery efforts, noting that they depended on "the priority of the industry or importance of particular housing, the supply of labor and materials, and the availability of substitute facilities and housing." Time would prove this skepticism correct, as widespread destruction made recovery in housing impractical if not impossible. Because of that, people left the cities en masse, abandoning jobs and their roots in search of food, shelter, and safety. Industry, too, spooked by their vulnerability in cities, dispersed without bothering to attempt reconstruction. Even if the people or industry tried to stay and rebuild, the totality of the fire's destruction eliminated the local supplies of raw materials. Finally, when the people left, the workforce disappeared with them, leaving no one to work in the remaining plants. The JTG held no illusions about the destruction to homes their plans entailed. Attacks "would kill or injure a large number of persons, disrupt utilities and transport services." From this "worker efficiency would decline due to overcrowding of dehoused persons . . . difficulty in reaching places of employment . . . and to general fatigue."[76] The one distinction made in these plans was to attack the homes of industrial workers, not random areas. They knew there were specific areas in the major cities where the workers lived, and they pushed to have the bombs fall there. Whether this came from a moral compunction is impossible to tell, but more likely it falls in the realm of efficiency: Why attack a useless target when a viable one sits nearby?

The decision to seriously analyze and recommend a course of action that laughed in the face of conventional bombing wisdom did not stem from a blithe acceptance of the COA's recommendation. The analysis considered the pros and cons of such a strategy and found overwhelmingly in favor of burning out urban industrial areas. The advantages spoke of both the efficiency and the effects of area attacks. Japanese cities were so vulnerable to fire that not burning them seemed the wrong course of action. The generalized production loss possible against Japanese cities came out to one and one-half times more than similar British area attacks on German cities, and that sounded like an understatement to the JTG. The greater physical destruction that Japanese cities would suffer would not only destroy the industrial plants themselves but restrict the flow of materials between plants and create "general administrative disorganization."

The second advantage reflected the same arguments made supporting urban-area attacks many times before. The complementary effects when paired with precision attacks made it possible to push "industries to their critical point."[77] While some overlap of the efforts was bound to occur, the use of area attacks to intensify the damage, chaos, and recovery effort of precision attacks made the efforts more than worth it. An added advantage mentioned here dealt with dispersal. Not understanding the degree to which the Japanese came to rely on the plan to protect their livelihood, the JTG saw destruction of industrial space in general as a positive step toward hampering the dispersal efforts.

The final advantage of note reflected the operational issue experienced by the B-29 crews. Opening the target parameters up to the size of a city section instead of a single plant returned radar to the playbook as a viable aiming method. With the adverse weather conditions over the islands and focus of crews on radar training, any way to return to the use of the technology behooved the war effort.[78]

Attacking urban areas was not a foregone conclusion, though, as

92

it had its disadvantages, albeit only a few. First in the minds of planners was the diffusion of loss inherent in area attacks. No one industry suffered specifically or severely or received the death blow that strategic-bombing doctrine demanded. For example, when a specific plant could not be destroyed with precision means, the workers operating it could be attacked to prevent them from going to work. The shortcoming identified by the JTG in this scenario centered on attacking only the homes of the workers at the plant: "Unless this is done, it will be necessary to destroy the bulk of all housing occupied by workers in various industries, in order to achieve substantial absenteeism in the industry against which attack is being directed."[79] Tremendous effort, then, may be required achieve results, a tough sell in a situation where the countdown to invasion marched onward.

The second concern also centered on diffusion of effort, but this time the obviating of the work done by the precision attacks. Switching from precision to area attacks risked giving the plants and industries already bombed time to recover their operations. One of the tenets held by the COA from the beginning entailed seeing a target group to its destruction. This meant that bombers needed to apply continuous pressure to an industry, even after it appeared defeated. Area attacks threatened the application of this continuous pressure by taking up available sorties, even if it did complement the precision strikes to an extent by making that recovery impossible.

Finally, area attacks did such widespread and varied damage that assessment of the effects and successes proved difficult. Without knowing the specific damage done, planners did not know what to hit next or again, and the overall effect on the war effort of these activities remained a mystery.[80]

The extensive planning and analysis done by the Air Force and civilian authorities in the two and a half years leading up to deployment of the B-29 tried to frame the war against Japan in the same way the theory of strategic bombing worked and with the lessons learned in Europe. The point missed at the time, because they sat so close to the subject, was that Japan did not operate as a fully industrialized economy like Western countries. The Japanese still relied heavily of smaller-scale operations and did not fully mobilize for the war they started. For this reason the list of viable targets remained short and often pointed to the need for destruction of large areas to clear out these small-scale operations that sat interspersed with the residential neighborhoods of the cities. Added to this came the undeniable vulnerability of Japanese cities to large-scale fires. Despite repeated attempts to identify specific bottleneck industries against which precision bombs would cripple the economy and bring the victory theorists postulated, none ever emerged except wholesale destruction of the industrial areas. The bottleneck they made dealt less with what they produced than with their compact physical location. Instead of finding a single specific industry, the COA, JTG, and supporting organizations identified the physical concentration of industry itself as the weak point of the Japanese economy.

The intent of the theorists and strategic-bombing adherents remained satisfied. With a bottleneck found and an industrial target selected, the argument that this campaign held to the tenets of the United States' strategic-bombing policy remained true. Maybe it took a bit of convincing or careful following of logic, but the planners ensured that the integrity of American airpower remained intact by attacking urban industrial areas, even though such actions entailed the collateral damage of destroying people's homes.

1. Maj. Gen. Curtis LeMay (*left*) and Brig. Gen. Haywood Hansell (*right*) after LeMay arrived in the Marianas to assume command of the 21st BC. Hansell would receive the Distinguished Service Medal for his time with the 21st BC, and LeMay would lead the bombers to the epitome of their destructive potential.

2. Gen. Curtis E. LeMay, the commander of the 21st BC and the man who implemented Japan's destruction.

3. (*Opposite top*) Frontal view of the Wright R3350 air-cooled radial engine used to power the B-29. All eighteen cylinders are visible in this view. The rear cylinders, peeking out from between the front bank of cylinders, had an especially difficult time receiving cooling air. The lines on each cylinder are fillets for increasing the surface area that cooling air will pass over, preventing overheating.

4. (*Opposite bottom*) Ground crew prepares a B-29 from the 500th BG, 73rd BW. Armorers load .50-caliber ammunition into the top quad turret, prepare 1,000-pound bombs, and perform engine checks. The size of the sixteen-foot, seven-inch propeller required to pull the plane through the air can be seen by comparison with the worker sitting on the hub.

5. (*Opposite top*) A B-29 ditched in the Pacific Ocean. The round-trip from the Marianas to Japan stretched the B-29's range to the maximum, limiting bomb loads and making any miscalculation of fuel consumption costly. Prior to the taking of Iwo Jima, the only choice for crews that ran out of fuel or succumbed to battle damage was ditching the plane at sea and hoping for rescue. The prospect of ditching took its toll on morale as much as the prospect of being shot down over the target.

6. (*Opposite bottom*) B-29 Flak Alley Sally of the 313th BW awaits refueling on Iwo Jima. The plane, along with seventeen others, stopped on their way back from attacking the Kobe urban area on the night of March 16–17, 1945. They burned 2.9 square miles of the city at the loss of only three bombers.

7. (*Above*) Planes of the 29th BG, 314th BW sit in hardstands at North Field on Guam. Slow construction and ever-increasing numbers of B-29s made all the airfields in the Marianas crowded and busy.

8. B-29s of the 29th BG, 314th BW flying in formation. Formation flying provided the accuracy and protection required for daylight precision bombing, but against area targets formations were optional, especially at night when it was safer for each plane to bomb the target area individually.

9. (*Opposite top*) A smoldering Tokyo seen on March 10, 1945. Smoke still rises from the sixteen square miles burned out (white areas). Good bomb dispersal and a driving wind helped the fire spread on both sides of the river (*center*), although the Imperial Palace (*top center*) was spared destruction.

10. (*Opposite bottom*) Tokyo up close after the 21st BC attacked. The densely packed wooden structures were incinerated and the masonry structures gutted. The firestorm created almost total destruction, taking homes and industries alike.

BURNING TOKYO 3-10-45

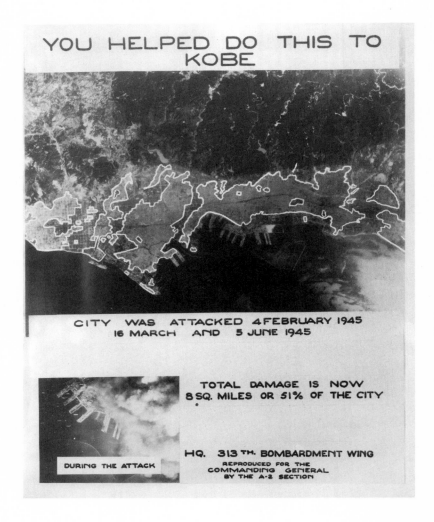

YOU HELPED DO THIS TO
KOBE

CITY WAS ATTACKED 4 FEBRUARY 1945
16 MARCH AND 5 JUNE 1945

TOTAL DAMAGE IS NOW
8 SQ. MILES OR 51% OF THE CITY

DURING THE ATTACK

HQ. 313 TH. BOMBARDMENT WING
REPRODUCED FOR THE
COMMANDING GENERAL
BY THE A-2 SECTION

11. The 313th BW generated flyers to show the flight and ground crews the positive impact they had on the war. The 313th had been in the theater since December 1944 and had participated in the tough missions of January and February, when the results did not equal the effort. After the start of incendiary attacks, morale rose as targets were destroyed. This sheet shows how in three missions half of Japan's fifth-largest city, Kobe, was burned down.

12. The 313th BW flyer advertising the results of the one strike sent to Yokkaichi, a small city on Japan's east side. Its harbor areas and oil refinery made it an important target but not one that could be effectively attacked with precision bombs.

YOU HELPED DO THIS TO
HIMEJI
DAMAGE TO CITY TOTALS
1.38 SQ. MILES OR 71.8%
TOTAL BUILT UP AREA

ATTACK OF 3-4 JULY 1945

HQ. 313TH BOMBARDMENT WING
REPRODUCED FOR THE
COMMANDING GENERAL
BY THE A-2 SECTION
B 313TH WING
PHOTOGRAPHIC LABORATORY

13. The 313th BW flyer for the city of Himeji, which was twice the target of the B-29s. The July 3–4, 1945, mission did the most damage, bringing the total amount of built-up area destroyed to 71 percent. While a small city, it contained an important railroad terminal, producers of electrical equipment, and a Kawanishi aircraft plant.

YOU HELPED DO THIS TO
HODOGAYA CHEMICAL WORKS

ATTACK OF 12 APRIL 1945
HEADQUARTERS 313TH· BOMBARDMENT WING
REPRODUCED FOR THE COMMANDING GENERAL BY THE A-2 SECTION

14. Important precision targets also received recognition. Here the April 12, 1945, strike on the Hodogaya Chemical Industries in the city of Koriyama is highlighted. The plant produced, among other chemicals, tetraethyl lead, an important additive to gasoline for improving engine performance. The bombing stopped production for a month, after which the plant struggled to reach 25 percent of its previous production level.

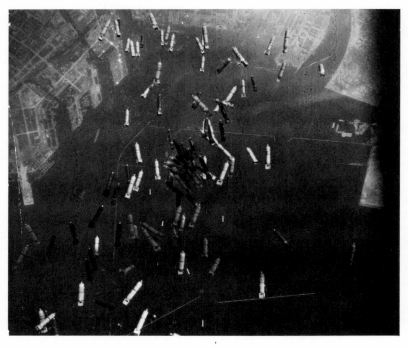

15. (*Opposite top*) M23 500-pound incendiary clusters await loading on a
B-29 of the 499th BG, 73rd BW. Each cluster could carry thirty-eight M-69
incendiaries, and each plane could carry forty of the clusters, making a total
of 1,520 individual incendiaries per plane.

16. (*Opposite bottom*) M-47 100-pound incendiaries rain down on the already
burning harbor area of Osaka, June 1, 1945. Using hook and cable adapters,
each B-29 could carry 240 of the M-47s.

17. (*Above*) The coastal city of Kagoshima prior to attack by the 21st BC.
Kagoshima was the major port on southern Kyushu. It also contained an
important railroad repair shop, an electrical equipment manufacture, and
two ironworks. One of the works, the Yashimi Iron Works, produced small
boat engines, an important component of suicide boats that the Japanese
intended to swarm on the American invasion fleet.

18. (*Opposite top*) Kagoshima after the 21st BC incendiary mission of June 17–18, 1945. The white areas are the burned-out parts of the city. In one mission the B-29s destroyed 44 percent of the city, which was roughly comparable to Richmond, Virginia, in size.

19. (*Opposite bottom*) A Japanese Ki-45 Nick dives away from a B-29 of the 314th BW after making a head-on attack. The prevalence of head-on attacks prompted the addition of two more .50-caliber guns to the forward top turret of the B-29s.

20. (*Above*) A B-29 flies above the clouds. Clouds were especially prevalent over Japan during the months the 21st BC was in operation. Clouds made visual bombing almost impossible and ensured a reliance on the ill-prepared radar bombing capabilities of the B-29s.

21. (*Opposite top*) The Nakajima Musashino aircraft engine plant just outside Tokyo. Designated as the main target for the 21st BC, it became the test for high-altitude precision bombing against Japan, a test that produced poor results.

22. (*Opposite bottom*) The Nakajima Musashino aircraft engine plant after nine attacks, culminating in the April 7, 1945, daylight mission by the 73rd BW in which the bombers came in at medium altitude and finished off the plant, eliminating it as a viable production facility. The importance of specific industries kept precision bombing an important tactic for the B-29 wings.

23. (*Above*) August 1–2, 1945, all of Toyama burns. The 73rd BW destroyed 99.6 percent of the city, which was roughly the size of Chattanooga, Tennessee. Toyama was believed to have the largest aluminum refining plant in Japan, as well as steel and chemical plants. The bombers suffered no losses on the mission.

24. A 315th BW plane flies overhead, clearly showing the large blade antenna of the AN/APQ-7 "Eagle" radar. The APQ-7 was an improvement over the standard AN/APQ-13 radar, creating better images of the target. The improved radar allowed the 315th BW to strike precision targets, primarily oil refining and storage, with radar. These targets were well suited for radar attack because of their location along the coastline, which gave good radar returns. Note the dark undersides and absence of gun turrets characteristic of the 315th's planes, which operated primarily at night.

4

Hansell's 21st Bomber Command

GEN. HAYWOOD HANSELL'S TENURE as commander of the 21st BC had never gone well. Not due to his lack of ability—he was one of the leading staff officers in the Air Force at the time—but because of the overall complexity of what General Arnold asked of him and the 21st BC and his dedication to the principles of strategic bombardment. From the time the first plane landed on Saipan on October 12, 1944, the push to succeed at all costs commenced. Whereas the 20th BC passed its failures off to a new plane, new organization, and basing in a remote and politically chosen area, the 21st BC received everything it needed to succeed from the start—or so it seemed. The bases in the Marianas, on Saipan, Tinian, and Guam, sat unfinished with runways not long enough to accommodate the B-29 and not enough hardstands on which to park the planes.[1] The plane, now based in range of Honshu and the Japanese industrial heartland, still suffered from engine problems that grounded the ones it did not crash. Six months into B-29 operations, the crews still went overseas with little time in a B-29 and an especially meager understanding of the plane's autopilot system and fuel conservation. Worst of all, the hopes of every airman and strategic-bombing proponent rode on the wings of the 21st BC. Everyone, including their commander, Curtis LeMay, wrote off the 20th BC as an effective fighting force. The logistics issues proved too great to maintain a force that could only reach the southernmost, and from an economic standpoint the least fruitful, areas of Japan. The future of the 20th AF rested on the shoulders of Hansell and his men. Failure, even initial failure, offered the Joint Chiefs of Staff the chance to rescind the independence of the 20th

AF, assign it to a theater commander just like in Europe, and demonstrate to the government that the Air Force did not deserve to be an independent branch of the U.S. military.

Even as the first planes staged at Chengtu back in June 1944, the push to change the direction of B-29 operations stirred in Washington. Brig. Gen. Emmett "Rosie" O'Donnell, a fighter pilot by trade before switching to bombers and gaining fame early in the war bombing a Japanese cruiser and destroyer escort in the Philippines as the islands fell, used his position on Arnold's "Advisory Council" to strongly urge downgrading precision attacks for the moment and instead sending the bombers "singly at night using radar to destroy and burn down the several large cosmopolitan centers" and "thereby striking a tremendous blow at civilian morale." This idea appealed to him, particularly since many Japanese cities sat in coastal areas and thus made ideal radar targets. This idea went nowhere, but O'Donnell found himself assigned as commander of the 73rd BW slated for deployment to the Marianas in the first wave of the 21st BC. Likewise, the commander of the 20th BC's 58th BW, Brig. Gen. LaVerne "Blondie" Saunders, and "perhaps a majority" of his staff favored use of the B-29 "exclusively as a night bomber." They believed that a moderate bomb load dropped by radar at night might be better than rated bomb loads in formation by day.[2] The difficulties with the plane's development and crew training, coupled with the slow pace of operations in China, drew planners toward cut-rate solutions that looked good on paper but possessed their own implementation issues. Both O'Donnell and Saunders acknowledged the limitations of daylight bombing, especially when feeling out a new plane, but reverted to a solution popular behind a desk, radar. Neither appears to have known (or at least admitted) that the radar presented few, if any, advantages over visual bombing. It just acted as a panacea to solve the precision-bombing problem.

Operations from China continued at their snail's pace as September 1944 progressed. Under LeMay's leadership the organization and efficiency of the 20th BC improved, but it ran into the ceiling of the limited logistics train and distance from targets that plagued operations from day one. Even with the improvements, the success of their strikes remained hit-and-miss. A return mission to the coke ovens at Anshan on September 26 resulted in no damage from the seventy-three planes that dropped their loads by radar. As if this did not appear bad enough, 109 planes took off on the mission but only 70 percent bombed the primary target, leaving 30 percent of the effort off the target area entirely. The lack of success after only four months led Arnold to contemplate abandoning Chinese operations and shifting all the 20th AF's might to the Marianas. The big bombers in the land of Chiang Kai-shek offered a nice gesture from the U.S. government, but the time for the Air Force to achieve results had arrived. The B-29s needed to be where they could do good in the war.

To that end, Hansell, recently the chief of staff of the 20th AF, took the brand-new 21st BC to the Marianas. The first target directive for the 21st BC, received November 11, 1944, put aircraft engine manufacturers and component assembly plants at the top of the list for attack by precision, with port areas and urban areas as "secondary and last resort targets, all suitable for radar bombing." An additional directive that day ordered the 21st BC to test incendiaries on a Japanese city, taking special care not to test from too high an altitude. Hansell's understanding of the primary directive held true to their intent, as he believed the primary target was aircraft factories thanks to European experience showing air superiority as "essential to strategic air operations as well as to surface operations and invasions." Eliminating fighters cleared the way for more bombers and provided near-real-time support of troops in other theaters who operated under threat from Japanese air attack. European experience in the carnage fighters wreaked on the 8th AF, the relative ease of the invasion at Normandy, and the continuing advance of Allied troops under the near-exclusive cover of their own planes made aircraft the logical choice as a primary target. After that, Hansell acknowledged, came selected targets to be destroyed by precision bombing, and urban targets such as "home-shop" facilities, to be destroyed by incendiary attack. Overall, the "initial primary air aims were practically the same as those in Germany—the paralysis of the military, economic, industrial, and social structure supporting the will and the ability of the Japanese nation to wage war." The 21st BC would strike at the bottlenecks of Japanese industry and society, crippling it and bringing the war to an end.[3]

The one part of the directives that Hansell seemed to try to avoid regarded the test incendiary raid. As a founder of the Air Force's precision-bombing doctrine, Hansell saw a switch to area raids, even ones ostensibly targeted at small, home-based industries, as a complete reversal of everything he and the rest of the Air Force had fought for. It did not help that the request came at the same time he received orders to destroy the aircraft industry by precision, and before his command dropped any bombs on Japan. Using the mantra professed for the previous year by planners, like the COA, to concentrate on a target and destroy it before moving on, Hansell balked at the idea of taking away sorties from a fledgling precision campaign to test a theory. As a good soldier, though, he complied with his orders, if only the letter and not the intent. On November 29 he dispatched twenty-nine planes to the industrial area and docks of Tokyo with incendiaries, giving them a legitimate target to bomb, but sending them in at 22,000 feet. Only twenty-three actually bombed the primary target, by radar nonetheless, expending a measly 6,800 pounds of bombs each. The results came back as negligible, only a tenth of a square mile destroyed. Thinking he had completed his task, Hansell focused again on the precision campaign. Unsatisfied by the lackluster effort, Norstad pressed Hansell for a real effort in testing the incendiary theory. He subtly let Hansell know his concerns—and those of the 20th AF in general—in a November 29 personal letter which revealed that "Washington seemed to think too much reliance was being placed on HE [high-explosive] bombs." Subtle prodding aside, Norstad wrote again on December 7 to "reassure Hansell that he had 'the utmost latitude in accomplishing [his] mission,' but latitude extended only to 'the dates that you select, the size of force, and the sequence of targets within the priority list.'"[4] Hansell's future as commander rested on his exercising his free will to follow orders, not create his own. Regardless of his reservations, Washington wanted firebombing, and his responsibility to comply with their wishes came in a worthwhile test raid.

Hansell's woes grew when LeMay sent the 20th BC against the dockyards of Hankow, China, on December 18. Responding to a request from theater air commander Gen. Claire Chennault, LeMay put eighty-four planes with 500 tons of incendiary bombs (11,900 pounds per plane) over the target at medium altitude. The fire burned for three days. Arnold felt enough pride in the results to inform Secretary of War Henry Stimson that "60% of the 400 acre target area [was] destroyed, including more than 100 warehouses, factories and office buildings." He continued by pointing out that this widespread destruction constituted a "vital factor in limiting the speed, effectiveness and scope of Japanese operations in China. There is no doubt as to the efficiency of the Hankow strike from a long range as well as an immediate standpoint."[5]

This success prompted Norstad to press the issue with Hansell, sending a teleconference message on December 18 in which he requested a one-hundred-plane "full incendiary attack" at the earliest possible date against Nagoya. He made no effort to hide the intent of the mission, citing two purposes: "first, to destroy as much of the city as possible to reduce its industrial capacity; second, to determine the effectiveness of our incendiary weapons." He went so far as dictating the weapon type to be used (M-69s in aimable clusters), the portions of the city to hit, and the timing of the forces over target; he also specifically requested post-strike photography. He made sure his intent did not leave room for delay: "The performance of this mission is an urgent requirement in order that future operations may be planned with far greater assurance as to our capabilities than we now possess." Seeing the writing on the wall for both his required actions and the future of the precision campaign in the Pacific, Hansell fired back a response that cited both the practical and philosophical objections to such an order. "I have with great difficulty," he began, "implanted the principle that our mission is the destruction of selected primary targets by sustained and determined attacks using precision-bombing methods both visual and radar." Those methods just started paying off, he argued, finally doing real damage to the aircraft industry, but now "the temptation to abandon our primary targets for secondary area targets is great and I have been under considerable pressure to do so, but I have resisted so far. I am concerned that a change to area bombing of the cities will undermine the progress we have made." Yet ever the professional soldier, he accepted the order and scheduled the Nagoya mission as his next one. Norstad calmly replied that the rules of the game had not changed as much as a new play called. The Nagoya mission was a "special requirement resulting from the necessity of future planning." He got what he had wanted since August: a dedicated mission to see if incendiaries created the destruction the Air Force needed. After the war Hansell would deny he knew where the pressure for incendiaries really came from—Arnold, Norstad, COA—but he knew the outcome as well as anyone else: he sent planes to burn down Japanese cities.[6]

In his usual way, Hansell construed the requirement to fit his personal desires and sent eighty-two aircraft to Nagoya on December 22 armed with 5,500 pounds of incendiaries each, but targeting the Mitsubishi engine plant rather than simply the urban area. Criticism be damned, he would not throw the bomber at the man on the street. Flown in daylight from 30,000 feet, the radar-aimed bombing of the forty-eight planes that hit the primary target produced little damage and no validation of the principle of area incendiary bombing. Flying too high and with too few planes, Hansell scuttled the possibility of success, setting this test up to be another failure.

Hansell's case for precision strikes rang hollow in Washington thanks to the series of disappointments that started with his first mission. His first true hurdle was the same one identified by the COA and others in the year prior: a total lack of visual intelligence. Nobody had pictures of Japanese cities or targets, least of all Hansell and his planning staff. When told to strike the Musashino engine plant, he knew where it sat physically but not what it looked like from the air, so he could not direct anyone to it or tell them where to aim their bombs. Radar presented the same problem. Even if, from a technical standpoint, radar drops of bombs were comparable in accuracy to visual drops, there were no radar maps or radar screen images of the targets to show to bombardiers and radar operators. Not even offset bombing points existed. These points—known distances from desired targets—presented easily identifiable radar returns, enabling the radar operator to triangulate the plane's position relative to the target and determine a reasonably accurate drop time. In future operations this method proved invaluable against targets obscured by clouds but not distinct enough to appear on a radarscope themselves. But to determine these points, planes needed to first fly over the area and find them.

When the first B-29 photoreconnaissance plane (designated an F-13) landed in the Marianas on October 30, 1944, after its flight from the United States, the crew immediately refueled and flew to Tokyo to take pictures, making it the first Air Force plane over the Japanese capital in more than two and a half years. The pictures brought back represented a treasure trove of data to process. Concurrent to this, the phone from the United States rang off the hook with requests and commands. Hansell later lamented the fact that the radio equipment placed him at Washington's beck and call. He recalled: "The machine worked twenty-four hours a day all night, without stopping. Most of the messages seemed to consist of questions that I couldn't answer."[7] The most important question on Hansell's mind, though, was when his planes would first strike Japan. A series of shakedown flights and trips to Japanese-occupied islands did not answer Arnold's demand for *his* Air Force to enter the action in the Pacific.

The opportunity to start a precision bombing campaign finally came on November 24 when mission San Antonio I left after several false starts due to weather in the Marianas. Before the mission, with the difficulties of his own 73rd BW and the entire 21st BC fresh in his mind, "Rosie" O'Donnell again stepped into the picture. In a handwritten note to Hansell, O'Donnell suggested to his friend that the B-29 offered little chance of success as a high-altitude daylight bomber, and pushed for a switch to low-altitude night attacks. It seems O'Donnell's concerns revolved more around the utility of the radar bombing system than a doubting of the aircraft itself, but this did give him a chance to distance himself from failure. Hansell took the advice for its worth and sent 111 planes to the skies for the Nakajima Musashino aircraft engine plant just outside Tokyo. Traveling in formation at 30,000 feet and each carrying 5,000 pounds of bombs, a quarter of the plane's capability, 88 bombed a target: 24 the primary, 59 the secondary, and 5 something else. In the face of a 120-knot headwind, the accuracy earned the description of "poor."

In fairness to Hansell, who was barred from leading the raid himself because of his knowledge of the atomic bomb, even the vaunted European bombing campaign started slowly and inaccurately, and they waited awhile before venturing into the homeland of the Nazis. Nevertheless, higher command took notice. Lt. Gen. Millard F. Harmon, commanding general of United States Army Forces in the South Pacific area and the airman on the scene in the theater, wrote to Hansell the next day acknowledging that the mission "did not result in substantial destruction of [the] target" and directing a follow-up attack to be launched the next day.[8] The 21st BC dutifully complied and sent eighty-one planes back to Musashino on November 27. None of the eighty-one planes that got airborne bombed the Musashino plant, thanks to the weather. More embarrassing, a quarter of the planes dispatched never bombed a target at all, aborting the mission somewhere along the way.

Hansell strove to make the 21st BC more efficient and address some of the deficiencies of their operations. Realizing that takeoff weight had a huge influence on the ability of a plane to reach its target, damage the target, and make it back to base, he proceeded to strip the planes of excess baggage, taking 6,000 pounds off each aircraft. Weight affected every aspect of the mission. High takeoff weights threatened the planes with disaster if they did not clear the end of the still-unfinished runways, and strained the already temperamental engines on the ascent. Part of the mass of the early B-29 missions amounted to fuel. As mentioned before, the early mission carried only a quarter of the listed bomb load of 20,000 pounds. The balance of the 140,000 takeoff weight sat in the fuel tanks, and those inevitably came up dry as the planes neared the Marianas at the end of a mission. Even with the 4,100-pound bomb bay tank, which Hansell summarily stripped from the planes to save weight, one major cause of losses on missions fell to ditching at sea due to fuel exhaustion. Owing to inexperience and shortened training schedules, flight crews did not know how to efficiently fly the plane, especially in formation or on autopilot, and sucked up their fuel at higher-than-anticipated rates. For a plane capable of striking almost the whole of the home islands, the 21st BC in 1944 and early 1945 found the flight to Tokyo difficult to manage.

Not all the fuel issues fell on the crews, though, as the Japanese presence on Iwo Jima added miles to each mission in avoidance of the island. The taking of the island in February 1945 draws criticism today, as it was only an emergency airstrip with no tactical value, but the dividends came quickly to B-29 crews who no longer needed to avoid the island and its fighters, could land there if short on fuel, and received fighter escort of their own once long-range fighters arrived in mid-1945. The benefits in fuel came on both ends of the island. Planes that earlier aborted a mission early and turned back before reaching Japan because they had already exhausted their outbound fuel allocation pressed on to the target, confident that Iwo Jima lay ready to service them on their return. All this translated to increased bomb loads. Even with poor results, planes able to carry twice the 5,000-pound loads of November and December's missions stood to do twice the damage to a target. While this might amount to 8 percent rather than 4 percent of a target destroyed, it doubled the effectiveness of the mission and cut in half the number of follow-up trips needed to do comparable destruction.

Hansell soldiered on through December and into January, sticking to the precision game plan he arrived with in the Marianas. In seven December missions he sent his planes to Musashino two more times and to Mitsubishi plants in Nagoya three others, augmenting it all with two attacks in force on Iwo Jima. With the exception of two of the Nagoya missions, results continued to be poor, and even the Nagoya attacks did not show decisive results. The most successful of the attacks saw nearly three-quarters of the bomb tonnage dropped on the Mitsubishi no. 2 and no. 4 engine works strike the plant area and damage or destroy 35 percent of the roof area of the plant. Since damage assessments relied heavily on roof damage as an indicator of total plant damage, it looked like small returns for a much-vaunted heavy-bombing force. Worse, while losses due to combat stayed steady, enemy fighters started to appear in greater numbers and attacks increased. On December 3 alone, over Musashino, the Japanese made 523 recorded attacks on the seventy-five bombing aircraft. Only three bombers fell to the enemy guns, but the intensity of the air battle started to resemble the fights over occupied Europe.

Reinforcement gave Hansell and his staff little consolation. Elements of the 313th BW started arriving at the end of December when the 504th and 505th BGs landed on Tinian. Their training and operational readiness proved so bad they needed to engage in a five-week training program just to bring them up to fighting capability. So until the end of January the 21st BC relied on only one bomb wing for operations, even though the force continually grew with new elements. A telecon message received on January 3, 1945, from the commander of the 20th AF illustrated the issues faced by all units flying the B-29. Using data from the 20th BC, the analysis determined that 14–19 percent of planes failed to bomb their primary target because of mechanical reasons—a stark contrast to the 4–6 percent failure in the 8th AF. Not surprisingly, half the failures were attributed to engine issues.[9] The issues in the field gained attention at the highest levels, but this did not help Hansell any when he needed to explain the sluggish performance of his units to the same high-level commanders.

The beginning of January brought Hansell into direct confrontation with Norstad and Arnold over the Nagoya incendiary test, the third such "test" mission. On January 3, Hansell sent ninety-seven planes to the Nagoya "docks and urban area" at 29,850 feet. Only fifty-seven hit the main target, each bombing visually to drop its 4,900-pound load of incendiaries. Despite the clusters opening at the much lower altitude of 8,000 feet to spread their individual munitions, their four-mile plunge already irrevocably dispersed them, so the results came back as minimal and inconclusive. Once again a test attack on an urban industrial area showed little promise as well as poor execution on the part of the commander in the field. The order fulfilled, Hansell moved on to his primary precision targets. Frustrated again, Norstad and Arnold, who wanted a maximum number of incendiaries over a target, looked for an alternative.

Here an interesting nuance crept into the command hierarchy of the 20th AF. In mid-January 1945, General Arnold suffered a severe heart attack and remained in convalescence for two months. During this period, Norstad, as deputy 20th AF commander, stepped in to command the B-29s. Resting in Florida, Arnold stayed largely clear of the day-to-day details of the Air Force in general, only communicating with Lt. Gen. Barney Giles and Norstad via periodic teletype message. Arnold's biographer Herman Wolk helps dispel confusion over the nature of this command arrangement, asserting that "Norstad certainly sat in for Arnold, but it is also clear that Norstad knew exactly what Arnold wanted and in no way was he about to issue any directive or guidance that he knew to be counter to Arnold's views."[10] This explains the sudden prominence of Norstad in the communications and decision making regarding operations from the Marianas, and why the tone and goals never changed despite the events in Washington.

An exchange between 20th AF and the 21st BC during early January sought to determine the maximum number of incendiary bombs a B-29 could carry to Japan. The estimates that came back stopped at 10,000 pounds owing to fuel considerations due to the inclusion of a supplemental gas tank in the forward bomb bay which took space and supplied the fuel needed to make the trip. It is hard to tell which aspect played more into these calculations: the belief that the planes would attack at high altitude or the inexperience of the crews that wasted gas. Both used up fuel and lowered bomb capacity, but the messages made no differentiation between the two. Yet the exchange stands out for more than just the perceived limit on the B-29's carrying capacity. It reveals a lack of bomb rack adapters to carry incendiary clusters by the entire force and a lack of the specified weapon to be tested, pushing testing of this more defined theory into February. In addition to Hansell's reluctance, the amassing 21st BC did not yet have all the required tools to carry out a well-refined test mission or exploit any successes it might bring.

After another poor performance against Musashino on January 9, Hansell smashed the Kawasaki aircraft factory at Akashi on the nineteenth. Sixty-two planes damaged 38 percent of the roofed area. Actually, they hit every important building in the engine and airframe branches, disrupting every aspect of the works and cutting production 90 percent. They only damaged 10 percent of the machine tools on-site but frightened the company enough to disperse almost all the remaining equipment, ending the site's utility in production. The plant dispersed first to a pair of spinning mills in other cities before ending up in tunnels outside the cities, where long setup time, poor working conditions, and an awful transportation network to the remote locations kept the efforts from succeeding. These ancillary effects would not become known to the Americans until after the war, but visual results revealed a glimmer of hope for the B-29 force.

Successes of this sort gained attention in Washington and earned recognition. In a transmission dated January 16, the 20th AF reiterated the target priority of the 21st BC as aircraft engines, with no mention of other target groups. The directive went so far as praising the efforts of the 21st BC, citing the "considerable damage" done to the two engine plants believed to produce 75 percent of all Japanese engines: the Mitsubishi plants in Nagoya and Musashino. Damage assessments credited the 21st BC with destroying one month's production at each plant, not an inconsequential contribution if the intelligence reports were right and planes went directly from the plants to front-line units.[11]

Alas, despite the sudden success, the trials and tribulations of Haywood Hansell ended on January 20 when Curtis LeMay stepped off a plane to take command of the 21st BC. Arnold offered Hansell the opportunity to stay on as second in command, an offer Hansell wisely refused, preferring to simply hand over power outright to LeMay. Upon his transfer, Hansell wrote a personal letter to Arnold describing the four major problems he experienced as commander in the Marianas:

1. converting the 73d Wing from a preference for radar night bombing to a belief in precision bombing
2. improving bombing accuracy, which was "deplorable"
3. reducing the abortive rate, which had reached 21 percent of sorties
4. reducing the number of aircraft ditching and improving air-sea rescue[12]

He also attributed the abort issue and excessive ditching to maintenance issues and believed he drove his men too hard. These were all valid assessments, after all; the crews he received arrived with minimal training in visual bombing as well as radar bombing, and the planes he used were delivered with a laundry list of issues not yet resolved. On top of this, he was operating out of an airfield complex still under construction and staffing up. Yet like his previous pleas all fell on deaf ears in Washington, where results matter most.

Craven and Cate, in the official history of the Army Air Forces in World War II, summarized Hansell's replacement by noting that "Arnold was not a patient man" and that "perhaps in the last analysis Hansell's chief fault was in adhering too strictly to the 'book'—to

doctrines of precision bombardment which he had helped formu-
late—in the face of a growing interest in area incendiary bombing
evinced by Arnold's headquarters." Hansell agreed to a degree with
the belief in Arnold's changing interests, rationalizing his demise by
saying, "Time was not on the side off the XXI's Commander. Gen.
Arnold wanted and demanded measurable results at once" and was
"heavily influenced by bomb tonnage instead of target destruction."
He then fell back on his European experience, noting that "many
more tons of bombs could be dropped at night using radar bombing than in daylight. By day the force had to fly in formation and
operate at high altitude to defend itself against Japanese fighters."[13]

Actual experience revealed the hollowness of Hansell's victim-
hood, as the fighter problems over Japan made a strong showing at
first, and then tapered off, and the requirement for formation bomb
runs in the daylight versus solo ones at night fell to the training of
the crews much more than the limitations of the equipment. In the
light of day everyone expected the planes to actually hit a target,
and with limited numbers of experienced or lead crews all planes
in a formation dropped on the leader rather than try to aim their
own bombs. At night, where accuracy came as a luxury more than
a requirement, each plane's abilities met the need of hitting an area.

The one place Hansell hit the mark in his argument was regarding the interest in tonnage versus accuracy. Tonnage mattered more
to Arnold than accuracy, because he lacked the former and could
generate more of the latter. If the independent Air Force failed to
hit targets and dropped few bombs, it had no chance of standing on
its own after the war. At least big numbers of bombs showed power,
even if that power dissipated quickly. In this way Hansell was short-
changed by the lack of intelligence on Japanese targets after his missions. He is partially right when he says the 21st BC destroyed the
aircraft industry early in the campaign but "we were not able to prove
it, and the proof was not apparent to anyone until after the war." Postwar analysis showed that by the start of the area attacks in March
1945 engine production dropped from a peak of 5,090 in July 1944
to 1,695 in February 1945. Airframe production dropped in the same
way from a September 1944 peak of 2,572 to 1,391 in February 1945.
True, bombardment only contributed to these declines—dispersal,

raw materials shortages, and skilled labor shortages all helped—but results are what really mattered. The Japanese aircraft industry slid on a decline with no real hope of recovery, but this was not evident to the intelligence community.[14]

In the end, though, Hansell lost his command owing to more than just poor results, or a belief that LeMay gave the command a better chance at execution. Hansell's stubbornness on the issue of incendiary attacks doomed him and presented him in a bad light to his superiors. A strong adherent to precision bombing and a loyal officer, Hansell made every effort to execute the orders he received regarding test incendiary raids but always made sure to conduct them his own way, a way that ensured their failure. Historians will defend Hansell, saying he "never even hinted at resigning or disobeying orders. If area bombing was what it took to stay in command, Hansell would have continued to do as much of it as Arnold told him to."[15] In a way this is true, but Hansell read into the orders what he wanted, not what Arnold intended. Despite their friendship and previous working relationship, Arnold, like any other commander, could not tolerate a situation where he had to spell out in explicit detail his orders. Hansell's repeated responses showed him not to be the one to execute the orders from above, at least not as intended.

After the war LeMay earned accolades for his innovations in tactics, but Hansell earned and deserved few for his performance in the Pacific. On missions designed to see whether the Air Force could saturate a Japanese city in fire at high altitude he sent planes shorthanded, with minimal bomb loads, and against specific industrial aim points in place of known urban concentrations. Each mission scattered its firebombs all over the place with no concentration and failed miserably. Yet he fulfilled his duty enough to report back to Washington that he completed the mission as ordered. Norstad in particular appears to have grown tired of this game, repeatedly resubmitting the order for a test raid in the hopes of getting an honest effort.

This does not aim to tear down the character of the man, but Hansell showed himself as obviously not the right man for the job the 21st BC needed to accomplish. The compressed schedule of operations, lack of precision targets, flammability of Japanese cities, and operational advantages made incendiaries the future. Hansell's training and personal ethics did not allow him to spread destruction out-side the specific targets that supported the war effort. A great plan-ner, Hansell stood totally unprepared for the horrors of a total war.

LeMay inherited a command fraught with technical problems, supply problems, bombing problems, and worst of all, low morale. Improvements in performance existed, but they developed so slowly that they went unnoticed by any but the most optimistic. The morale problem did not escape the medical community on the island, which generated the undated report "Human Elements of the Operations of This Command." Despite maintenance improvements, the planes still worried the crews, who trusted their lives on a twelve-hour mis-sion over open waters entirely to its reliability. When this was mixed with combat and poor bombing results, optimism ran short and led to crews resorting to just doing the "flying of missions" with what Bartlett Kerr summarized as "a dull emotional tone, lacking in enthu-siasm and hope for eventual success." The conclusion of the report summarized the malaise that settled over the crews as one of sur-vival of condemned men, devoid of hope. Advocating for a mission count that led to rotation home, the report went on to say, "Symbol-ically this 'something to shoot for' was not connected with waging the war or defeating the enemy but with home, security and reward for the dutiful completion of a hopeless task."[16] The 21st BC sat in a rut, unable to achieve success and devoid of hope. The bad times inherent in establishing a command failed to dissipate, and opera-tions stagnated.

LeMay ignored all the speculation and started work on improv-ing operations across the board, a sure way of getting results and improving morale. The day he took command he fired off a one-line message to Arnold requesting any available data on incendiary damage done to targets in Europe and what bomb types they used. Knowing the interests of the 20th AF commander, LeMay immedi-ately began preparing. Just to be on the safe side, though, Norstad gave LeMay the same reminder on target directives on January 23: "I cannot overemphasize the importance of illuminating this objective [aircraft engines] at the earliest practicable date."[17] LeMay received the job not because he offered a change in tactics but because he was a commander who got results regardless of the situation.

LeMay followed through on his orders to keep the pressure on the aircraft engine factories, striking the Mitsubishi plant in Nagoya on January 23 and the Musashino plant on January 27. But he did no better than Hansell, achieving no significant hits and seeing only 19 percent of his planes hit the primary targets. Obviously, a new commanding officer did not make a difference on its own, so LeMay started to institute changes. Lead crew training stepped up, and increased integration with the naval units that ran the islands the B-29s sat on brought improvements in performance and living conditions. An emphasis on flight discipline started, holding the wings responsible for their crews flying the briefed routes and bomb runs and for dropping properly on the cue of the formation leader. No longer would lax adherence to procedures be tolerated.

LeMay evaluated the problems that had plagued Hansell and came up with responses and answers to the concerns of his superiors. Regarding radar bombing and navigation, he freely admitted that "my radar personnel are unable to operate with the efficiency necessary to accomplish our mission." This boded ill for operations, since the weather over Japan forced 38 percent of all bomb drops to occur by radar. The future looked worse according to LeMay, with the visual bombing conditions over the next four months falling to below a third of the time. Like it or not, bombing Japan required radar as both a navigation aid and an aiming device. Avoiding excuses, LeMay resorted to a plan that had served him well throughout his career: training. The principal program he instituted was to train qualified radar operators, not the enlisted gunners currently being pulled in to operate the equipment; they would be taught by skilled personnel from the training units in the States. The way out of the bind came with education that should have been received before deploying; now that training needed to come to the troops in the field.[18]

Most important, LeMay altered the maintenance scheme the 21st BC used, focusing on making aircraft available for missions and not failing while flying. Based on suggestions from his chief of maintenance, Col. Paul "Stan" Emrick, LeMay shifted responsibility for maintaining individual aircraft around, concentrating specific tasks in the hands of the most skilled individuals rather than plane-specific crews. He set a goal of 120 hours a month flying time per plane, four times that achieved by bomber crews in Europe and twice as many as the command currently supported. As the effort gained speed the availability rose markedly, so that by the end of March aircraft availability rose to 114.9 hours per month. This fit nicely with the rising crew abilities, which topped out at an ability to fly 95 to 100 hours per month, and the crew-to-plane ratio of one plane for every one and a quarter crews. The differences showed in mission success as well. The failure of planes to hit the primary target fell from 22.7 percent in January to 17.4 percent in February, and sank again to 9.6 percent in March, where it stabilized. And while parts availability always presented a problem for the crews in the Marianas, with a new system where planes from the States ferried in a steady stream of replacement components, the ground crews never ran out. This work on the ground to prepare planes efficiently showed dramatically in the number of planes grounded for want of repairs. In December, 12.7 percent sat idle in the Marianas, while in January only 4.6 percent waited around unable to fly. When April came along, with an ever-expanding number of planes available in the islands, the number sank further to 1.3 percent before dropping to 0.3 percent two months later. During a period of increasing tempo in operations, LeMay's changes cut the number of planes missing the primary target due to mechanical issues in half and reduced the percentage of grounded planes by 98 percent over the numbers experienced by the command before his arrival.[19]

Despite the improvements gathering steam, at the beginning of February the planning side of the 21st BC still expected anemic sortie rates and bomb loads. When planning for ammunition requirements they used current figures of 7.5 missions per plane per month, with only half the planes tactically available. They also calculated an average bomb load of four tons, less than half the plane's capability, though slightly more than that carried regularly on missions. At first the split of ordnance ordered appears as a harbinger of things to come, but the 60-40 split between conventional bombs and incendiaries represented normal operations only. Even when precision bombing, the B-29 usually carried some incendiaries to start fires and burn rubble. Having incendiaries on hand became a necessity, especially when they occasionally flew as the sole type of ordnance or the idea of testing their feasibility against specific targets, like aircraft factories, floated around as a solution to the woes of command.[20]

This increase in available planes coincided with the ability of the 313th BW to participate in missions, completing their needed in-theater training period. The 112 planes LeMay got airborne for Kobe on February 4 marked the highest number since the first attack on Musashino in November the previous year. Weather and navigation errors threw off nearly half the force, so only 69 planes spread 159 tons of M-69s (5,000 pounds per plane) over the city at 24,100 feet. The minor reduction in altitude over previous tests did little, and only 0.15 square miles of the city burned. On the bright side, three important industrial targets also burned, showing the potential for fire to wipe away the list of targets assigned to the strategic bombers. Again Norstad felt disappointed: he wanted three hundred tons placed in the city. As before, he ordered another test, this time against zone one of Nagoya, to obtain conclusive results. The follow-up test orders arrived on February 12, with Norstad apologizing for going "into tactical detail that properly is your responsibility" to create a "conflagration" in Nagoya. This directive stood second only to continued pressure on the engine plants.[21]

Unlike Hansell, who accepted the failure of the incendiary raids as validation of the precision doctrine, LeMay was "not satisfied with the concentration achieved with the M-69" at Nagoya. A few years before he died, Robert McNamara, the former secretary of defense and member of the 33rd Statistical Control Unit in the Marianas under the command of the 21st BC, reflected on the Curtis LeMay he knew. As a member of the unit that compiled the numbers which showed in black and white the successes and failures of the 21st BC, McNamara got to know LeMay and his approach to leading a bomber force. He said that LeMay "focused on only one thing, target destruction. He was the only person that I knew in the senior command of the Air Force who focused solely on the loss of his crews per unit of target destruction." Sending planes to a target and not destroying it did not sit well with the man and demanded correction.[22]

While he planned his next move against the urban areas, LeMay sent three more missions after the aircraft plants from high altitude. Again clouds hid the primary targets, so the planes hit the secondary targets, Tokyo's port and urban areas. The failings of the mission to Musashino on February 18, the seventh overall to the plant, pressed home to LeMay the futility of fighting the weather. Attempting to bomb from 32,000 feet, only 1 percent of the bombs landed within 1,000 feet of the aim point because the weather disrupted the formation, allowing only 25 percent of the planes airborne to reach the primary target. The official history of the Army Air Forces in World War II addressed this crucial point: "The mission merely added to the cumulative evidence that precision bombing under existing conditions was not paying dividends. Though still unwilling to launch the all-out incendiary attacks against major cities until the B-29 force had been built up, Washington wanted more experimentation with fire bombs." LeMay explained it more succinctly in his biography: "It began to seem that this high altitude stuff was strictly for the birds."[23]

A new target directive arrived at the 21st BC headquarters on February 19. The new directive reinforced the existing primacy of the destruction of the aircraft engine plants as part of the larger goal of destroying Japanese airpower. This new directive coincided with the U.S. invasion of Iwo Jima, the first major campaign in the Pacific since the retaking of the Philippines the previous year. This meant that the principal engine plants that appeared on previous target lists remained top priority until destroyed. The secondary mission of the 20th AF as a whole consisted of supporting "planned Pacific operations," a mission executed by "attacks directed against the primary targets listed" earlier in the target directive. Thus, no secondary target group appeared on the list, but secondary targets for visual or diversionary reasons did warrant listing after aircraft plants. These were "(1) Selected urban areas for test incendiary attack as directed" and "(2) Principal aircraft assembly plants." Also, listed as a final option, the "target clusters" were suitable for radar bombing conditions. These six areas consisted of groups of known target buildings in a concentrated area that offered a decent radar return and would be susceptible to carpet bombing by high explosives. The one thing the directive did not order, or even authorize for that matter, was a full-scale incendiary campaign. Any efforts undertaken came explicitly from 20th AF orders, leaving the timing up to the exigencies of the theater and the commander there. Arnold and the 20th AF did not stand ready to pull the trigger on a full-blown incendiary campaign, especially with no data to back up their theories of success.[24]

Before Norstad's requested Nagoya test mission occurred, missions in support of the Iwo Jima landings took precedence. Instead of bombing the small volcanic island, the 21st BC supported by hitting targets in Japan on the initial days of the assault. Required to make a maximum-force strike on or about February 25, LeMay looked at engine plants in Tokyo and Nagoya and found clouds and winds beyond practical limits for precision bombing. In classic LeMay fashion, he made a decision and ran with it. Following the second part of the target directive received six days earlier, he filled his planes with M-69 incendiaries and sent them to Tokyo. For the first time all three wings were represented in the 231 planes that took off, by far the largest mission yet for the command. Out of this aerial armada, 172 planes reached Tokyo to disperse their 411 tons of firebombs, varying their altitudes from 23,000 to 30,000 feet. The daylight attack burned one square mile. Craven and Cate give the best one-line description of the mission when they say that the "results, like the size of the effort, exceeded anything achieved before." In the grand scheme of things, both in Europe and in future Japanese operations, one square mile seems small, yet for the time in the Pacific it validated the long-held belief that Japanese cities would burn, and burn vigorously. The pilot of the lead plane on the mission, Maj. David Burchinal, described what they accomplished on the mission based on photo reconnaissance: "We realized we had burned out a pretty respectable chunk of Kawasaki, the first area we hit. So we knew the effect was there; Japan would burn if we could get fire on it."[25] Now to actually do it.

5

Losses Per Unit of Target Destruction

AMONG THE MULTITUDE of boxes brought ashore in the Marianas to support the 21st BC, several brought harbingers of a future world concerned with data management. In these crates came the IBM punch card machine of the 33rd Statistical Control Unit (SCU). Originally conceived out of a contract Harvard University held with the Air Force, the SCUs sought to analyze and explain the actions and trends of units in combat and to determine more efficient ways of achieving the military objectives. Combining standard statistical processing methods with advanced data sorting and punch card computing, the SCUs supported both theaters of war.

In the 21st BC, the 33rd SCU processed personnel reports and determined the best method of utilization for the men on hand, analyzed maintenance and parts availability to enable more aircraft to be combat ready, and prepared presentation materials and analysis for briefing up the command structure of the 20th AF. Their most important function, though, centered on the operations statistics—the collection, auditing, compiling, and analyzing of combat data. The data formed a picture of operations over Japan and the weaknesses of the command as they attempted to pound Japan into submission. The various monthly activity reports, graphic summaries of operations, command books, aircraft utilization reports, and staff planning reports painted a depressing visual story of the 21st BC through February 1945.

After a little over a month on the job, the 33rd SCU put on paper what LeMay already knew at the beginning of March: "We had not accomplished very much during those six or seven weeks." Looking at the numbers, the failures seem evident, despite LeMay's changes and personal élan. In terms of putting planes over the primary target, only 49.4 percent achieved that goal in February, a slight increase over January. Sorties themselves rose in the two months from 669 to 1,011, a 50 percent increase, but the bomb tonnage carried stayed close to the same percentage increase. Bomb loads remained at a steady at 2.4 tons per sortie. When taken with the rate of sorties per aircraft assigned, 3.0 in January and 3.1 in February, and the sorties per crew assigned, 2.2 in January and 2.5 in February, it becomes obvious. The increases in sorties only came from the increase in total aircraft in the command, the addition of the 313th and 314th BWs.[1]

Despite the maintenance fixes, even with the small bomb loads, engines still caught fire and fuel exhaustion continued to send planes into the ocean. But the weather remained the worst of all. The jet stream played havoc with planes and bombsights, and the clouds obscured every target. Surely, Clausewitz did not have this in mind when he spoke of the fog of war, but it definitely made understanding the battlespace difficult. As explained earlier, cloud cover was light enough for visual bombing only on a handful of days a month over Japan. The command book from February 1945 estimated seven days of visual bombing possible in March, six each in April and May, and only four in June. Despite several weather-strike missions a day, predicting the days of clear weather still involved guesswork, practically guaranteeing a failure to exploit some of these opportunities. The weather in particular bothered LeMay: "How many times have we just died on the vine, right here on these islands? We assembled the airplanes, assembled the bombs, the gasoline, the supplies, the people. We got the crew set—everything ready, to go out and run the mission. Then what would we do? Sit on our butts and wait for the weather. . . . So what am I trying to do now? Trying to get us to be *independent of weather.*"[2]

And finally, bombing accuracy remained poor. Recent successes represented the exception and not the rule up to that point. The forced reliance on radar aiming because of the weather contributed to the inaccuracy, but the altitude did more. Up to the end of February the mean bombing altitude of the missions from the Marianas stood at 29,000 feet. Lt. Col. Robert McNamara wrote a report that came to the same conclusion as one written by the 8th AF in Europe: increased altitude led to decreased accuracy in bombing. At 12,000 feet in combat conditions, 44 percent of bombs dropped landed within one thousand feet of the aim point. At 18,000 feet that number halved to 22 percent. By 27,500 feet of altitude, 5 percent made it into the thousand-foot circle.[3] The technology to calculate a bomb drop from extreme altitude did not exist, plain and simple. The increase in variables overwhelmed the analog computation capability of the Norden bombsight or the resolution and computation ability of the AN/APQ-13 bombing radar. An added disadvantage to the altitude was that it held the planes above the clouds. A reduction in bombing altitude increased the chance of staying below the clouds, obtaining a good visual identification of the target, and staying out of the drift-rate-increasing jet stream. While the B-29 crews trained in radar bombing, coordination between the bombardier and radar operator could increase the chance of putting bombs on target, so having a visual on the ground made a difference. And in the event of a radar failure, a visual solution with the Norden came into play again now that the airspeed and corresponding drift rates returned to normal levels.

An additional advantage came with lowering the bombing altitude and a shift to incendiary attacks: eliminating the need for formation flying or precise aim points. It would be safer and more practical to have the bombers fly over the target individually at night, only having to aim at the existing flames or by radar relative to an easily identified offset aim point. These changes offered reduced fuel consumption and less emphasis on a level of precision not yet available.

While operational losses tended to decrease over the existence of the 21st BC, combat losses increased. By mid-February 1945 operational losses had come down from a peak of eight planes in December, to four in January, and five in February so far. During the same period, combat losses spiked up from nine in December, to sixteen in January, and four up to that point in February. All this occurred as the total number of sorties increased: 415 planes flew on five missions in December, rising to 469 sorties in six missions in January, and jumping to 345 in only three missions by mid-February. The 33rd SCU attributed the shift to greater enemy activity, better maintenance, and greater experience on the crews' part. Still, if one moderately bright spot remained at the end of February it came from the Japanese themselves, who, after all, offered little resistance compared with the fears felt early in the campaign. Understandably, enemy aircraft and flak still accounted for over 80 percent of aircraft losses, but when viewed in light of the per-mission overall loss rate the numbers were small. In January 1945, 3.4 percent of airborne planes fell to enemy action; in February that number plummeted to 1.5 percent. These numbers accounted for all sorties, and the numbers for bombing missions looked worse, at 4 percent. Fighters made a strong showing early in the campaign but then tailed off. Attacks from fighters still occurred, though no mission came close to the 984 attacks that came over Musashino on January 27, yet the interceptions met with little success. The altitude of the bombers provided safety, and the gun system worked well. To dispel any myths about the utility of the remote turrets, LeMay stepped forward in his autobiography to praise it in a way only he could: "By the time the B-29s came along, we had such a system, and it was functioning. Poor gunnery in the Orient was never the dreadful bugaboo [as in Europe]."[4]

Flak appeared as mostly heavy guns, but often in moderate amounts and mostly inaccurate—still a threat for sure, but more a hazard of the job than a samurai sword in the sky. The one thing the Japanese did not seem to field was medium flak guns. Good for altitudes above 5,000 feet but below 10,000, these high-slew-rate weapons covered the crucial gap between high-altitude strategic bombers and menacing low-altitude fighter bombers, and in all the intelligence reports, photographs, and espionage sources they never appeared.

With all this to mull over, LeMay threw one last factor into his decision making with a report he sent Norstad at the beginning of February. Evidence suggested the Japanese had begun dispersal of operations at the Nakajima plants in Ota and Katsumi. The movement of precision targets raised the real possibility of losing track of them, or worse, their reestablishment in locations immune to bombardment. That made the time to act and destroy the targets now, before their precious machine tools and equipment disappeared. Norstad took the news in stride, even citing the movements as "conclusive evidence that both the pattern and the effectiveness of our operations against Japanese aircraft industries have been established." Still, it created great urgency in operations over the next sixty days, where "our mission must be to destroy essential machinery and machine tools while they offer concentrated targets." LeMay no longer had time on his side. The Japanese reaction demanded a counterstrike, and four precision ones did arrive over aircraft engine plants during the next thirty days, but not enough. The counterstrike needed to strike a decisive blow.[5]

The pressure on LeMay hung as heavy as it ever did on Hansell. Arnold could fire LeMay just as easily, and LeMay knew it. As far as planning in Washington was concerned, the countdown clock for invasion ticked ominously, making the time for strategic bombing to make a difference a dwindling number. Failure now threatened the invasion forces and threatened the existence of an independent Air Force. In a roundtable discussion with other leaders from the campaign years after the war, LeMay said, "We were still following the European pattern. At that rate we could get missions off doing high-altitude bombing, but the weather wasn't going to let us do the job; we weren't going to finish the job before the invasion. So we had to do something radical." LeMay looked at the evidence before him and made the decision to go in at low altitude, no guns, maximum strength, no formation, all incendiaries. Others before him had toyed with the idea and did not possess the power or will to implement it. LeMay took that power and wielded it. Historian Michael Sherry expressed a similar sentiment when he described LeMay's decision as one in which "he grasped a weapon others were free and encouraged to use." The burning of Japan's cities came as not a question of if, but when. LeMay's arrival answered the question.[6]

At low altitude the medium flak presented a danger, and while no evidence existed to prove it actually existed, that did not mean it was not there.[7] Low altitude also left the planes open to the heart of the Japanese fighters' performance band, and LeMay took the gun turrets off the planes. The reduced weight translated to more bombs, and the Japanese did not have night fighters. Plus, no guns meant no fratricide among the bombers in the confusion of darkness. A maximum-strength mission, including one of the first major actions for the 314th BW, undertaken with no formation, threatened to scatter planes all over the Pacific. Without definite ties to other planes the individual aircraft could save gas, but each must perform flawless navigation to reach the target, bomb the target, and return home. With no lead crews to save the men, each crew would have to bomb on their own and the result could be erratic. All incendiaries had been tried before, but this time they would be delivered from 7,000 feet, where their concentration would be maximized. All of these were chances others had declined to take, but LeMay took high risks, and the possible rewards were huge.

"In any case it was my decision and my order which sent the B-29's to the task in the manner described. . . . *My* decision and *my* order," LeMay asserted with authority after the war. When he floated the idea with some of Arnold's subordinates, some agreed and some did not. LeMay then famously asked Norstad, "'You know Gen. Arnold. I don't know him. Does he ever go for a gamble? What do you think?' . . . [Norstad] did opine that he thought Gen. Arnold was all for going in and getting the war won. Certainly Larry didn't say enough to convince me that I'd get off scot free if I made a mistake. But I did gain the impression that being a little unorthodox was all right with Hap Arnold."[8] LeMay saved Arnold the blame in the event of failure by not informing Washington of his plans until the day of attack, when he knew no one would see the message until it was too late to cancel the mission. Any failure fell squarely on LeMay's shoulders; any success became the benefit of every Allied serviceman.

On March 8, 1945, LeMay sent the invitation to the Meetinghouse as Field Order 43, target Tokyo, no specific plant or industry given, just the city.[9] Without a guise of a specific target, the 21st BC threw itself against the industrial complex of urban Tokyo. The planned bombing altitude—below 10,000 feet—spread concern among crews, especially when informed that they would attack individually at night. To those trained and indoctrinated in high-altitude bombing, some with dramatic experience from Europe, the move to low/medium altitudes did not appear to be a good idea at all, in fact almost a death sentence.

It all worked better than anyone imagined. A cold, dry wind blew over the city the night of March 9–10 when 279 of the 334 planes dispatched arrived. The destruction surpassed that of an atomic bomb and killed almost as many as both A-bomb blasts combined. Six-teen square miles of Tokyo burned to the ground, and 100,000 peo-ple died. A firestorm developed, driving the flames across the city, creating enough ambient heat to ignite hair and boil standing water. Within thirty minutes of the first bomb drop, the fire department of Tokyo lost control of the situation, and in the conflagration lost ninety-five fire trucks. Firebreaks and canals did little to stop the flames, as incendiaries fell on all sides and the driving wind pushed the flames and embers through the metropolis. By the next morn-ing over a million Tokyo residents were homeless and 82 percent of the explicit target zone was destroyed.[10]

In the air, the hot updrafts sent bombers on rises and plunges that rivaled the best roller coasters. The light of the burning city glowed for miles behind the departing aircraft, and the smell permeated the nostrils of the crews. In one fell swoop at least sixteen targets came off the list, destroyed, and eighteen significant installations lay in ruins. One night's effort did the job of dozens of individual precision missions, and created chaos in the capital of the enemy.[11]

On the ground in the Marianas, LeMay and the rest of the com-mand waited fitfully to know whether the gamble paid off or resulted in a massacre of vulnerable planes. He took a moment and spoke to the 21st BC public-relations officer, telling him, "If this raid works the way I think it will, we can shorten the war. We've figured out a punch he's not expecting this time. I don't think that he can keep his cities from being burned down—wiped right off the map." Radio silence prevented early results, forcing the wait to last until the crews stepped off their planes and started debriefing. All but fourteen planes returned for a 4 percent loss rate, comparable to daylight missions, and only two of the losses fell to fighters, validating the removal of the guns. The report from the dedicated observer on the mission, who circled the city during the attack to track the damage, validated everything LeMay gambled on. Tokyo lay in ruins as the victim of the worst urban fire in human history. Photos taken the next day showed destruction of 18 percent of the industrial area, 63 percent of the commercial area, and the heart of the residential areas in cinders.[12]

Arnold sent his compliments along to LeMay, telling him, "Con-gratulations. This mission shows your crews have got the guts for anything." Accepting the message as both a compliment to him and his men and also as tacit approval of his tactics, LeMay realized, "I couldn't sit around preening myself on that. I wanted to get going, just as fast as was humanly possible."[13] Now carrying with it the blessing of the commander of the Air Force, the campaign moved into full-scale operation.

Nagoya appeared next on the list of six cities the COA created so long ago, and it received an application of fire on the night of March 11–12. As the other home of the Japanese aircraft industry it held second priority only to Tokyo. Already hit six times with precision attacks and one of Hansell's incendiary missions, it was ripe for the burning by the B-29s. Believing that the fire had burned well but in too concentrated an area in Tokyo, the 21st BC modified its tactics to prevent oversaturation. The 313 planes sent to Nagoya split into two groups, with the second one arriving an hour later to hit areas missed by the first. Also, the release interval of bombs increased from fifty to one hundred feet to spread the pattern over a wider area. The changes failed, if two square miles of burned area may be called a mistake. Failing to understand why the Tokyo fire reached the intensity it did, the bombers lost concentration of force. Tokyo burned because of a combination of a heavy saturation of bombs, overwhelming and destroying the firefighting infrastructure, and a fortuitous wind that powered the flames. At Nagoya the interval between strikes allowed ground recovery, and the increased inter-valometer settings spread the bombs too thin. With no heavy winds to help spread the flames, the initial fires came under control before the second wave arrived and started their fires.

The daily intelligence summary of March 12 reported initial results of the mission to Nagoya and provided rationale for the mission as Nagoya having "congested industrial districts and densely crowded residential sections," with "workers' quarters in the vicinity of the industrial districts." In addition to the workers living next to the plants, the target zone included the industries too small and dispersed to be considered individual targets but which "tend to cluster in congested residential, industrial sections where they are exposed to spreading fires set by incendiary attacks." Victory came from both burning the industries and the homes of the workers, diverting their attention from work to survival during and after the attack. The next day's intelligence summary listed the industrial targets damaged in the Nagoya mission. The Aichi Aircraft Works, believed to be the main plant for the company's fuselage construction and final assembly, lost 13.6 percent of its total roof area, and its main assembly building was "completely gutted." An electrical steel plant, a chemical plant, a machinery company, and a duralumin mill all received damage, along with one of the four major arsenals in Japan, the one at Atsuta, which suffered losses to the small shops surrounding the main arsenal.[14] Rather than sending bombers to each site, the area attack hit them all.

Next the planes visited Osaka on the night of March 13–14, burning out 8.1 square miles of the city. When they returned to their bases the wings received a message from LeMay outlining the intentions of the command regarding future operations. Contingent on the success of the next couple of incendiary missions, the 21st BC would maintain the frequency of their fire missions. Never one to reject a good idea, LeMay determined to take incendiary missions as far as they could go. Further in this memo we read that if the incendiary attacks failed, the fallback plan consisted of "night demolition attack . . . from low altitude."[15] LeMay did not just believe in area incendiary attacks over continuing precision attacks in adverse weather; he seems to have wholly rejected the futile attempt to hit specific targets day in and day out. Low-altitude missions now became the way to go, if only to drop high-explosive bombs. The paucity of Japanese resistance to the night attacks and increasing utility of radar bombing during both day and night relegated the high-altitude missions to the past.

The last two missions of the effort visited Kobe and Nagoya on the nights of the March 16–17 and 18–19, respectively. Kobe suffered 2.9 square miles destroyed, with Nagoya losing a tick more at 3.0 square miles lost. By this point the incendiary supply started running low, with the planes forced to carry the unpopular AN-M50s or even top off their loads with high-explosive bombs under the partial guise of disrupting firefighting efforts with the explosions. Regardless of the intentions, the supplies in the ordnance dumps simply did not support continued operations. Even the fastest vehicle requires fuel to run, and the incendiary campaign acted no different, sputtering to a premature halt for want of ordnance. After the second Nagoya mission the 21st BC ran out of sufficient incendiary bombs to continue.

With the final glow of the embers dying the tallying of the results from the effort began, starting with the thirty-two square miles of Japanese city burned away. Early estimates showed thirty-nine "important industrial targets totally destroyed or damaged," including oil, chemical, steel, wire, communications, machinery, and arsenal concerns, spreading the damage across the breadth of the Japanese war-making industries. Having been on hand on Guam during the Tokyo mission and seen the initial reports firsthand, Norstad offered his congratulations on a campaign well done upon arriving back in Washington, telling LeMay, "I was greatly impressed with the progress you have made in the last two months towards establishing an effective fighting unit." He went on to relate the overwhelmingly positive response of other members of his traveling party not connected to the 20th AF as a sign of the obvious and outstanding quality of work LeMay and his men performed. Even the Navy sent their kudos to the 21st BC, saying they were "proud to operate in the same area as a force which can do as much damage to the enemy as your force is consistently doing. May your targets always flame."[16] The 21st BC, and 20th AF for that matter, now rode on a wave of success and achievement unthinkable a month earlier. They went from the also-ran of the theater to leader of the effort to knock Japan out of the war literally overnight.

To the rank-and-file members of the 21st BC the explanation of the change in tactics centered on weather as a limiting factor and low altitudes solving those issues. Incendiaries came as a logical weapon for low-altitude attacks, though "it should be emphasized that the decision to mix up the strategy against the enemy was not a decision to throw out the window high altitude precision daylight bombing."[17] While risks were involved, the command felt they were negligible or surmountable, and the decision went forward. While a couple of pages in the 21st BC newsletter sufficed to convince the air crews involved that so much destruction was the correct course of action, LeMay and his staff recognized the need for a more formal review of the events of early March. They prepared a report to analyze the effort and draw conclusions on why it succeeded. The analysis started with defining the why behind the incendiary effort. Just as important as lauding the successes came the explanation of why changing tactics made sense at all.

The problem, simply put by the document they generated, was that for operations up to that point "the results were unsatisfactory." Weather dominated the list of causes for this performance, an issue illustrated in the analysis in a cartoon of a weather officer standing in front of six betting windows each labeled with different weather impediments and a sign above all the windows saying "High Altitude Derby—Only 6-Race-Parlay Bets Taken." As the caption reads, "The odds do *not* favor the weather officer."[18] To complete their job the 21st BC needed to become independent of the weather.

Night missions solved some of the weather problems and minimized the other risks inherent in a bombing mission. Lower altitudes put the planes below the impeding clouds, while night missions guaranteed the bombers returned in daylight hours, a counter to the deteriorating weather in the Marianas. An added bonus, the long-range navigation (LORAN) radio signal came through stronger at night than during daytime hours, making single planes better able to navigate on their own.[19] Also, Japanese fighter response was rated as weaker at night than during the day, and gun-laying radar for anti-aircraft fire was inefficient.

From here the report shifts to what had gone right and wrong on the missions and how the command adapted to the situations to create the efficient machine that came out of the campaign. The five sequential missions allowed planners to understand the outside forces influencing the results of their efforts and make changes accordingly. While earlier incendiary missions occurred one at a time with long periods between execution, the March attacks went off at one- to two-day intervals, placing an emphasis on quick adjustments to stay ahead of the game. The surprising success of the initial Tokyo mission gave an impression of false superiority, one that dissipated after the letdown following the Nagoya mission two nights later. The lesson learned from the "failure" centered on concentration of bombs and planes. The Nagoya mission spread the attack out too much and gave firefighters the chance to control the fires before they formed a full conflagration. This lesson translated immediately into the subsequent missions, which strove to push the bombers over the target area within a two-hour window and concentrate their attack.

The low-altitude missions also answered some lingering questions about where and how the B-29 should operate and gave the command what the report refers to as the "high cards." Low altitudes and the dissolving of formation flying eliminated the issue of high winds and allowed pilots to fly most of the mission on cruising power, thus saving fuel and reducing mechanical failures. On the five incendiary missions, 91 percent of aircraft airborne reached the primary target, compared with only 36 percent on the preceding five high-altitude missions. Also, the lower altitude enabled the planes to carry more bombs and minimized timing errors when dropping bombs, tightening their pattern over the target area and increasing overall accuracy. On high-altitude formation missions each plane only carried 35 percent of its potential bomb load, a number that jumped to 100 percent if attacking singly at low altitude. Even radar performed better at low altitudes, giving a better picture of the target and being less inclined to break completely before the target area.[20] The incendiary missions and their tactics made the B-29 the bomber the Air Force and Boeing believed it to be, fulfilling the promise of the most advanced bomber in the world.

The March attacks also reversed the silent but crucial decline in morale that plagued the 21st BC. Heavy losses due to enemy action and their own planes' mechanical failure, coupled with poor bombing results, had driven the efficiency and enthusiasm of the crews down to near a breaking point. In a way, if not launched to achieve a military victory, the March missions were almost needed to give the men a chance to show they could destroy something, that they could do a lot of damage. Before March the 21st BC had settled into a mode of "flying the missions," a lusterless and mechanical series of motions that marked off missions but made no effort above and beyond the minimum required to achieve the goals of the command. Cases of "flying personnel disorders," a term referring to fatigue or the physical effects of the fear of flying the mission, hovered around ten cases per week, or 1 percent of the crews reporting a unique instance. In fact, in mid-February the number of cases spiked to over twenty in one week as the command flew four missions in seven days. But when the lower-altitude tactics went into effect and the success they brought spread to the men, the instances of fatigue dropped dramatically. The cases per week fell back to just above ten and the instances of new disorders fell to only 0.2 percent of the men—all this as the number of men and planes in the command grew and the tempo of operations increased dramatically as full-effort missions launched every other night. The pace of operations almost doubled, increasing the risk for the crews twofold and doubling their schedule of exhausting fourteen-hour flights, and still the proportion of men pulling out of missions decreased. LeMay, his subordinate commanders, and countless crewmen all recount the newfound bounce in their step as they saw the images of Tokyo destroyed, the fruits of their labors finally paying off. LeMay and his tactics got the most out of his crews and showed that contrary to popular understanding they could be pushed far beyond what Hansell and high-altitude tactics had done.[21]

Not everything worked properly, though, and the report points to corrections and further analysis needed for future operations. Achieving the desired pattern while attacking individually presented the greatest problem. Despite using radar aim points, crews still tended to drop bombs off target, a flaw that on at least one mission was attributed to "complete disregard for the prescribed aiming points." Crews started bombing by looking for areas not on fire, trying to spread their destruction but often dissipating the force of the attack. The analysis determined that "not until the fourth mission (Kobe) was it realized that visual distribution methods, which are in fundamental contradiction to the principles behind the selection of aiming points, were largely responsible for the failures of previous attacks." From this point on, crews had to understand that visual correction could only occur after acquiring the aim point and for making minor adjustments to hit that point.[22]

Another important factor to take into account on future missions centered on wind speed. On five out of six of the missions actual damage failed to meet expectations, often by a large margin, and the underlying factor coincident to each of those missions was a lack of wind. The one mission that exceeded expectations, that first night over Tokyo, benefited from strong winds fanning the flames and increasing the damaged area by almost a third. Future missions needed to account for this factor, as it could "compensate for insufficient concentration or uneven coverage of the area."[23]

The report closes with a blunt statement about the future of operations in the Pacific: "Precision attacks from 25,000 feet or above against pinpoint targets are unsuited to operations in this theater. Radar operates inefficiently at high altitude. Weather conditions—high wind and poor visibility over the target, scattering of formations when penetrating fronts on route—interfere with navigation, render bombing inaccurate and require highly skilled crews." From now on the preferred tactics centered on low-altitude missions, preferably at night. Even ways of hitting precision targets would be investigated, as well as daylight incendiary missions. The analysis closes with the promise that "immediate steps are being taken to requisition adequate supplies, aircraft, and crews to permit the maximum employment of our new tactics."[24]

The Statistical Control Office validated the success of the 21st BC in its calculations, which it submitted to Norstad on April 4. According to the statistics compiled by Lieutenant Colonel McNamara, during the single month of March the 21st BC dropped 96 percent of the bomb tonnage previously dropped by the entire 20th AF. They did this while achieving a sortie rate of 6.7 per aircraft for the month. This figure included all the wings, even the recently arrived 314th and 315th. The veteran 73rd BW flew an even more impressive 7.2 sorties per plane, 80 percent more than the previous planned rate of 4.0 sorties per plane per month. Increased sortie rates alone did not account for the massive tonnage, though, as increased bomb load thanks to the low altitudes contributed to the number. The command averaged 6.8 tons of bombs per plane, more than double the 3.1 tons carried on high-altitude precision missions. The lowered altitude, delayed rendezvous, and other factors pertaining to the nature of night missions allowed reduction in plane weight through removal of fuel and miscellaneous weight (guns), and meant weight for bombs. The overall takeoff weight of the planes when they left the Marianas actually increased one thousand pounds, but more efficient operations made it possible to complete the missions and do more destruction than before. As if these numbers did not sell the future of operations as a copy of the March efforts, the reduced losses to planes sealed the deal. Improved maintenance put more planes in the air and reduced failures to bomb the primary target from 19 percent and 11 percent in January and February, respectively, to only 6 percent in March. Once over the target the losses also dropped dramatically. In March the 21st BC cut their February loss rate of 3.3 planes per 100 combat sorties down to 1.3 planes. The quantitative facts did not lie: operations improved greatly when the tactics changed for the B-29.[25]

While on the surface it seemed the 20th AF departed from the strategic-bombing doctrine of attacking the specific industrial targets that fueled the enemy's war machine in favor of indiscriminate area attacks, at the highest levels this idea met total rejection. Norstad wrote privately to LeMay at the beginning of April admitting his increased respect for the 21st BC's abilities and how the events of March represented a compromise between industry and a "susceptibility to fire." He expressed his confidence that the 21st BC, "more than any other service or weapon, is in a position to do something decisive." He emphasized this position to his staff as well, telling them that the destruction wrought by the fire raids "alone might break the will of the people to continue to fight. This may be the thing that will bring home the futility of continuing the war to the Japanese people as well as to the leaders of Japan."[26]

Behind the scenes, when the subject of bombing the Imperial Palace surfaced, a popular target for hawks to advocate despite the disadvantages such an action entailed, Arnold clarified the policy of the entire 20th AF: "Bombing policy of 20th Air Force remains in force; i.e. to attack specific assigned targets."[27] This shows that Arnold, and the Air Force in general, perceived the urban-area missions of earlier in the month as attacks on industrial targets, even if very large ones. This falls in line with the COA's and JTG's understanding that these urban areas represented a distinct target system, worthy of attack and not outside the moral restrictions of strategic bombing. But how to reconcile the cost to the Japanese people with the necessity for such destruction? For historian Michael Sherry,

One solution was the resort to a rhetoric of cost-benefit analysis, contrasting the B-29's strikingly low loss rates with stunning statistics: "1,200,000 factory workers . . . made homeless" and "at least 100,000 man-months" of labor lost to Japan and "369,000,000 sq. ft. of highly industrialized land . . . leveled to ashes" in the Tokyo raid alone. Of course the human carnage was implicit in such statistics, but they kept the emphasis on the economic objectives of precision bombing. Of course there was no denial that incendiaries were the weapon and great conflagration the result, but incendiary attack was simply "the economical method of destroying the small industries in these areas . . . of bringing about their liquidation." When asked about "the reasoning behind this switch from explosives to incendiaries," Norstad denied any switch because the mission still remained "the reduction of Japanese ability to produce war goods." Was there any change in "the basic policy of the Air Forces in pin-point bombing [and] precision?" "None."[28]

Arnold informed LeMay by teleconference on March 28 that the JTG found no strategic bottlenecks in the Japanese industrial or economic system except aircraft engine plants, but "the enemy's industry as a whole was vulnerable through incendiary attacks on the principle urban areas." Under that assumption, the 20th AF sent a JTG study to the 21st BC on additional urban areas worthy of attack. While listing certain industrial targets of high importance as precision targets, by late March the JTG also designated thirty-three urban-area targets in the comprehensive plan of attack. The targets fell into three groups: Phase 1 for the ten of highest industrial importance, ones including ground ordnance and aircraft plants; Phase 2 for the next twelve areas of industrial importance, ones including machine tools, electrical equipment and components; and the "Remaining" areas of lowest importance but still viable as area targets. The list did not consist of individual cities, but areas within cities that held concentrations of industries, making them legitimate strategic targets and not the object of wanton destruction. Of the original thirty-three areas, four lay in Tokyo, eight in Nagoya, and seven in Osaka; the rest were spread over five other cities. In essence, the JTG set up two target systems, one for precision targets and one for area targets.[29]

6

Down the Path of Destruction

IF CIRCUMSTANCES DID NOT allow him to send planes at night to Japan filled with incendiary bombs, LeMay looked for a way to use the dark for precision purposes. The opportunity to fly at low altitudes with heavy bomb loads and little enemy interference proved too good to pass up. He put his staff and those of the wings on the task of finding the best method for accurately putting high-explosive bombs on a specific target in the dark. Pathfinder aircraft dropping various types of incendiaries and flares to mark targets, or at least illuminate them for visual bombing, all received consideration if not actual operational test. All came up short. One attempt in particular, the mission on March 24, 1945, to the Mitsubishi engine works in Nagoya, started with pathfinders dropping incendiaries to illuminate the target, but they missed and only added to the confusion caused by the clouds and smoke. Results turned out negligible. While similar tactics had worked in Europe for the British, the 21st BC lacked the experience at this type of operation and the large incendiary bombs needed to effectively mark a target. In what starts to appear as a pattern, the 21st BC appealed to the 20th AF to expedite British-type marker munitions to the Marianas so they could take a second crack at night precision bombing. Until then the realm of hitting precision targets remained in the daylight under clear skies, just as it always did. As will be seen, the rapidly unfolding operations in the Far East pushed this request and associated intentions off to the side, for all intents and purposes ending the experiment of nighttime visual precision bombing.

Experimentation with different types of ordnance did not confine itself to incendiary munitions only; the 21st BC dropped various types of high-explosive bombs on Japanese targets, looking for the most effective method of destroying Japanese industrial and urban targets. By far the most prevalent conventional munition used was the 500-pound bomb, though 1,000-, 2,000-, 4,000-, and even 10,000-pound bombs found their way onto the B-29 for delivery to Japan. The primary targets of the conventional bombs, like the entire campaign, were Japanese industry. Attacks on industrial targets sought two primary goals. First came destruction of the physical plant, the buildings, towers, holding tanks, pipes, and other fixed structures on-site, all the large and heavy things that could not move. Second came destruction of the machines and tools inside the plant, from large presses and transformers to jigs and conveyor belts—everything that could move and enabled work at the site to continue inside the buildings. Actual products came as a bonus, though they were not the primary target. Strategic bombing seeks to destroy the ability to make and continue making war, not directly destroy combat units.

To this end the evaluation of the high-explosive bombs focused on their ability to blow up buildings and render the tools inside useless. Each type of bomb revealed advantages and disadvantages. The most popular type of high-explosive ordnance by far, the 500-pound bomb, came with positives and negatives. Small size allowed more per plane, up to forty, and in concentration they covered a target well. That same small size limited their blast effects, creating heavy damage to roofs and soft structures but requiring direct or close hits on structural members to damage them. And while individual structural members may break, the damage did not extend far enough to instigate a spreading collapse. The corrugated sheet asbestos commonly found on the sides and roofs of Japanese industrial buildings fared particularly badly, easily blown off the structures. The smaller and lighter 500-pound bomb allowed each plane to carry more pieces of ordnance and spread destruction over more of the target area, but it performed rather poorly at both of the crucial criteria. When fused with short fuses, the bombs often detonated as they hit the light asbestos-tiled roofs of Japanese industrial buildings. This blew the tiles off and mangled the steel roof frame but did not structurally compromise the building by damaging the support pillars or beams, and it did no more to the machines below than pepper them with shrapnel, insufficient damage to take the machine out of service for any considerable amount of time. In fairness, the relatively light construction of many Japanese industrial buildings at the time enabled them to survive bomb hits rather well. Oftentimes the buildings consisted of steel or concrete vertical supports with horizontal steel crossbeams, possibly even reinforced by a sawtooth roof. The sides and roof covering consisted of sheet metal or asbestos tiles. This meant that the overpressure of a bomb exploding blew the walls out but failed to damage the frame of the building. Repairs, then, consisted of simply reapplying the walls to the frame. Even explosions on the roof of these buildings, which gnawed the trusses apart, only collapsed the immediate areas of the roof over which they exploded. To actually damage the building, especially with a small bomb, a direct hit or very close near miss was required.

Bombs of 1,000 or 2,000 pounds did more damage than their 500-pound counterpart but still needed a lucky close hit on a load-bearing member to bring down a structure. Against steel-frame buildings the 1,000-pound bomb did extensive damage, but still not enough to distort the building and bring it down. The 2,000-pound bombs did much better, though, their air bursts knocking columns off their footings, severing girders, and bending overhead crane tracks, whereas ground detonations only shifted columns and distorted roof trusses. Against concrete buildings the 2,000-pound bomb was the only one that consistently penetrated the solid roofs to detonate inside and deform the entire blast space. According to the USSBS, the damage of a 500-pound bomb against a reinforced-concrete building only did 12 percent of the damage done by a 2,000-pound bomb on the same type of structure.[1]

In all cases, fusing played a crucial role in the success of individual bombs. Those set too sensitive detonated in soft areas. In particular, the most numerous type of bomb, the 500-pound, often received one-hundredth-second or zero-delay fuses, which detonated them as they hit the roof rather than letting them penetrate to or into the floor. Good at mangling the lighter metal parts of the building, it dissipated the majority of the energy outside the structure and not onto the contents of the target, causing the roof and sides to blow off but leaving the contents and structure intact. Damaging heavy machines inside buildings necessitated direct hits or delayed fusing to cause the bomb to detonate in the floor and break the machine bed or supports. To hurt lighter machines, blast and fragmentation did greater damage, but not definitive destruction. Collapse of the building itself often buried the machines but did not permanently disable them.

The step above 2,000-pound bombs came in a package twice its size. With a light case and explosive fill comprising 80 percent of the weight (normal bombs are only roughly 50 percent explosive and 50 percent casing), the 4,000-pound bomb relied on explosive power rather than shrapnel to generate its extensive damage to buildings, notably steel-frame and concrete structures. While they did not damage machines they did not directly hit, the debris and fire damage they caused tended to eliminate the productive capability of their target. Overall the 4,000-pound bomb achieved spectacular results, prompting the USSBS to comment that "the degree of its superiority over other types of demolition bombs becomes more conclusive as the weight of target construction increases." Yet the Japanese lacked heavily constructed buildings, and the bomb's impacts on machine tools "were not particularly outstanding compared with its potential power." The "collapsing structural members are comparatively ineffective in producing serious damage to machine tools."[2]

In one instance of 4,000-pound bomb usage, the attack on the Sumitomo Light Metals Industry plant, 104 bombs over two missions structurally destroyed 72 percent of the roof area of the plant, collapsing and distorting the buildings. Similarly, at the Aichi Aircraft Company, 43 percent of the built-up area was destroyed, with 51 percent more roof area blown off. Combined with the resulting fire from the bomb blasts, much of the tools, supply stocks, and work in progress was eliminated. The damage proved deceiving, though, as post-strike reconnaissance overestimated the damage done by 40 percent due to misinterpretation of the roof damage.[3] While the plants were put out of commission, the fire did more to destroy the tooling than the blast effects. Against incombustible targets the 4,000-pound bomb lost much of its punch.

The biggest bomb tested with any regularity was the 10,000-pound light-case high-explosive bomb. Though capable of a massive blast, because of its size this bomb represented more of a one-shot wonder than a viable weapon. Each B-29 could only carry two of the massive weapons under the best of conditions, as the weight of two equaled the maximum payload of the bomber. To that end, most of the tests involved individual planes or only a few aircraft each dropping one on a specific target. Capable of a 250-foot blast radius, the bomb was a force to reckon with, able to sweep away anything in the vicinity of its detonation. In one instance a locomotive ten feet from the explosion flew seventy-five feet from the force. Against residential structures the bomb blew the light construction apart but failed to severely damage the parts, allowing the people to collect the debris and reconstruct livable buildings again and defeat the purpose of destroying the workers' homes. In terms of damaging larger structures the big bomb did well, but like other high-explosive bombs it did not hurt the contents without something close to a direct hit. In one instance a can and drum manufacture experienced a hit only twenty feet away. The building collapsed but failed to catch fire, and half the machines inside survived enough for salvage. This made the 10,000-pound bomb only a very large high-explosive bomb, with no damaging effects beyond those proportionate to its size.[4] It should be noted, too, that these bombs were not dropped so much to test their blast effects as the USSBS would have one believe. The 10,000-pound bomb used the same case shape as the Fat Man atomic bomb. The B-29s that dropped them were from the 509th Composite Group training and refining tactics for the coming atomic bomb missions.

The overriding differences between the smaller high-explosive bombs carried by the B-29 boiled down to the options size created. The smaller bombs, which came with thicker steel cases, offered more penetration and fragmentation than the larger 4,000- and 10,000-pound weapons. In the same way, the number of each carried varied by weight. With a 20,000-pound maximum load, under the best of conditions each plane could carry forty 500-pound, twenty 1,000-pound, or ten 2,000-pound weapons. The dispersal over the entire target by a formation of planes dropping the heavier bombs did not create enough critical hits to damage the vital machines inside the buildings. While the larger ordnance caused more structural damage and collapse, these conditions did not ensure the destruction of the contents of the buildings. Any way the mission planner calculated the situation, it was difficult to load planes with the proper ordnance to achieve first-pass target elimination.

Understandably, solid conclusions regarding which weapon worked best in which situation proved difficult to come by based only on post-strike photos. After the war the USSBS concluded the 4,000-pound bomb to be the best, followed by the 10,000-pound in terms of destroying industrial buildings. Yet even they admitted this data proved little based on the variety of targets each bomb hit and the variations in types of damage done. Another, yet unnoticed, variation in the data came from the timing of the attacks. The larger bombs all fell near the end of the war, when experience and opportunity for success reached their peak, resulting in more hits on the target by the more powerful bombs. Even if these conclusions emerged during the campaign, little could have been done about it, as the majority of conventional bombs available in and on their way to the Marianas weighed 500 pounds.[5] Unlike the incendiary campaign, use of anything but 500-pound bombs never had a chance to expand. Whereas the ammunition dump of the 21st BC always carried at least small stocks of incendiaries, and this ordnance figured directly into precampaign plans and standard operating procedure for precision attacks, larger high-explosive bombs needed to prove themselves in testing before regular use. The tempo of operations simply did not allow for intense testing when real destruction was needed.

Further complication to the question of which high-explosive bomb to use stemmed from the confusion caused by the preponderance of roof detonations and the damage they did. Typical post-strike photo interpretation determined the effectiveness of attack based on the square footage of buildings damaged or destroyed. The detonation of many of the bombs on the roof created the impression of more area, or "roof area" as it sometimes appears, having been destroyed. In some cases this resulted in drastic overestimation of the damage done, as at the Aichi Aircraft Company mentioned earlier, or in other cases undercut the bombers by not showing how a small number of holes caused the gutting of the building by shrapnel and fire. Unfortunately, high-altitude pictures offered the only

urban industrial incendiary raids dovetailed with the chaos of dispersal nicely, possibly even ensuring its failure as the USSBS believed. The widespread damage of the fires disrupted transportation and supply lines, displaced workers and caused absenteeism, and spread construction materials thin. More important, as Norstad and LeMay envisioned, attacking the cities, all the cities, kept the pressure on industries by burning them out even after their dispersal. Those companies that dispersed in their home city suffered like Mitsubishi Heavy Industries did when the March 18 fire raid on Nagoya burned the Matsuzakaya department store where the dispersed experimental and research data resided. Worse still, dispersal to smaller cities failed to immunize production to the destruction of fire. The Hitachi Aircraft Company, which moved some of its production facilities to the smaller city of Chiba, suffered the loss of sixty-six machine tools and 7,950 square feet of plant area when the 21st BC burned out the city on July 7, 1945, and damaged the girls' school, technical school, and university buildings where the operations had been reconstituted. The propeller division of Sumitomo Industries lost the operation it dispersed to a brewery in Nishinomiya when the 21st BC burned down 2.8 square miles of the city on August 6. By spreading the destruction to the smaller cities the Air Force started forcing redispersal of establishments, like the Kawasaki Aircraft Company, which first moved its operations from Kagamigahara to Ichinomiya and Gifu, both of which fell under the flames of the 21st BC, necessitating a second dispersal to forest workshops outside the urban environment.[9]

The true effects of dispersion appeared after the war when careful analysis of Japanese industry showed that by the end of June 1945 half the Japanese aircraft production capacity was idle due to dispersal. This amounted to loss of production large enough that the USSBS believed it accounted "for practically all of the drop in production of aircraft in the summer of 1945."[10]

· · ·

While precision bombs remained the mainstay of the strategic-bombing campaign, and incendiaries were executing a separate thrust all their own, a third prong of the B-29 offensive lay beneath the surface waiting for an unsuspecting ship to happen on it so it could detonate. Air-dropped sea mines helped finish the blockade on Japanese imports implemented so spectacularly by the Navy's submarines. The credit due to the mines for helping strangle Japan coastal and inter-island shipping lanes never matches the space it receives in accounts of the bombing campaign.

As he did with any operation that pulled bombers away from strategic objectives, LeMay reacted cautiously to any plan that ended with his planes' sorties doing the Navy's job. In short order, though, he came around to the value mining offered the war effort and the value his large planes offered the mining effort. With its large carrying capacity and radar aiming ability the B-29 proved ideal for the low-altitude seeding of minefields, and the mission offered good practice in night operations and radar guidance.

The campaign, appropriately called Operation Starvation, embraced three main objectives: (1) prevent importation of raw materials and food to Japan; (2) prevent supply and movement of military forces; and (3) disrupt shipping in the Inland Sea. This translated to mining the Shimonoseki Straits between Kyushu and Honshu (where troops and supplies moving south for the defense of Kyushu needed to pass); mining the ports on the Inland Sea, Tokyo, and Nagoya; and mining the ports used for the Korea/Japan trade. Using a mixture of magnetic, acoustic, and pressure mines, the planes of the 21st BC created a web virtually guaranteed to ensnare any large or metallic ship courageous enough to run the silent blockade. The Japanese, as always, deficient in countermeasures and technology, sat helpless to clear paths with enough certainty to permit traffic. This prevented imports from reaching their destination but also held ships already inside ports from leaving to transport goods, effectively paralyzing Japanese shipping.

In forty-six missions (1,528 sorties) the 21st BC dropped over 12,000 mines. Starting in late March 1945, as the incendiary fires dimmed, the bombers first bottled up the remaining Japanese fleet at Kure-Hiroshima and started seeding the Shimonoseki Straits to slow traffic between the islands and cut off the repair facilities situated in the Straits. After plugging the Straits the bombers moved north, sealing off ports, achieving a near blockade by the end of July. Mines not only accounted for tons of shipping sunk but forced inter-island shipping onto the railroad system, taxing that resource to near the breaking point and making it an ideal bottleneck target for future bombing. Long reliant on ships to move goods up and down the coast and between the main islands, the Japanese were forced to fall back on constructing more small wooden ships as the only type of vessel able to safely ply the mined waters; they lacked the capacity or numbers to support the needs of the wartime economy.[11]

Mining operations by the 21st BC pulled out the last slack in the tightening noose around Japan. Mines augmented all the other efforts to squeeze the life out of the islands, taking away the last options for survival. They supported U.S. Navy submarine efforts and gave the surface fleet more independence of movement by isolating the Japanese fleet in port. Against the industries of Japan, the mines helped shut off the flow of supplies and raw materials into the production facilities and made an already critical food shortage for the Japanese people that much more dire. Finally, the mines pushed traffic traditionally carried by coastal boats onto the meager rail system, further clogging the arteries already heavy with dispersal efforts and increased wartime traffic.

In the course of a month, 20th AF's fortunes had changed completely. By diversifying operations, their combat effectiveness skyrocketed and the Japanese started to feel the effects of strategic airpower. The tactics were now in place to prosecute the air war: precision bombing when weather permitted, incendiary attacks when weather was bad, and regular return trips to keep up the minefields.

• • •

The unthinkable finally happened on March 27 when the 21st BC received orders to commence support of the Okinawa invasion. The dreaded call from the theater commander to focus the B-29s on tactical targets finally arrived. To reduce the threat of Japanese air intervention of the landings, the B-29s were directed to destroy the airfields on Kyushu. LeMay protested bitterly, citing the gross misapplication of airpower as well as the futility of slowing the flow of kamikazes by peppering the rudimentary airstrips with bombs. LeMay knew it did not take a genius to figure out that the Japanese stored the planes in hiding places around the airfields, and turning over the dirt on dirt runways only made a nuisance out of the massive bombers. He argued that the B-29 served the invasion better by taking the plants producing the planes out of the war rather than chasing the individual units around the home islands like a giant silver rendition of the Keystone Cops. The protests came to no avail, and for over a month the B-29s made near daily trips to the Kyushu airfields, but managing to sneak in attacks on the manufacturing plants as weather permitted.

It was on one of the intermittent returns to a strategic target on April 7 that the 313th and 314th BWs finally smashed the Mitsubishi plant in Nagoya. Attacking with 500-pound bombs and coming in at medium altitude at high noon, 154 planes dropped 2,456 bombs on the plant, putting a quarter of them in the target area, half of those striking buildings. When it was over, 90 percent of the plant's facilities were destroyed along with 20 percent of the machine tools. Many buildings lay in ruins, and output at the plant dipped from 129 engines in March to 15 in April, and then only 30 for the rest of the war. The same day the 73rd BW did the same to the Musashino plant with 2,000-pound bombs, eliminating it as a viable production facility. There the bombers came in at medium altitude and in daylight as well, achieving 26 percent accuracy in the target area, smashing the remaining machine tools at Musashino (those not already dispersed), and forcing the plant to cease engine production. The biggest aircraft engine manufacturer in Japan no longer played a role in the fight and fell off the 21st BC's target list.[12]

As much as LeMay continued to itch to increase the operational tempo as he did in early March, the resources just would not allow it. The layoff for Okinawa support gave the entire 21st BC a chance to evaluate their success and plan the future. What worked needed little explanation; from a plane and crew perspective, the tactics kept both from increased losses. The biggest question of all, that of which altitude to send the big bombs in at, now appeared forever settled. No longer did the planes need to fly at 30,000 feet for protection, as the Japanese defenses did not warrant such precautions. The 21st BC's A-2 Section (Intelligence) submitted a report in early April confirming low to medium altitudes as the area in which to fly. Looking at European experience as well as the 21st BC's own, the report concluded that no altitude gave immunity to flak (a slight jab at the B-29 itself), but because of the benefits that came from bombing at lower altitudes they recommended daylight bombing levels anywhere from 18,000 to 25,000 feet, numbers commensurate with the efforts performed in Europe. At night, when the Japanese defenses faltered most, heights as low as 7,000 feet were permissible. LeMay's gamble now came officially endorsed; low altitudes at night represented the way to go.[13]

Owing to the dramatic turn of events in the Pacific air campaign, April saw a flood of updates made to JTG planning documents in an effort to maximize the effectiveness of the bombing campaign. The "Japanese Aircraft Industry General Analysis" received update and still found the target system the most important in Japan. By the JTG's estimation, 1,305 to 1,750 combat aircraft still came off the assembly line each month, only a 17–38 percent decrease from three months earlier and not a whole lot for the primary target of the entire bombing campaign. The positive indication came from the evidence showing an 80 percent production loss in army single-engine aircraft production, resulting primarily from the destruction of the Nakajima New Ota plant in February by the 21st BC. These figures belied the fact that, according to the JTG, only 30 percent of Japanese aircraft production now supported the army, the other 70 percent going to the navy.[14]

The importance of this target group remained at the highest possible rating. "Aircraft losses to the JAF [Japanese air force] continue to fall and there is lessened resistance to the continually rising scale of Allied effort." No firm cause could be drawn, though theories existed regarding shortages of planes and pilots, gasoline going to tactical units, or, more likely, a "policy of conservation of aircraft on the part of the JAF as a result of past and anticipated attacks on their production facilities."[15] The rationale proved wrong, but the assumption on the policy was dead-on. The Japanese began saving planes as part of a massive retaliatory effort for when the first Americans hit the beaches of Kyushu or Honshu. After the Okinawa campaign, ongoing at the time, the Japanese strove to increase the net number of planes available for defense, refusing to use them up piecemeal.

A long-anticipated but chilling trend also emerged as the bombing increased and the intelligence community increased their collection of target-area photos. The Japanese ramped up dispersal on a large scale, moving the equipment and production of aircraft to other suitable locations. The report cites the new discovery of a converted textile mill near Himeji believed to produce George fighters at a rate of thirty-five to seventy-five per month. This defied several standard assumptions of the bombing campaign, as a textile plant sat near the bottom of the list regarding desirability to hit and Himeji lay well outside the cities understood as the concentrations of industrial production. If taken as an indication of a growing trend, suddenly the focus of the 21st BC needed to expand all over Japanese islands and to all of Japan's cities.

The JTG's "Japanese Urban Areas General Analysis" received update in April as well. Cognizant of the flaws of the earlier version of the report, and the limitations imposed by ignorance in February, this analysis fully embraced area attacks as "an integral part of the program recommended by the Joint Target Group for overwhelming of Japan's productive capabilities."[16] Their enthusiasm only extended to the effects on industrial concentrations, and to that end the revised report included a list of thirty-three concentrations designated as viable area targets. These concentrations sat in eight different major Japanese cities, six of which appeared on the original COA list of six cities suitable for incendiary attack. So the conversion of the JTG to embrace area attacks did not entail much of a shift from earlier conclusions, just a tighter grip on the strategy.

The report went further, defining on paper the strategy that LeMay already sought to implement. Understanding that "a great deal of priority industry lies outside urban industrial concentrations," this industry needed destruction lest "area attacks have limited effect." Thus area attacks complemented, not supplanted, precision attacks of the vital aircraft and industrial plants. To this end the JTG gently molded air doctrine to meet the ultimate goal to "progressively weaken the most formidable strengths of the enemy." Departing from the long-held belief that individual choke points offered the best chance to strangle the enemy's war-making ability, the JTG condoned an all-out attack on that ability by hitting it at every level. In their interest in the belief that Japan's "most formidable strengths lies in her stores of munitions, her transportation system and particularly in her productive capabilities," they stepped up to the reality of the war at hand, and that pressure existed throughout the supply pipeline in Japan. Cutting off the source did not end the flow of supplies entirely until that in the pipe flowed out too. Now, at the end of April, the list of options for ending the war obviously started to grow short, and the realization set in that the academic issue of the number of planes or shells produced was about to translate into a real equation for deciding how many soldiers and marines died on the beaches of the home islands. Urban-area attacks earned acceptance as a "program of comprehensive attack on Japan's end product industry would be formidable if it were not for the heavy concentration of industrial capacity in urban areas at risk from incendiary attacks. This makes urban area attacks an integral part of the program for overwhelming Japan's reserve position."[17]

To address any concerns regarding these attacks as indiscriminate bombing of the Japanese people, the JTG provided rationale. The highly concentrated nature of Japanese cities made this strategy feasible, but only the industry itself should be attacked, not "residential structures." This allowed the "destruction of capacity important to the continued production of war material and de-emphasize[d] reliance on production loss resulting from absenteeism or disorganization." To this end target areas received selection according to degree of concentration and contribution to the war industry and effort. This made these areas legitimate military targets, and there was no violation of the strategic-bombing doctrine. This represents the first expansion of said doctrine outside the gates of the actual plants themselves, acknowledgment that an economy runs on much more than specific individual parts and instead relies on the whole living being to function. As quantitative evidence to support their argument the JTG noted that in the thirty-three areas outlined, "30% of aircraft assembly, 42% of aircraft engines, and 56% of aircraft parts are located in the 33 areas. The same areas include over 50% of all types of electrical manufacturing, 51% of machine tool production, 75% of general metal working capacity, and over 25% of armament manufacturing." The human consequences did not escape the JTG as they drew their conclusions. Burning out these smaller plants would directly affect the people in target areas by causing them "loss of homes, injury, etc.," the "etc." referring to death.[18] But the benefits of destroying some plants and immobilizing the others trumped the human cost in Japanese lives.

With Okinawa support still the order of the day, a new target directive arrived on April 4 with Musashino and the Mitsubishi engine works in Nagoya still the top priority, followed by the six highest-rated Phase 1 urban areas. Norstad then told LeMay, "If the AAF destroyed the next group of targeted areas within a reasonable time, 'we can only guess what the effect will be on the Japanese. Certainly their warmaking ability will have been curtailed. Possibly they may lose their taste for more war.'"[19]

LeMay took full advantage of the directive and worked in strategic attacks whenever possible. Precision strikes on aircraft plants still occurred when the weather allowed and the weather over the Kyushu airfields conveniently cooperated and stayed cloudy. More pertinent to the discussion here, by mid-April the Marianas accumulated enough incendiaries to mount three night fire missions against Tokyo and Kawasaki. The first mission, on April 13, targeted the arsenal section of Tokyo, long seen as a target too small for effective precision attack but in need of destruction to support the overall war effort. In all 11.4 square miles went up in smoke along with the Japan Artificial Fertilizer Company and precision piston ring maker Physico Chemical Industries; several other war-industry sites received minor damage. Two nights later the B-29s returned to the Tokyo area, eliminating another 6.0 square miles of Tokyo and 5.1 square miles in the Kawasaki-Yokohama area just to the south. Among the 240,000 buildings destroyed by the attacks of April 15, seventeen important targets were in or adjacent to the burned area, among them power stations that helped supply electricity to the metropolis and the Tokyo Measuring Instrument Works, one of the typical tooling plants so necessary for industrial production but too small to target for precision attack.[20] And then the missions ceased again for want of incendiaries.

The renewed success of the incendiary campaign showed the tactics viable and repeatable and brought up the issue of how far to take such an endeavor. Despite the JTG's list of urban industrial areas worthy of burning, and the obvious success in the tactics, the question of their utility remained. Did attacking urban areas really qualify as strategic or even ethical? This brought the argument back to the origins of the doctrine and the idea of aiming at the enemy's morale, which could be destroyed resulting in a reduction of their will and ability to fight. The doctrine allowed for this as a last resort. After the precision targets were eliminated and the war dragged on, then the assault on morale entered play as a way to push the enemy nation over the edge to peace. The bottom line in Japan was that as an industrial nation they never conformed to the Anglo-European mold that the doctrine was created to counter. The Japanese entered the war with enough industry and technology to fight a war of colonial conquest and never possessed or mobilized industrial capacity to conduct a full-scale modern war. That the Pacific fight lasted as long as it did comes as a testament to the overwhelming size of the area over which it was fought and the tenacity of the Japanese fighting man. At no point before or during the war did Japan have a chance of competing with the industrial might of the United States, much less an Allied coalition. By April 1945 the precision targets in Japan worth the effort to hit no longer existed. The few targets in that category which existed at the beginning of the campaign now lay in ruins or on a very short list for the next clear-weather days. The rest of the precision targets constituted excess capacity or sites so small and individually insignificant to not warrant specific attack. The time for adding morale to the target list had indeed come.

On April 10, Col. Cecil Combs, founding staff member of the 20th AF who worked both the planning and operational sides of the organization, recommended to Norstad intensified incendiary bombing immediately after V-E Day. The tide toward a full-scale tactics switch started to turn, a move in which historian Michael Sherry sees incendiaries as going from a backup measure to supplement precision attacks to the reverse, with the cities burned and then the rest picked over by precision. Around this time LeMay told Norstad that in the "present stage of development of the air war against Japan . . . for the first time strategic air bombardment *faces a situation in which its strength is proportionate to the magnitude of its task.* . . . [D]estruction of Japan's ability to wage war lies within the capability of this command, provided its maximum capacity is exerted unstintingly during the next six months."[21] Between those lines read the plea to send LeMay the final tools he needed to burn down the rest of Japanese industry and bring the war to an end. Finally, the planes, crews, and tactics all came together to give strategic airpower the force needed to fulfill its destiny, and the only thing standing in its way was a series of empty bomb dumps.

An analysis of the evolution from precision to incendiary attacks requires inspection and understanding of the incendiary ordnance on hand in the Marianas and on their way. The ammunition dumps in the Marianas contained both high-explosive and incendiary munitions. The high explosive's purpose is obvious for a precision bombing unit; the incendiary ordnance was used interspersed with the high explosive to ignite debris and flammable structures and for specific test missions. As of January 1, 1945, the depot on Saipan held 6,211 tons of M18 cluster units of M-69 incendiaries.[22] At an expected loading of four tons per plane this equated to 1,552 sorties of incendiary-only missions. Keep in mind that incendiaries also were expected, from a planning perspective, to compose 40 percent of the load for precision missions to ignite the debris and vulnerable buildings in the target area. Based on 6.5 missions per month and eighty-one planes per mission, both 21st BC averages, with a ratio of two incendiary test missions and eleven precision missions the incendiary usage breaks down as shown in table 2.

This left a healthy margin for practice missions, weather/recon missions, slight increases in bomb tonnage as efficiency improved, and conducting six missions to burn the six cities identified by the COA for urban industrial attacks. It must be noted that these numbers reflect only M-69 units, which were by far the most numerous incendiary munitions on Saipan at the time. Small stocks of M-47s and M-17s also existed, but not in numbers great enough to be used as a primary weapon on any mission. Viewing these numbers as a snapshot in time, the 21st BC's incendiary stocks supported both regular precision operations and the long-planned campaign against the six cities, but no more. This leads to the conclusion that the urban industrial areas only represented a single target system, no different from any other. Striking the six cities, contingent on test raids proving the feasibility of fire as a weapon, was an end in itself. After their destruction the B-29s would move on to the next system on the list.

Table 2. Prospective incendiary usage

	Missions	Load	Split	Planes	Total (tons)
Precision	11	4 tons	0.4	81	1,425.6
Incendiary	2	4 tons	1	81	648.0
					2,073.6

Everything changed starting on March 9, 1945. The success of that night's incendiary raids and the follow-up missions to other cities in the first half of March raised several issues. The 21st BC ran out of incendiaries, and it only struck four of the six cities listed as targets. LeMay later insisted that he would have continued his offensive had he the weapons to do so. After the first round of attacks, he said, "If we'd had more fire to pour over the enemy industry we would have poured it. But we didn't have it, though it had been requested well in advance."[23] Yet there is no evidence to suggest LeMay's intent to continue the destruction beyond the six main cities. He never made any statements to this effect, and he still needed to finish the job at hand. This brings up the second issue: regardless of the estimated density of incendiaries required to destroy the target areas, by the time they ran out of weapons two cities sat untouched, Kawasaki and Yokohama, and the other four sat incompletely burned. Combat experience showed the variability of results that different weapons, intervals, weather, and altitude combinations created. Just to finish the job on the existing targets the 21st BC needed more incendiary munitions. The situation turned more critical as the planes carried drastically more bombs on low-altitude missions than anyone estimated. Previously, expenditure and procurement planning occurred predicated on a load of 4.0 tons per plane, per sortie. The initial Tokyo mission on March 9–10 went 20 percent above that to 5.3 tons per plane. By the Kobe mission on March 16 that number almost doubled the estimates, rising to 7.0 tons per plane. Looking at the incendiary expenditures versus receipts for March, it becomes obvious that the ordered and shipped incendiaries did not account for the success or increased usage of weapons that LeMay's men achieved. The 21st BC received 4,486 tons of incendiaries in March to replenish their stocks and account for the increase in planes assigned to the theater; they used 10,763 tons. Instead of maintaining expenditures to plan, they went right through their allotment. The diary of the chief of staff of the 33rd SCU summarized the situation from a numbers point of view in a March 17 entry: "Prior estimates are now no longer effective due to the new tactical concepts and use of the B-29, which double and in some cases triple the former incendiary loads."[24] Obtaining more incendiaries, or any weapons for that matter, involved a sea of approvals and a trip across the sea before receipt. Figure 2 illustrates the complete process flow for obtaining more ordnance.

All requests were initiated at the BC level, where they ended up in the hands of Army Air Force Pacific Operational Area (AAFPOA), who contacted the Commanding General of the Army Air Forces (CGAAF) to release the ammunition and deliver said ordnance to the port of embarkation. Likewise the AAFPOA contacted Commander in Chief of the Pacific Operational Area (CINCPOA) to allocate the needed shipping space to transport the ordnance from the port of embarkation to the requesting command. The process took weeks to accomplish, stopping at AAFPOA, where requests were scrutinized for actual necessity; with the CGAAF, where the actual ordnance needed to be located or manufactured; and lastly with the CINCPOA, whose shipping schedules defied interruption and the journey of ships from San Francisco to the Marianas took weeks regardless.

Incendiary shortages were nothing new in the Marianas. As early as November 1944 mission planners realized that the bomb bay rack configuration of the B-29, like that of other heavy bombers, failed to accommodate smaller munitions effectively, such as the 100-pound M-47 incendiary. The racks needed adaptors to carry multiple pieces of ordnance, and the 21st BC did not carry enough in its stocks. It was only through the intervention of Arnold that the requested adapters arrived in a timely manner. The events highlighted a shortcoming in the use of incendiary munitions by the 20th AF. Most firebombs came in units much too small to warrant individual use, and required cluster kits or rack adapters, or both, to hang multiple units on the B-29's bomb stations designed for 500-pound conventional bombs. The planes and the ground crews sat unaware and unable to equip

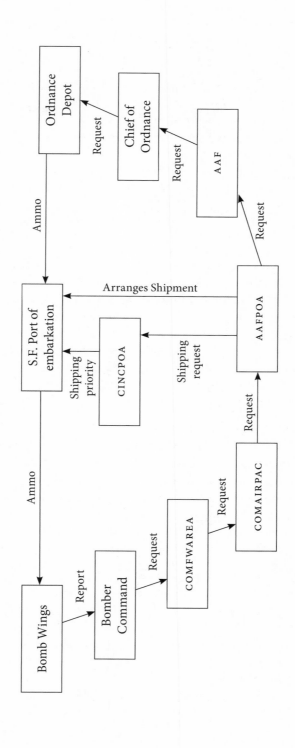

Fig. 2. Process for incendiary delivery

the bombers appropriately. A form of just-in-time engineering and high-priority parts requesting made sure the planes flew with their required loads, hardly a sustainable system for long-term operations. It is doubtful that if ordered to start full-scale incendiary operations before February, the 21st BC held it in their power to comply. The 20th BC, which does not appear to have ever delved into the intricacies of using a variety of incendiary bombs, surely had no chance of answering the call to start incendiary raids. A better reason for this shortcoming by the 20th BC was that all its planes flew from bases well out of range of the six cities chosen for fire raids.

In accordance with the identified need for additional weapons and accessories, the AAFPOA submitted ordnance needs for the entire theater on December 17, 1944. The estimates for the 21st BC usage reflected the increasing number of planes available to the command as it grew to four groups (one wing) in January, eight groups (two wings) in February and March, and twelve groups (three wings) in April, May, and June. The estimations came close to reality with the 313th BW entering operations in February to add the second expected wing, but the 314th BW joining a month earlier than expected, in March. The request assumed 40 percent of all B-29 sorties to carry only incendiaries, further breaking down that number into individual types of incendiary clusters.[25] A bit of ambiguity arises here. Does the 40 percent figure indicate that the estimators believed that nearly half the B-29 missions would carry only firebombs, or that 40 percent of the perspective tonnage consisted of incendiaries? Two pieces of evidence point to the solution. First, as mentioned earlier, notionally 40 percent of each 21st BC load contained firebombs as augmentation to the high explosives' destructive power. Second is the percentages they allocated to B-24 and B-25 missions for incendiaries. The same request that pegged B-29 usage at 40 percent planned on 45 percent of B-24 sorties and 30 percent of B-25 sorties as consisting of incendiaries. Since B-24s and B-25s did not undertake any large-scale firebombing campaigns, and often stayed relegated to inter-island attacks on Japanese base areas, the estimates obviously refer to overall bomb usage more than the way those bombs were loaded for any particular mission.

Unfortunately, these numbers never passed through the 21st BC for concurrence. While this appears an egregious miscalculation, the actual ill effects amounted to little. The 21st BC they would have passed through was still in its infancy and fell under the command of the incendiary-wary Hansell. He did not intend to conduct extensive incendiary operations anytime soon, and he was totally unaware of future actual expendable rates, so input from the 21st BC would not have materially changed the estimates of the AAFPOA. Even if, by some shocking turn of events, Hansell dispatched his precision targets in short order, neither he nor his staff understood the actual requirements of incendiary ordnance until a successful test raid occurred. By the end of December only one such test occurred, the pitiful mission to the Tokyo dock and industrial area of November 29, and the execution taught the command nothing regarding the proper use of fire weapons on a flammable area.

Based on theater inputs, the Air Force set production requirements as of March 11, 1945, with the assumption that ammunition expenditures by the 21st BC would only consist of 33 percent incendiaries, the rest consisting of high-explosive ordnance, mainly 500-pound bombs.[26] No explanation is evident for the inconsistency between the requested numbers and the prepared units, but the ordnance orders do lead to two conclusions. The Air Force as a whole, with Arnold as its leader as well as leader of the 20th AF, held no intention of changing its overall strategic-bombing strategy from precision to incendiary for anything more than striking preordained urban industrial areas. They did not procure incendiaries in any quantity greater than was sufficient to maintain the planned operations tempo for high-altitude precision daylight bombing. This especially holds true for expanding the campaign to all the sizable cities of Japan. The incendiaries ordered as of March 11 absolutely *did not* accommodate an expansion of the operations. The second conclusion is a refutation of Sherry's assertion that the dearth of incendiaries on hand represented a further sign of Washington's hands-off approach in the decision making in the Marianas. "Washington issued no formal directive sanctioning the planning and execution of the Tokyo raid, and Arnold remained a convalescent substantially out of the command picture," writes Sherry. "LeMay was apparently blessed by an extraordinary suspension of control from Washington." Sherry goes on to include the ambiguous actions of the president and Joint Chiefs of Staff, all of whom knew of the plans and possibility of fire attacks on Japanese cities but took no active participation in the decision-making process. "The destruction proceeded with accountability beyond LeMay's, poorly fixed," he writes.[27] The reality is that the powers that be in Washington did not so much leave LeMay to his own devices in the Marianas as much as establish general goals for the destruction of Japanese industry, and not supply a large incendiary campaign. The independence LeMay enjoyed was typical of commanders in the field. The decision to execute on the urban industrial target system only fell in line with the fulfillment of the target priority structure in effect for the previous year. Most importantly, the paltry ordnance order that passed through the Air Force command structure gave no consent or even indication of a desire to conduct a campaign comprised heavily with incendiary raids. Washington did not leave LeMay the tools for Japan's incineration and walk away expecting him to start the campaign he did; nor did they even establish a supply train to accommodate greater success in the execution of authorized urban industrial attacks on the six cities. Washington did nothing out of the ordinary, never expecting or desiring the fundamental mission of the B-29 to change.

The overwhelming success of the March fire campaign necessitated a revision of incendiary planning numbers. Accounting for both the increased number of sorties flown (ten in March alone) and increased bomb loads, the 21st BC revised its bomb needs. The number of sorties per plane increased to nearly eight per plane, and the load per plane doubled to almost eight tons. The divergence from normal planning came with the command's assertion that the expenditure could consist of entirely high explosive or entirely of incendiary bombs, so it needed on hand in the Marianas sufficient weapons to conduct all one type of operation or the other. A postwar study summarized the situation: "After careful consideration the XXI Bomber Command decided that the optimum possible level for VHB [very heavy bomber] ammunition in the Marianas was a two months stock level of both incendiary and high explosive bombs. Based on an expected expenditure of 10,000 weight tons [long tons] per wing per month."[28] All told, the 21st BC asked for nearly four times the ordnance it previously planned on receiving. This carrying of concurrent stocks of both conventional and incendiary munitions gives the first indication of a willingness by anyone, most notably LeMay as theater commander, to consider using fire ordnance as the primary weapon of the strategic-bombing effort over Japan.

Norstad endorsed the request, saying, "It is realized that the quantities listed are very large; however, the successful operations of the past months indicate these requirements are not only possible but probable, therefore recommend that every effort be made to furnish this ammunition so that no mission has to be changed or cancelled because the desired munitions are not available."[29] This shows an early willingness at the theater level, and approval at the headquarters level, with incendiary missions at a heavy pace in the future. But this does not guarantee, or even on Norstad's part endorse, an increasing campaign of firebombing. As noted earlier, by the time they depleted the stocks on hand in March, four of the six major cities of Japan lay damaged but not destroyed, and two sat untouched. Incendiaries at the ready for everyday use only ensured completion of the destruction of the "urban industrial" target group already defined, with an option for utilizing the successful strategy later against other cities as necessity demanded.

The 21st BC further refined their numbers in April. The requested tonnage delivery for May and June comprised more than 75 percent incendiaries, replenishing stocks expended in early March. By July, and for each subsequent month, the requested amounts of ordnance remained even between conventional and incendiary types, and full supplies of each. These increased planning factors did little to generate immediate results, as April's ordnance supplies had already started on their long journey from the United States to the Marianas. In fact, the receipts of ammunition in March, April, and May largely originated from orders requested before March. To state it another way, contents in the supply line lagged far behind the changing tactical situation.

Reflecting the current and long-standing belief in incendiaries as a mere component of a large precision-dominated strategic-bombing campaign, the six ships that which docked in April 1945 brought 8,653 tons of incendiaries and 14,000 tons of high-explosive bombs, nearly the inverse of the 21st BC's revised request. These paltry numbers did little to ease the hunger for firebombs. After the last trip to Nagoya with firebombs on March 18, the 21st BC took a forced month off from the tactic until supplies replenished enough to send 352 planes to the Tokyo Arsenal Area and burn out another ten square miles. Strikes on the Kawasaki and Tokyo urban areas over the next two days followed before lack of weapons, and the theater request for support of Okinawa operations, shifted all the priorities of the 21st BC.

In May, supplies finally caught up with demand, and the incendiaries received accounted for more than half the weapons delivered to the Marianas. Alas, requirements for Okinawa support continued into May, leaving any new incendiaries off in a corner to wait. When the support request lifted in early May, LeMay and his planes sought to finish the job started in March of torching the major cities of Japan. They returned to Nagoya and Tokyo, as well as visiting Yokohama and Tachikawa for the first time before the month ended, spreading charred debris in their wake. During those May missions 72 percent of the incendiary tonnage received that month fell on Japan, leaving the situation as dire at the beginning of June as it was at the end of March and April. By one estimate, only enough incendiaries for four full-strength missions remained when May ended.[30]

Fortunately, in mid-June the emergency shipments of incendiaries began arriving and a new phase of the campaign started. LeMay enlisted the marines to unload weapons from the ships, and the bombs never saw the bomb dump, going straight to the hardstands and the planes, and the campaign hit its full stride again.

At the same time, questions arose from the CINCPOA. They rejected the necessity of the 21st BC possessing ammunition in numbers that equated to twice its possible expenditure rate. To this end, Air Inspector Maj. Gen. Junius V. Jones went to the Marianas in June to see for himself the ordnance situation and needs. His findings, published in a memo on July 5, 1945, found that the "present supply of bombs on hand, both IB [incendiary bombs] and GP [general-purpose high-explosive bombs], is adequate for operations during the months of July and August."[31] Based on his inspection of sortie rates, supplies on hand, and storage capacity, the islands held more than enough ordnance to complete their tasks. To that end he recommended that supplies be maintained at present levels with a ratio of three high-explosive bombs for every two incendiary weapons.

LeMay's response came five days later to tear apart Jones's findings and reveal some of his intentions. He categorically denied the assertion by Jones that the weather in July and August offered conditions ill-suited for incendiary bombing, countering with the knowledge that the low and middle cloud cover over the summer months precluded pinpoint precision bombing much more than the more liberal targeting of incendiary bombing. LeMay correctly pointed to his latest target directive of May 12 directing the 21st BC against aircraft plants and major urban industrial areas. He stated, "The method of compliance with this directive is dictated primarily by weather considerations." To that end, "As in the past month, this headquarters anticipates that at least 80% of its effort will be incendiary attacks against urban industrial areas." To refute the belief that targets suitable for burning no longer existed, LeMay pointed to "a list of 180 urban industrial areas which are now in the process of being evaluated to determine which areas constitute profitable targets for incendiary attack," at least one hundred of which "definitely . . . are of sufficient importance." This led LeMay to conclude that the entire effort of the command could focus on incendiary attacks if the situation and weather so warranted.

LeMay rejected the other crux of Jones's findings—that the supplies of ordnance on hand in the Marianas constituted plenty for planned operations—as a total misunderstanding of the original 21st BC request: "Such conclusion requires acceptance of the condition that the command's tactical decisions be governed by type of munitions on hand, which is precisely the condition which this command is seeking to avoid."[32] Never again would LeMay allow the momentum of the campaign stall due to supply issues, as happened in March. To LeMay's dismay, Jones's findings were based more on previous operations than on future tactical plans. The 21st BC looked forward to growing in size and power, and utilizing the advantage it discovered over the Japanese in the form of fire, yet it continued to do all within its power to carry on the strategic campaign against specific, vital targets through precision bombing.

LeMay eventually lost the argument, when the stocks ordered

immediately after the March raids reached the Marianas and supply fulfilled demand. Since the 21st BC never resorted to all one type of mission over the other, the ordnance on hand and arriving met the overall needs of the unit, and no missions ever needed postponement again due to a lack of the proper weaponry.

The overall point here is obvious: nobody in the Air Force, from top to bottom, anticipated that incendiary attacks would take the level of precedence that they it did. Burning Japanese cities seemed obvious, but never as a primary form of attack or against as many cities as the campaign eventually encompassed. The weapons for such destruction only flowed into the Marianas once the March raids proved the concept and the possibility of continued execution loomed as possibility but not a certainty. To that end, LeMay wanted on hand enough bombs of each type to shift his focus at will. If LeMay, or any of the many layers of Air Force planners and decision makers, all the way to Arnold's level, insisted on or planned at any point to dedicate the efforts of the B-29s to firebombing as a primary or sole tactic, they would have given the units in the field the tools to carry out that mission, and they did not.

7

Death Throes

THE WEEK OF MAY 7, 1945, proved monumental for the 21st BC and the world. On Tuesday, May 8, Germany surrendered, ending the war in Europe, and on Friday, May 11, the support of Okinawa operations officially came to an end. The war now focused on the Far East and the pending final act of Japan's defeat. With Okinawa operations complete, LeMay received updated orders by which to set his priorities. "Current target directives remain in effect until changed as the situation requires," the directive stated. It went on to specifically direct that "the primary mission of the Twentieth Air Force is to complete the destruction of the major aircraft production and to destroy the principal Japanese urban industrial areas in the shortest possible period of time." The message closed with an open-ended admonition about winning the war as soon as possible: "It is extremely important, in order to capitalize on the present critical situation in Japan, that your effort be concentrated to the utmost on those targets which will contribute most to the defeat of Japan."[1] The intent comes across as obvious: hurt Japan as much as possible to end the war.

The aircraft targets remained easy to execute on. One simply needed to wait for a clear weather day, and the 21st BC would flock to them. The urban industrial targets created a slightly larger question. The JTG originally identified thirty-three areas as targets for firebombing, but that number seemed small and largely concentrated itself in cities of the original six designated for incendiary attacks. A broadening of the air campaign to eliminate principal areas and push the weakened Japanese over the edge to defeat needed more than just hitting the major cities again. It neither provided the pressure needed

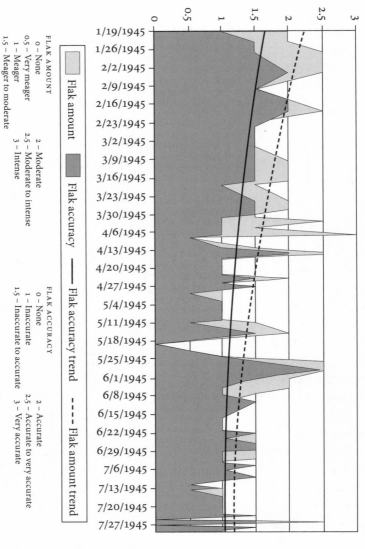

Fig. 3. Flak experienced over Japan

FLAK AMOUNT
0 – None   2 – Moderate
0.5 – Very meager   2.5 – Moderate to intense
1 – Meager   3 – Intense
1.5 – Meager to moderate

FLAK ACCURACY
0 – None   2 – Accurate
1 – Inaccurate   2.5 – Accurate to very accurate
1.5 – Inaccurate to accurate   3 – Very accurate

Flak amount
Flak accuracy
———— Flak accuracy trend
------ Flak amount trend

nor offered enough targets for the growing B-29 force to feed on very long. With the crucial tipping point for the Japanese people seemingly in reach, the time came for taking the destruction to every city and level of the enemy's society.

Expanding the incendiary campaign carried with it risks. The low-altitude tactics that took the Japanese by surprise months earlier might not work again owing to Japanese adaptability and concentration of defenses as their empire shrank. To this end it became important to evaluate the defenses in general and see whether the risk to the bombers increased since their March success. Flak accuracy and intensity decreased noticeably as 1945 progressed. Figure 3 uses postmission crew debriefings to determine the flak situation.

In January 1945, flak intensity experienced by crews hovered above moderate, just below the moderate-to-intense level. In terms of accuracy, they felt it equated very close to accurate. At the time, flak threatened the aircraft and created real concern among crews. In February both the intensity and the accuracy of the flak started tapering off until it settled in a gradual slope around March toward meager intensity with inaccurate firing. The switch to lower altitudes, inside the medium flak zone, lessened the intensity of the fire available to the defenders, a condition magnified as summer progressed and the bombers started hitting targets outside the industrial centers and away from flak gun concentrations. Accuracy also suffered over time as an emphasis on night attacks robbed the Japanese of visual gun direction. While searchlights at night helped frame the bombers for flak to hit, this did not compensate for a lack of radar. The shifting bomber tactics placed them in the blind spots of the flak defenses, and the lack of sophistication of the Japanese defenses and their slow response to evolving situations limited U.S. concerns over the possibility of sudden improvements in their defenses. Flak still presented a danger to the bombers, but nowhere near as great as when the campaign began. With continued caution and use of evolving countermeasures, such as the radar-reflective metal strips called "rope" used to fool enemy radar, flak would not truly bother the B-29 any longer.

Likewise, fighter opposition decreased as operations over Japan continued. The April 5 daily intelligence summary pointed out that

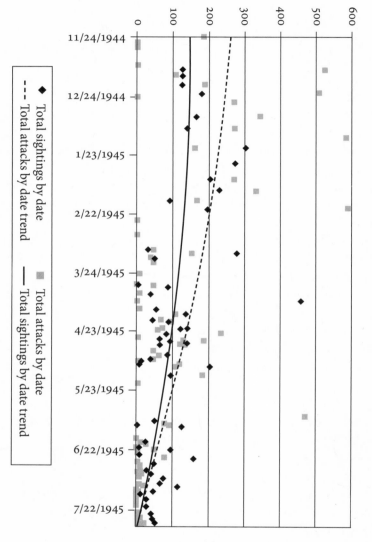

Fig. 4. Fighters encountered over Japan

Legend:

◆ Total sightings by date
■ Total attacks by date
- - - Total attacks by date trend
— Total sightings by date trend

the "strategy of the Japanese high command seems to be to nurture its airforce [sic] for a last all-out hard strike when the tactical and strategic situation demands it, and in the intervening time depend on antiaircraft, unfavorable weather, and devine [sic] winds for defense of vital home areas." Ten days later, 21st BC intelligence added that the Japanese made "little more than a token defense except at Tokyo. The situation is reminiscent of the days when the Luftwaffe started retrograde." A review of fighter encounters over the course of 1945 reinforced this finding, showing the Japanese defenses as deteriorating to almost nonexistent as spring turned to summer. Total sightings per mission dropped from an average of 150 in November 1944, at the height of the precision campaign, down to half that and declining by the start of June 1945. Attacks per mission dropped even more dramatically, losing more than half its average 275 per mission in November to equal the sightings per mission at roughly 75 by the beginning of June, and eventually down to no attacks at all by early July. The straight statistics in figure 4 do not convey the enormity of the change, though. During the first six months of full-scale operations by the 21st BC, the number of B-29s over Japan increased dramatically, as did the number of targets hit per day, increasing the chances of encountering an enemy airplane, yet the number of encounters continuously dropped. Likewise, the bombers started going in at night, obviating the enemy's response because of their lack of night fighters. One thing that does not come through in the figure but appears in the intelligence summaries that provided the data is that as time progressed the attacks became less and less aggressive. Whereas early Japanese response to the bombers entailed pressing attacks to distances where accidental ramming occurred, as time went on the attackers stayed at standoff ranges and appeared less and less inclined to actively engage the bombers. So while the average at the beginning of June may read 75 attacks experienced per day by the 21st BC's bombers, those attacks often fell far short of the effort required to bring down a bomber.[2]

All this information boiled down to one thing: the Japanese no longer effectively defended their homeland. The 21st BC tried every type of mission possible, day or night, high or low altitude, and all the combinations, and the defenses came up short every time. Now, no matter how LeMay chose to send his planes in, he knew they need not worry about enemy response. The Americans held all the cards.

Given the results of the March attacks, the disarray of the Japanese economy, and the impunity with which planes flew over the empire, in late May planning for the Empire Plan began. The B-29s needed an answer to the cloudy period of late spring and summer, and while they already carried on their docket the JTG's thirty-three areas, they needed a longer-term solution to the problem. The 21st BC told Washington that by the end of June they anticipated destruction of all thirty-three of the JTG's "Selected Urban Industrial Concentrations" as outlined in the "Japanese Urban Areas General Analysis" published at the end of April. The correspondence emanated from a belief by the command in the Marianas that "the destructive effects of these urban incendiary attacks is cumulative—each successful additional attack of this kind adds to the dividends to be derived from all previous attacks." As always emphasized by planners, concentration of force kept pressure on the enemy and increased the destructive power of each attack. Stopping at the thirty-three areas removed the pressure on the enemy. So, "this factor is worth especial emphasis at this time when there is a possibility of achieving a decisive effect with air power."[3] To maintain the level of effort and destruction on the Japanese, the targeting needed to expand to other cities, even ones not already identified as industrial centers.

The 21st BC recommended expanding incendiary operations to twenty-five additional cities. Their selection weighed on the priority/number of war industries in the designated target areas, looking closely at trying to destroy not only a specific industrial plant but also the surrounding area that housed workers and supported the larger concern. They believed that attacking these areas did the same amount of damage to the industry as removing an individual target and came with the added benefits of social dislocation and transportation tie-ups that inhibited the larger economy. Burning out areas churned up the day-to-day lives of the Japanese, accelerating the destruction wrought by the strategic-bombing effort and giving the reasonable impression that soon the lives of the people would be so disrupted and fractured that the only option left would be to sue for peace.

Under this new plan, secondary industrial cities received a visit from the B-29s on cloudy days, with precision strikes occurring anytime the weather allowed, which in April meant only five times, three in May. The small size of cities allowed splitting up the command so wings hit separate cities on a single day. The idea of attacking multiple targets at one given time, while partly a local decision based on the number of planes available and size of the targets, also stemmed from a study done months earlier by the JTG. Looking for ways to improve bombing efficiency, the study understood that conditions over Japan varied greatly from those over Germany. The concentration of Japanese industry and challenges of continual cloud cover over Japan offered many targets and few opportunities to destroy them. The smaller size of each target also limited the amount of ordnance needed for complete destruction. To this end, smaller formations of planes over a target increased accuracy. For example, with fewer than fifteen aircraft attacking a target, 22 percent of bombs fell within five hundred feet of the aim point, while if fifteen to sixty planes attacked that number fell to 11 percent, and nearly halved again to 6.5 percent if more than sixty planes attacked. In practical terms, this meant that if each plane carried ten bombs, the fifteen-aircraft formation placed thirty-three within five hundred feet of the target, the middle group (thirty-eight planes, splitting the difference between fifteen and sixty) hit with only nine more than that, and the sixty-plane formation put only thirty-nine in the target area. Clearly, the smaller group created much more efficiency in bomb deliveries. Without drawing explicit conclusions about why this was the case, the implication remained clear: a large formation of planes is unwieldy to control and spread out to such an extent that some of the planes never physically pass over the aim point. That is why the study suggested either designating multiple aim points or simply reducing the number of planes over the target. These figures, the study argues, paid the greatest dividends on smaller targets, like those in Japan, where individual hits matter the most and also proved the hardest to achieve.[4]

The 20th AF responded to this plan with a new target directive three days later. It once again put aircraft up at the top of the priority list, lauding the considerable damage done already, but warned that many targets in the system still existed, including some newly identified ones. The 21st BC needed to maintain the pressure on the target system "to the point where attrition can be maintained greater than production . . . [and] effective new weapons must be prevented from being used in large numbers." After that, the tone of the directive changed from previous orders. When it gave the second priority as urban industrial areas it placed their attack not in terms of the aircraft industry but the reverse: "The above targets [listed aircraft plants] will be attacked when logistical support is not available for incendiary attack on urban industrial areas or when weather forecasts indicate a reasonable certainly that visual daylight bombing conditions will exist."[5] Read with an open mind, this wording almost placed urban industrial attacks above the precision attacks. Whether this is because of the practical understanding that the bombers had a five times greater chance of hitting an area target than a precision one on any given day is not given, but the indecision reached an end and area attacks on industrial targets joined precision attacks as a full-fledged strategic-bombing tactic for the Americans.

LeMay and his command, long waiting for this opportunity, went right to work on executing the plan. Ever since the successes in March he had been pushing for more training in the tactics of dropping firebombs and for more bombs period. In the intervening months he asked for use of the small Marianas island of Rota as a practice target for perfecting incendiary tactics. At the same time, he and his staff started lobbying for more incendiaries to arrive in the Marianas as soon as possible. While the supply and ordering issues regarding these weapons was covered earlier, it is helpful to understand that the 21st BC started a very vocal campaign of message traffic looking for ways to increase its weapons stores without waiting for the usual bureaucratic mess to subside. They inquired about spare munitions in other theaters, asked for supplies and instructions to create their own oil bombs out of fifty-five-gallon drums, and wrote stern messages regarding pending weapons shipments. One such memo, written on April 18, 1945, as the 21st BC chomped at the bit and planned its next great phase of operations, admonished the chemical officer for the Pacific Operational Area that "five ships of incendiary bombs to arrive [in the] Marianas before June 20, 1945 will not ful-

fill tactical requirements of this command. Shipments of incendiary bombs should arrive [in the] Marianas Islands prior to June 1,
1945."[6] Finally, in mid-June the waiting paid off. The planes, crews,
bombs, and timing all came together to launch a second round of
incendiary attacks.

On June 15 the last major city on the JTG's list received its dose of
fire, and on June 17 the smaller cities started to feel the heat of the air
campaign. Nightly, each wing received an assigned city so that when
the sun rose the next morning another group of Japanese metropolitan areas came off the target list thanks to results "greater than the
average results of the four-wing missions against the major cities."[7]
Whenever planes sat ready and radar conditions proved favorable,
the mission went off. This made it harder and harder for the mission
planners, as daily they needed to assemble, for each new city, target packages that contained pertinent and well-considered details
such as bomb type, numbers, aim points, and all the other helpful details intelligence provided. It also made it harder and harder
for the Japanese, who saw their entire civilization upturned by new
calamities each night.

As the second round of fire raids ramped up in mid-June the
JTG released a summary of "Current Developments" regarding their
"Japanese Urban Areas General Analysis." This summary reads like
the citation of a commendation to the 21st BC, giving an accounting of estimated damage done by the command during their March
attacks. The attacks destroyed an estimated 29 percent of the industrial buildings in the six cities designated for urban-area attacks, or
8 percent of the industrial area in all Japan. While precision bombing accounted for nearly all of the three months of aircraft production lost through the destruction of 30 percent of the building area
of engine plants, the urban-area attacks supported the effort against
aircraft by burning out several propeller plants.[8]

Along with this came the incineration of 50 percent of houses in
the six cities, dehousing roughly 10 percent of Japan's population
(1,267,000 dwellings housing 5,748,000 people). Dehousing forced
absenteeism among the population as they skipped work to rebuild
their lives. According to estimates by the JTG, this equated to six to
fifteen days of lost production in the six major cities. Quantitative fig-

ures for absenteeism gave credence to the belief that attacks on urban industrial areas paid multiple dividends by destroying equipment as well as taking the workers out of the economy of the unburned areas. Even if the main plant sat immune to the firestorm it sat idle for a period after an attack for want of workers.[9]

Summer also brought the invasion of the home islands into the realm of reality. The land forces lacked further islands to hop, and with the war in Europe over, a supply of reinforcements boarded ships for the journey halfway around the world to the Pacific. The apparent settling of the question of strategy led the JTG to focus its planning on supporting such an endeavor. This meant eliminating the precision targets most valuable to the Japanese war effort in sequence. The 21st BC took exception to this recommendation on the grounds that as the command on scene they better understood the situation. Weather, that ever-present factor, dominated their argument against dedicating the force to precision attacks. Even using radar, though much improved since the beginning of the year, the planes could not bomb through the clouds effectively. This, and probably a bit of pride and fear of a European-style coup like that which hijacked the strategic-bombing offensive before D-Day, prompted the assertion that "the strategic bombing program should be planned only with due reference to, but made contingent upon, invasion plans." Neither concerns over control of the independent 20th AF nor a change of tactics to negate the most viable evolution in bombing doctrine yet experienced, attacks on urban industrial areas, was allowable simply because of an invasion planned for months away.

Attempting to deflect interference to plans already in motion, LeMay wrote to Gen. Lawrence Kuter and agreed in practice with the two-pronged assault of precision and area attacks but refused to limit himself to a schedule of missions when both he and those in Washington knew so well how much the weather dictated everything. With that limitation understood, the list of thirty-three targets designated as urban industrial targets offered too little to the 21st BC commanders and they revealed that they intended to expand the incendiary campaign to all of Japan, which they had just started a week earlier: "Rapid destruction of a large number of Japanese cities is resulting in the loss to the enemy of much of his industrial capacity not presently listed in current intelligence reports." When combined with precision attacks as possible, this complete expansion of the incendiary campaign "may create such a depression of the overall Japanese economy that the enemy's capacity to resist may cease to exist or be tactically ineffectual." It worked within the framework of the existing doctrine so that the use of "parallel targets exploit[s] the capabilities of the strategic air forces to the utmost within the operational limits imposed in this theater and provides flexibility consistent with the capabilities of VHB [very heavy bomber] aircraft."[10] To put it another way, the B-29 forces were doing the best job possible in circumstances very different from those in Europe, and planners in Washington needed to recognize that.

Some of the focus on pushing precision bombardment came from a continued belief in the viability of radar as an everyday combat tool. The thing not recognized outside the Marianas regarding radar was that it still did not work well enough to see through the Japanese overcast and precisely hit targets. Despite the use of offset radar aim points and the introduction of the 315th BW, who carried the AN/APQ-7 "Eagle" radar and spent their training period gaining proficiency with it, radar technology and the crews using it still saw a mess on their radarscopes hardly indicative of a specific target or building. LeMay continued: "Under radar conditions, with present equipment, pin-point targets cannot be effectively attacked and it has been necessary to designate urban industrial areas for radar strikes." The letter went on to mollify any concerns regarding the indiscriminate nature of attacking the urban areas by outlining the five criteria used for selection of these areas: flammability, presence of war industries, incidence of key transportation facilities, size of the city, and visibility on radar. Attacks on cities meeting these criteria fell subject to the "attendant results of area incendiary attacks . . . deprivation of food, housing, transportation, proper health and sanitation facilities to civilian workers, all of which tends to lower to a considerable extent the productive capacity of an entire urban industrial area."[11]

This ran contrary to the JTG's directions, which put the objective of attacks as urban industrial concentrations instead of predominantly residential "congested areas." Given the opportunity, the JTG would probably have recommended high-explosive precision attacks for each important target, if not for the effectiveness of the incendiaries. This same rationale drove LeMay's decisions on the front lines. In one night his planes could obsolete or destroy every precision target, those known and unknown, in four whole cities. Now that the race to invasion officially started, waiting for the weather's cooperation or scouring the thinned economy of Japan for specific targets still viable, worth striking, and requiring an air force worth of bombers to destroy no longer appeared worthwhile. The level of the total war now sank down to the people and their direct day-to-day effects on the war effort. Every city housed industries large and small, provided sustenance for workers and future combatants, and became a legitimate target. The ultimate goal became "maximum overall destruction of industrial capacity, rather than a very high level of damage in particular establishments. Incendiaries destroy combustible buildings or contents far more economically than HE, and a high production of Japanese urban industry (an estimated 50% of total floor space) is combustible."[12]

• • •

When June rolled around, with the mining and burning campaigns well under way against Japan, the USSBS reports from Europe started to be released. The initial findings advocated land and water transportation as targets, not area bombing. The *European Summary Report* referred to the attack on transportation as "the decisive blow that completely disorganized the German economy." Stopping raw materials from reaching factories and preventing finished goods from reaching the front lines negated the production capability of Germany. In the same vein of cutting off supplies to the production sites, the USSBS in Europe admitted a failure of the European bombing campaign in which electrical power received too little attention, noting that the "German electrical power situation was in fact in a precarious condition from the beginning of the war and became more precarious as the war progressed." And while the USSBS eventually owned up to the fact that the Germans feared night raids more than daylight attacks and that the air campaign as a whole undermined their faith in the Nazi government to the point that "if they had been at liberty to vote themselves out of the war, they would have done so

well before the final surrender," it challenged the ability of bombing to break the enemy's morale since it did not work in Europe.[13]

The 20th AF rejected these recommendations, preferring to stay
the course on the three-pronged strategy of bombs, fire, and mines
from the air that systematically ground the Japanese nation down.
Acting as though the findings in Europe represented an absolute
doctrinal shift that required heeding, some historians have expressed
shock and dismay over the unwillingness to implement the changes
in the Pacific. One focuses on the Pacific campaign as one of area
bombing alone and calls it "psychological inertia" that caused the
European results to be pushed aside. The resources already allocated, the fear of admitting waste in previous area attacks, and
worst of all the fear that the analysis which pointed to urban-area
attacks would be invalidated led to the rejection of the European findings. Besides, with the growing amount of resources in the Pacific,
both goals could be achieved simultaneously. After all, a pressure
existed in the military organization at all levels "to be tough, or at
least not appear soft and idealistic."[14] This argument focuses on the
psychological argument within the U.S. command structure, the
need to stay the course lest they admit personal failure, but it fails
to embrace the physical differences between the war in Europe and
the war in the Pacific.

Attempting to transfer the lessons of Europe directly to the Pacific
makes the same mistake that theoreticians made when they assumed
that all industrial economies functioned the same and hence contained the same needs and choke points. Experience over Japan alone
showed this to not be the case. The Japanese economy ran at a much
slower and less sophisticated pace than its Western counterparts. It
relied less on electrical power, oil, trucks, and large plants to produce
the goods it needed to wage war. Operating over Japan required an
open mind and willingness to see a different perspective than that
contained in a textbook or lessons learned from Europe.

A case in point relates to the utility of attacking transportation
targets. The memo from LeMay to Kuter mentioned earlier also refers
to these targets as gaining interest in discussion of the effects of
bombing on the Japanese war economy. The transportation system
of Japan presented unique challenges for bombers. Much of the intra-

island freight moved on boats owing to the anemic nature of the Japanese rail system. Only two rail mainlines extended the length of the main island, Honshu, with only one of the lines developed for heavy traffic; passengers made up most of the cargo for the rail system. Outside the main industrial areas the number of trunk lines dropped to two or three connecting the industrial centers to each other and their sources of supply. Loss of the coastal shipping ability due to mines and submarines shifted that traffic onto the already overburdened rail system, clogging it further. Likewise, the highway system remained "primitive," with intercity truck and bus transportation completely undeveloped.[15] This dearth of development kept the transportation network, outside mining, low on the priority list for the B-29s. Besides, attacking transportation targets was a tricky question of timing. In Europe the big push against the rail network of France came just before D-Day, seeking to inhibit reinforcements from reaching the beachheads. Attacking too early allowed recovery time and tipped one's hand about the location of the invasion; attacking too late risked leaving targets untouched. The same concern hung over planning against Japan. The European USSBS and prudence demanded the destruction of the enemy's ability to move raw materials, parts, supplies, and personnel as the war crept closer to direct land confrontation, and not to reject the idea entirely plans were in place for the 20th AF to take up such attacks in late August and September as the invasion neared.

This is not to say that the 21st BC ignored terrestrial transportation targets entirely during their tenure; they just did not attack them directly. The urban-area attacks rarely damaged the tracks themselves, but made the railroads suffer through destruction of rolling stock, warehouses, repair shops, loading docks, railroad yards, and the electrical lines that powered them. For a society reliant on the rail system to move people, the loss of the main power lines and overhead electric train power lines proved especially crippling. Without electricity, the intercity trains ceased to move, stranding workers and keeping them from their jobs. In the same attacks, the roads system suffered as well when trucks succumbed to the flames, making it more difficult to move goods away from rail stops.

The severity of the actual damage of the area attacks on transportation remains in doubt. Different USSBS reports give different interpretations of the outcome, ranging from "little effect on mainline rail operations" and reduction only to the cushion in the system stemming from the loss of the industry the rails served, to a belief that Japanese army ordnance suffered greatly from a lack of local transportation, a situation exacerbated by the area raids, all the way up to the damage to the railroads being "by no means moderate" with 5 percent of the nation's track, 14 percent of its locomotives, 28 percent of its electric cars, and 52 percent of its main repair facilities destroyed by air attack. If nothing else, the increase in number of displaced people from air raids added a huge strain to the rail network as the trains needed to move the people out of the cities to resettlement areas. When they needed to carry supplies, they carried refuges. In Tokyo's case, some 63 percent of the 6.5 million inhabitants left the metropolis by the end of the war, filling the transportation network in their effort to escape the destruction.[16]

The one thing all sources agree on, American and Japanese, was that attacks on the transportation network in conjunction with the mining campaign would have brought the opportunity to push the Japanese economy over the edge. The Americans referred to the failure to attack the railroad system when forces became available as resulting "in the loss of a major opportunity." Without ships, the Japanese relied heavily on their rail system to move everything: "life could not be accomplished without the rails." The Japanese transportation officials agreed, telling surveyors after the war that "serious disruption of trunk rail lines by earlier strategic bombing would not only have denied mobility to military operations but would also have brought industry to as quick and effective a standstill as the extensive attacks on the factories themselves." While undoubtedly these statements come with a basis in fact and experience, they do not offer an end unto themselves, as the Japanese exhibited an ability to adapt to the wartime conditions and continue fighting. One only needs to review the dispersal plans that placed factories in tunnel systems to understand the drive behind their war effort. So attacking transportation targets, while profitable, did not guarantee success or earlier cessation of hostilities. The recent studies of D. M. Giangreco show how the Japanese long anticipated the destruction of their transportation network and started moving divisions south to Kyushu months before an expected invasion. They anticipated that once land operations started, troop movement would occur on foot, at night, and on secondary roads. Under these conditions they anticipated a sixty-five-day journey for two divisions from Kyushu moving north to reinforce defense of the Kanto Plain. Adding to this situation came the acknowledgment by the U.S. intelligence community that their deception plans, similar to the ones used so successfully in Europe to tie up German divisions before D-Day, offered little against Japan, which lacked the large unit mobility and prepositioned their troops in such a way that they could support areas in trouble always moving by foot.[17]

Another interest of U.S. strategic-bombing adherents in the European campaign, which struck at the heart of the industrial economy yet gained little traction with the British or the Europeans, came from the black gold of oil. Always low on the priority list for bombing against Japan, oil gained significant attention late in the war in Europe, and this carried over to the Pacific campaign as well. The reliance of the modern war machine on oil made any industrialized nation beholden to it, whether it came from the ground or emanated in a synthetic form from a plant. In the Pacific one could say oil caused the war. With no domestic oil source or synthetic oil industry to speak of (and never to develop one), Japan relied on imports. Yet the imports they so needed also proved their undoing, as the ships carrying this oil easily fell prey to U.S. submarines plying the trade routes to the home islands.

This blockade made strategic bombing of the Japanese refining and storage capacity largely unnecessary, and both the COA and the JTG ranked it low on the list of priority targets.[18] The B-29s did not even attack the industry directly until May 1945, partly out of necessity and partly out of opportunity. The necessity revolved around the need to absorb the remaining oil in the home islands, preventing further refinement and destroying the meager existing stocks. Doing so limited the supply available for defense, especially for aircraft. The opportunity arose from location of the oil refineries and the arrival of the 315th BW with their "Eagle" radar. Japanese oil refineries sat on the coast, with excellent visibility from the air and clear radar contrast between the land and water. The 315th BW trained from the start to use radar and attack at night, so they came with no guns save the tail turret. With the virtual absence of defenses over Japan, this made these prime targets and an excellent opportunity to show how accurately the B-29 could bomb. When they arrived in the Marianas in May the 315th BW came to see through the dark and weather and reinforce the precision part of the 21st BC's three-part bombing offensive.

Dropping high-explosive bombs for their smashing and penetrating abilities, the 21st BC unleashed 40,085 bombs on oil targets in fifteen missions. Of these bombs 16.5 percent struck their target, slightly higher than the 12.6 percent achieved against European oil targets over more missions and under more stressful conditions. Out of these fifteen missions, three flew in daylight and sighted visually; twelve occurred at night and bombed by radar. Here the disparity with European experience and technology becomes apparent. The 21st BC's visual bombing scored hits with 41.5 percent of its bombs, compared with only 26.8 percent on European visual bombing missions. Using radar, the 315th and their improved "Eagle" units hit with 13.5 percent of their ordnance, 2.5 times more than the European radar bombing. While this led the USSBS report to conclude that "the results indicate that from the standpoint of accuracy radar cannot yet compete visual sighting methods," the viability of radar as a bombing method earned validation against the oil targets.[19]

The question of how much damage was actually done by these attacks generated enough debate that a postwar evaluation straddled the argument, concluding that "in the absence of adequate intelligence on the actual state of Japan's war economy, the strategic bombing attacks served as a guarantee that the oil industry had been eliminated." The low priority of oil targets suggests that planners recognized that refining lay deep within the Japanese economy, easily hurt by eliminating much earlier processes such as shipping; yet the need to eliminate all vestiges of the oil industry as the war progressed led them to err on the side of caution and send the bombers best suited for the mission to bomb the refineries. The fact was that the Japanese went to war with their oil-storage tanks just three-quarters full and only depleted them as the war progressed. By May 1945 the flow of oil into the country virtually ceased, creating increased surplus in both storage capacity and refining capacity. So even though by the end of the war bombs fell on every important refinery and nearly 84 percent of refining capacity lay destroyed, the contribution to Japanese defeat by the bombing was "negligible." And while storage tanks also received many of these bombs, they often sat empty to start with, simply absorbing the bombs with no effect.[20]

The immediate postwar assessment missed one crucial point regarding the Japanese fuel situation: while exhaustion of supplies kept many storage tanks dry, that was not the only cause of the fuel shortage. As discussed in chapter 2, when the Japanese recognized the danger of impending invasion they started stockpiling fuel in small hidden caches strategically placed for use against invaders. So while destroying the refining capability and main storage capacity of the industry benefited the overall war effort, it did not eliminate the resource so valuable to mechanical or airborne warfare. When U.S. troops hit the beach they still would have faced the retaliation of a modern military foe and not one cast into the pre-industrial age for want of gas.

The new round of incendiary missions brought success in terms of physical destruction the likes of which few had ever seen. At every level the Japanese nation and economy suffered terribly. Incendiary raids tried to take advantage of the nearness of Japanese industrial plants, the homes of their workers, and the subcontractors and home industries that supplied the plants. As one would expect in a modern industrial economy, subcontractors played a vital role in the creation of larger products, spreading the effort and specialization out to the most capable and qualified people available. The size of these producers varied from a few individuals in a home that also produced parts to several dozen people in a dedicated structure manufacturing components. The reliance of these smaller units on the prime contractor supplying expertise, tooling, and even raw materials in the heavily rationed economy ensured their physical location close to the main concern. The Japanese used this methodology to their advantage, and the Americans likewise used it against them.

The importance of the home industries cannot be overstated when it came to the American belief in the system. From the beginning of the war discussions of Japanese industry included, and even emphasized, the urban nature of the industrial system. The Air Force and its civilian counterparts identified the Japanese industrial economy by its use of small feeder shops. This remained a belief throughout the bombing campaign, providing a major justification for the classification of urban areas as urban industrial targets. Despite change in the Japanese economy as the war progressed, the interest was not without justification.

In Tokyo, for example, as of October 1944 there were 41,548 plants in the city. Out of these establishments, 58 percent employed one to nine workers and 38 percent employed ten to forty-nine workers. These two categories accounted for 54 percent of the industrial workers in the city. And while in reality much of the home industry dried up by that time, the work only migrated into slightly larger and more dedicated shops. Since 1940 the shops employing one to nine workers dropped in number by 70 percent, while the plants with ten to forty-nine workers grew in quantity by 83 percent. The Japanese economy evolved slightly but still concentrated its efforts in the same areas identified as urban industrial targets. The American planners did not realize this shift, and understandably so; with the Japanese economy under lockdown conditions since the late 1930s, information only trickled out and did not paint a clear picture of the modernization of the Japanese empire's economy.[21] The planners made their assumptions based on the believed preponderance of small industrial shops, which made the urban industrial areas lucrative targets.

In general, subcontracting accounted for a huge amount of the work done by industry. A breakdown of aircraft, for example, shows that 35 percent of airframe work, 24 percent of engine manufacturing, and 16 percent of propeller work came from subcontractors, numbers increasing as the war carried on. Still, all these manufactures used home industry to some extent, with roughly 8.2 percent of the industry's labor coming from homes as of February 1, 1944. Because these specific areas were too small for direct attack and were concentrated in groups near the product's final assembly point, burning them out meant a quick solution to dilemmas of immediately cutting off parts supplies to main plants and eliminating the raw

materials and components already in the system. Using this rationale, the USSBS tells us that U.S. planners "believed that the effect
of such destruction would be immediately and seriously felt in the
war economy." They did not miss the mark by much. Area attacks
on Tokyo, Nagoya, and Osaka curtailed the supply of electrical parts
and instruments to the Mitsubishi airplane manufacturing arm, an
especially hard hit because of the lack of alternate sources for the
parts. The company also experienced the theoretical "bottlenecks"
in the supply of electrical parts, leak-proofing material, and mount-
ing parts to attach Baka suicide rockets to bombers for both its Betty
and George aircraft production owing to the air attacks on suppliers.
Although not directly affected by the area raids, Nakajima's production of the Frank fighter suffered at its Ota plant when area attacks
in Tokyo and Kawasaki curtailed deliveries of important parts like
engines and oil-coolers. Their Omiya Works also suffered from distant
urban fires when it lost its supplies of friction plates and heatproof
angle tubes thanks to attacks on Kawasaki and Tokyo too. Even the
urban-area attack on Hamamatsu eliminated three Nakajima subcontractors, albeit not crucial ones. The overall outcome achieved
the goal set for urban industrial attacks and curtailed parts production and supply to the larger plants, which were then attacked with
precision ordnance to eliminate their work in process.[22]

The USSBS would have one couch the success against subcontractors in terms of individual industries, so while the overall damage
done was extensive, it varied considerably depending on location and
industry. In Tokyo, where over half the industrial output at the start
of the area attacks came from operations employing fewer than fifty
people, by the end of the fires and their concurrent effects 71 percent of the operations no longer functioned. When this is added to
the damage done to the larger operations, the *Effects of Air Attack
on Urban Complex Tokyo-Kawasaki-Yokohama* reported the losses
in Tokyo's overall production due to bombing as 75 percent of its
potential. Three-quarters of the largest component in the Japanese
economy lay burned, ruined, and scattered on the Kanto Plain. The
all-important aircraft industry suffered terribly from losses to suppliers. Some manufactures, especially those making communications equipment, almost completely shut down, and after March

1945, "damage from air raids sharply cut into all subcontract production in the second quarter of 1945."[23] The abrupt end to the war in the summer masked some of these effects, though, as the use of the parts entailed a one- to three-month lead time, so the effects were not immediately felt, but the impact loomed ready to strike as the battle hit its crescendo during the late-year invasion.

Despite the stunning physical destruction generated by the firebombing, it meant nothing if it did not hurt the industrial capability of the Japanese, principally the industrial plants that assembled the final products. As mentioned earlier, about the only way available for gauging the damage done to specific buildings or sites came in terms of roof area destroyed. This method offered both a solid rule of thumb for estimations and also came with inherent inaccuracies that hid some damage and overemphasized others. Along these same lines, after burning a city the disappearance of specific buildings entailed total destruction and elimination as a target. More ambiguous, though, were the effects on dispersed factories or factories not yet identified in the smaller cities. If the incendiary campaign counted for anything, it needed to destroy all of these targets. So while they could not prove it quantitatively, the 21st BC believed, based on the overall destruction accomplished, that it was achieving this goal. Postwar investigation proved them right.

The destruction started with the initial missions in March where the aircraft industry, the main target of the campaign, experienced heavy damage across the board from the fires. Mitsubishi, one of the largest aircraft concerns in the country, experienced at least ten separate attacks in five cities against sites at its no. 3 works and branches alone. During the initial series of attacks in March, the mission to Nagoya destroyed its wing-assembly shop and 263 associated machine tools, the tools not yet dispersed to alternate assembly locations. The Aichi Aircraft Company also suffered during the early attacks on Nagoya, with its Eitoku plant suffering extensive damage from the flames, losing several buildings and 20 percent of its machine tools.[24]

More important, the larger plants suffered from the damage done by the incendiaries to the local utilities. Gas and water lines ruptured, but worst of all the electrical power distribution system collapsed. While the light incendiaries failed to penetrate or ignite modern generating plants and substations built of fire-resistant materials, "of much greater importance was the large amount of indirect damage by incendiaries which caused urban area conflagrations that destroyed, along with everything else, poles, lines, distribution transformers, and other such facilities."[25] Despite the growing power surplus in the islands, no way remained to supply it to the surviving plants. As with the loss of workers or parts, the damage to the utilities worked as well as direct hits to stop the war industries.

The direct damage became acute as the incendiary attacks made their stuttering restarts in April and May and expanded to smaller cities. The Mitsubishi no. 5 works lost the entire Ichinomiya plant, which at the time produced parts for Ki-67 Peggy heavy bombers and Ki-83 fighters, when the B-29s burned 0.65 square miles of the city of Okazaki.[26] The Mitaka Company, builders of carburetors and never the primary target of any attack, lost part of its main office and tool warehouses when the bombers returned to burn Tokyo on April 15 and May 25. The same series of follow-up attacks on Tokyo and the surrounding area cost the Hitachi Aircraft Company 1 million square feet of its Omori works in Kawasaki as well as its foundry in Kawasaki. Just as planned, the industries themselves in the urban industrial target areas chosen by the JTG fell to the flames, along with their neighborhood support structure.

Outside the big cities the companies suffered too. Sumitomo Metal Industries suffered a 90 percent loss of productive capacity at the Kanzaki propeller plant when Amagasaki burned on June 15. Like so many others, it never appeared as a primary target for any mission but was caught up in the larger destruction. Nakajima Aircraft saw half its Matsuzaka engine accessories plant burn when the city burned. The flames took half the machine tools and 80 percent of a month's production of oil pumps, a severe blow to the ailing engine industry. Everywhere the bombers hit the enemy, industry felt the pain.[27]

Even the chemical plants, spread throughout the country and normally immune to the incendiaries thanks to the thick metal used for pipes and containment vessels, suffered extensively from the fires as wooden support structures and maintenance shops burned. Worst of all, as materials became scarce, wood took a more prominent place in these facilities. Floors, equipment supports, and even vats started to be made out of wood. When they ignited, the fire easily grew strong enough to melt the metal containers around them, either destroying the equipment, lighting the contents on fire, or both. "Although the actual damage to the chemical plants wrought by incendiary bombs was limited," the USSBS noted after the war, "from a broad standpoint of the total effect on the chemical industry and national economy the incendiary bomb was a very effective weapon in Japan."[28]

Another feature of note regarding the damage dealt by the fires deals with the efficiency in destruction they wrought compared with precision bombing. It only took one incendiary mission to destroy an aircraft plant, as opposed to the repeated precision missions required to knock out production at a facility. The attack on the Ogaki urban area early in the morning of July 29 destroyed 92 percent of the Mitsubishi no. 16 Engine Works; 539 of the 819 machine tools were destroyed, and the plant's productive capability stopped. The same occurred after the Fukui urban attack on July 19, when 90 percent of the Fuji plant burned, taking with it 193 of the 227 machine tools.[29] Plants unknown to the intelligence groups or too small to warrant individual attention disappeared in the flames, fully engulfed by the indiscriminate fires. The destruction proved so complete that rarely did a city need a follow-up attack, its production ability eliminated. And, unlike in Europe, even a single blow to a plant virtually guaranteed the end of its utility, as the Japanese made little effort to repair sites and fell back on dispersal to protect their remaining assets.

Overall, the fire missions produced the desired results against targets of all types and in all locations. In addition to grinding down the aircraft industry and its assorted supporting industries, the fires damaged other high-profile target systems. The arsenals, long a concern for planners, lost 44 percent of their production by the end of the war, three-quarters of which occurred after the area attacks started and began touching the industry's plants embedded in the urban areas. Spillover from area attacks even helped destroy one-quarter of the yard space for the shipping industry and reduced its production capacity by 10–15 percent. While the numbers against shipyards are shared with naval attacks, they were vitally important against the Japanese, who desperately needed the yards to produce more ships or repair those damaged by the blockade. Even the leftovers of the incendiary raids hurt the Japanese war economy.[30]

From the standpoint of destruction of specific targets, if the flames did not touch the workers and their homes the strategy still proved successful. The industries that needed destruction received it in a direct sense, and those outside the urban areas lost their suppliers and supporting industries to the flames. The final piece, though, remained the workers. No stone could stay unturned in the war, and the flaming plow did not discriminate between building types.

As important as the destructive effects of fire on the physical plants themselves were the disjointing effects on the workers whose homes and families lay in cinders. By dehousing the people, the fires resulted in absenteeism of the workers from their jobs, slowing or shutting down plants not directly touched by the fires. True, the Japanese civil defense plans accounted for the potential need to evacuate, but they were based on the belief that attacks could not be delivered on a large scale or for an extended period. When square miles ignited at one time, the plan became oversaturated and the "exodus from urban areas was for the most part haphazard and was caused by panic conditions which upset planning and had a deleterious effect on the war economy."[31] Making matters worse, the civil authorities failed to implement recovery operations after attacks, leading the displaced to fend for themselves, either moving in with neighbors whose homes still stood or, more likely, heading to the countryside where shelter and food existed.

The absence of workers had a direct effect on the productivity of industries. Like any business, Japanese industry went through the daily struggle of getting all employees on a shift on the job. The struggle grew harder in the latter half of 1944, before any bombing started. Food shortages, worker illness from malnourishment, and the black market in labor all drew people away from their job sites. The food situation in the home islands as the war progressed grew more and critical. Rice production fell from 10,027,474 metric tons in 1942 to 8,783,827 metric tons in 1944, with grim estimates made for the 1945 crop due to weather issues and fertilizer shortages. When taken with the reduction in fishing catches, the Japanese diet shrank from 2,000 calories a day in 1941 to a mere 1,680 calories in 1945. Malnutrition both sapped the physical energy to work harder as the war progressed and made the people susceptible to diseases like tuberculosis and beriberi, dragging them down further.[32]

Regarding the black market in labor, the government tightly controlled the employment of individuals and industries. Once placed in a job, a worker had little or no way out of the position, regardless of the availability of better employment elsewhere. Companies in need of workers that the government denied them would surreptitiously hire workers away from other firms (often with food payments), forcing the workers to go AWOL from their assigned job.

Bombing and urban-area destruction made the absenteeism problem worse, often shutting down the local industries for several days to a week after an attack. The loss of homes, loved ones, power, and water and the disruption of the public transportation system all contributed to the absenteeism experienced by worksites. In Tokyo a survey of "thirty essential factories" conducted by the Japanese after the initial March attack showed a marked influence on the working population by the fires. The day after the firestorm only half of the workers showed up to the businesses surveyed, reducing production for the day by over half. Similar numbers occurred, though worsening slightly, after the follow-up missions in mid-April and late May.

A similar pattern is seen in the man-hours lost by the Kawanishi Aircraft Company's Konan plant outside Osaka. After each area attack the hours worked plummeted by 50 percent or more for about three weeks before jumping back up to "normal" levels, only to be cast down by another attack almost immediately. Two things jump out from the numbers compiled by the USSBS on this subject. First, the "normal" level rarely reached the previous high. This indicates a cumulative effect of wearing down the population, with them never bouncing back as well as or better than a previous attack. Second, the drops in output correspond to attacks from all over. The plant sat in the Honjo Village fifteen miles from Osaka, and significant drops in production occurred not only when Osaka burned but also when the planes attacked Kobe and Amagasaki. The ripple effects of missions reached beyond the borders of just one city.[33]

The effect even reached the smaller cities attacked later in the war. The Nakajima Handa plant in Nagoya saw many of its workers' homes destroyed by the fire, resulting in an 80 percent absenteeism rate in the week after the attack, decreasing slightly to 65 percent over the next two weeks. A similar attack on the small city of Hamamatsu on June 18 destroyed 70 percent of the city and pushed the daily absenteeism rate up to 46 percent.[34]

Probably the best illustration of the effect of area attacks on the production of local industries comes from a comparison of the worker output and absenteeism rates between a city that received incendiary attack and one that did not. In Osaka and Kobe, both recipients of several visits by the 21st BC, employment dropped 265,000 in five months in Osaka and 65,000 after a single raid against Kobe. In contrast, the cultural center of Kyoto, Secretary of War Henry Stimson's "unblemished virgin" (which he spared from all attack, including the A-bomb), lost only 22,742 jobs over the course of seven months during the bombing campaign. The contrast between two Nakajima aircraft plants is also instructive. At the untouched Fukushima plant absenteeism ran from 6 percent in March 1945, creeping up roughly one point a month to 12 percent in August. The Musashino plant outside Tokyo, in contrast, went through March 1945 with 27 percent of its workforce staying away, a number that climbed to 41 percent by August. While Musashino is not the best example of urban attacks alone, since it received constant attention from precision bombers as well as area attacks in Tokyo (it did have a 21 percent absentee rate already in January 1945), it does illustrate the profound effects bombs falling on the workforce made.[35]

The area attacks did their job, disrupting production and throwing the economic and social systems into chaos. The numbers would not be tallied until after the war, but with the knowledge available on Japanese society, specific targets in and around the burned areas, and the obvious physical destruction seen in post-strike photos, one conclusion emerged: incendiary attacks worked and warranted continuation.

With the go-ahead implicit in the latest target directive to expand the fire missions, LeMay spread the word to the bomb wings in no uncertain terms:

Continuous bad weather over the Empire and the necessity for apply-

ing constant pressure on the Jap war economy prompts this headquarters to undertake the following course of action. Wings will be
scheduled to attack urban industrial areas with incendiaries when it
is known that units bust [must] bomb entirely by radar, often while
on actual instruments. Generally each wing will have its own urban
area and will not be called on to compress the time of attack in less
than one hour. In addition, wings may utilize altitude separation
between specified limits. To accomplish the desired degree of destruction, which is entirely within any wings' capabilities, thorough briefing using all available radar data must be given all crews.[36]

As soon as the renewed campaign started it achieved a pace all its
own. Every few nights four more cities fell off the list, losing an average of 50 percent of their total area to the flames. So thorough flowed
the destruction that only three of the sixty cities attacked in the second round required second missions to finish the job. The impunity
with which the B-29s moved over the home islands prompted LeMay
to start calling his shots, telling the people of specific cities to leave
before the 21st BC came. With Nimitz's help, LeMay dropped leaflets
declaring his target cities and then hit a subset of that list. On July
27, 1945. the 660,000 leaflets fell over eleven cities. The next night,
six cities felt the heat of the B-29's bombs. The Japanese defenses
barely acknowledged the pending presence of the planes. Seeing no
disadvantages to the propaganda coup just pulled off, they repeated
the tactic on August 1 and 4. Losses numbered seven planes. Leaflets added humanity to missions by warning people, saying in part
that "in accordance with America's well-known humanitarian principles, the American Air Force, which does not wish to injure inno-
cent people, now gives you warning to evacuate the cities named
and save your lives."[37] Leaflets also spread the message of total domination by the Americans. Contrary to popular belief in the home
islands, Japan was not winning the war.

With the war reaching its crescendo, any pretense of a surgeon's
precision fell victim to the need to finally push the Japanese out of the
war. Historian Ronald Shaffer notes that while Norstad and the JTG
disagreed about morale as a target, "Having eliminated most targets
of military and economic significance, the AAF moved increasingly

into political and psychological warfare." The push went to leaflets and the attempt "to destroy Japan's war-making industry, not the people of Japan."[38] More accurately stated, in the confusing myriad of events that occurred in the war, all of the violence, plans that came to ruin, missed opportunities, and varying strategies turned the battle over Japan from a careful and deliberate operation into an all-out war. Like every other battle against the Japanese during the war, all-out effort alone led to victory; any attempt at half effort fell by the wayside, quickly turning into widespread destruction and a disregard for the typical limits of "civilized" warfare.

As the second round of the incendiary effort started, Arnold visited the Marianas. After hearing LeMay and his staff brief on their operations and plans he dispatched LeMay to Washington to sell the plan to the Joint Chiefs of Staff. With the question of final strategy in the Pacific being settled, Arnold believed that the combined sea and air blockade could force the Japanese to surrender before ground troops were committed to any invasion of the home islands. LeMay flew the day and a half to Washington, briefed a dozing Gen. George Marshall to no avail, and returned to his command undaunted. Eventually, Washington chose both options and authorized an invasion of Kyushu for November while continuing the blockade and bombardment of the islands. Regardless, the United States committed itself to an epic land battle to end World War II in the Pacific.

While the Joint Chiefs of Staff did not buy the feasibility of the plan, the 20th AF still did. Now a general, David Burchinal related after the war how after hearing of the disinterest of the upper command, "from there on, we were going to fly max effort, logistically. . . . [W]e thought we could end the war. That's when the bombs came off the ships onto the hardstands and never got to the bomb dump. It was just max effort from there on out to knock the Japanese out of the war." When asked if he felt pressure from Arnold to prove something about airpower, Burchinal pointed at LeMay and said, "No. The pressure wasn't in Washington, it was right here." LeMay then chimed in, "I never felt that they were looking over my shoulder from Washington. That wasn't there; it was our own idea. I did the initial low-altitude attack on Tokyo without asking anybody. . . . I knew what was expected of me and why I was there. I had to produce some results."[39] The B-29 units now proceeded down a path that led straight to the end of the war, whether they knew it or not. Up to the official surrender announcement, increasing numbers of planes flew to Japan daily and unleashed destruction. With the war in Europe over, a new influx of equipment and personnel started arriving in the theater. The magnitude of bombing operations expanded beyond the over eight hundred B-29s available in the Marianas as the 8th AF transferred in from England. In light of these increased numbers and the joint nature of coming operations, the command structure of and over the 20th AF shifted. LeMay ceded command of the 21st BC to Lt. Gen. Barney Giles when he arrived in July to take command of the 20th and 21st BCs. At the same time another level of command emerged over 20th AF when the United States Army Strategic Air Forces in the Pacific was created under Gen. Carl Spaatz, with LeMay as chief of staff, as a way of absorbing the influx of European units and ensuring coordinated air support for the coming invasion. These changes did little in the short time they existed, as shortly after the atomic bombs dropped the Japanese surrendered, no invasion necessary. The final expression of Air Force power came the day the surrender documents were signed, when wave after wave of B-29s flew overhead, taking their rightful place as members of the victorious side.

8

Interpreting the Campaign

UPON REVIEW IT APPEARS evident that the switch in tactical doctrine to low-altitude area attacks occurred, but only to a point, because of expediency. To maximize the effectiveness of the bomber sorties and the destruction of Japanese war-making ability, the commander on scene, LeMay, focused a portion of his efforts on expanding the already sanctioned attacks on urban industrial areas. The decision to do so originated with him and received no objection from, and even more than tacit approval by, those above him in the chain of command. One must understand, though, that low-level incendiary attacks comprised only one part of a triad of strategies undertaken by the 20th AF, albeit the most publicized of the three. To accomplish the goals of the Air Force, from supporting the overall war effort through destruction of Japanese industry to showing independent spirit and capability by the air arm, the 20th AF used the means necessary, and one of those means was fire. This was a departure from prewar plans of high-altitude precision daylight bombing, to be sure, but it was still an expression of the intent of the doctrine for destruction of the enemy's industry and ability to make war. Amidst a total war against a country with minimal industry, and possessing minimal knowledge of the targets it harbored, a broad stroke made the most sense.

Out of all of this evidence the historian attempts to derive some larger motives, interpretation, or moral judgments. Sixty-seven cities burned, tens of thousands killed, and millions made homeless implicitly demand an explanation larger than expediency. Sadly, none truly exists. The chaos and carnage of war, by its very nature, defies

INTERPRETING THE CAMPAIGN

reason. Consequently, discussion of the incendiary campaign against Japan rarely focuses on the why and how, but on the how could they. How could the Air Force and the United States uses tactics so indiscriminate and destructive, especially in a war where they fought to maintain the moral high ground? Up until now the details of the decision-making process have taken a backseat to efforts to understand in the most basic terms why the U.S. military and government allowed destruction of this magnitude to happen. As a result, explanations of the campaign have been oversimplified, and the campaign has been characterized as unplanned, unguided, and even improvised. These misreadings not only gloss over details but misrepresent the facts. It has been seen here that from the beginning of the war, civilian and military authorities alike realized the vulnerability of Japanese cities to fire and actively investigated their options in exploiting this vulnerability. As the war progressed the primacy of strategic bombing as the tactic of choice clashed hard with the realities of executing such a campaign in Europe. After achieving a few hard-won victories in Europe, where Germany operated a fully industrialized economy, the strategy met another difficult challenge over Japan in terms of target selection.

The same planners who investigated the flammability of Japanese cities saw the difficulty of identifying not only Japanese industries worthy of destruction but also their location. No surprise, then, that attacks on urban industrial areas, with an emphasis on the industrial aspect, consistently rose to the top of the target list. When the planning ended and operations began, the grim reality set in: the B-29 force could not supply the striking power needed to drive the Japanese from the war using precision bombing alone. Unfortunately, no better expression of the Air Force's power and the primacy of strategic bombing existed than ending the war without ground intervention in Japan. Supplied with incendiaries and the approval from Washington from day one, the 21st BC held in its hand the tools to expand and prosecute the war to their full potential. Utilizing that potential entailed first bombing precision targets, which got off to a slow start and struggled to achieve results. Hansell preferred to concentrate his efforts on the doctrinal precision campaign and stuck with that plan until his dismissal. It is fair to say that "once Hansell had left the Pacific, no real advocate of precision bombing remained there," but one needs to acknowledge that the two remaining principal players carried little to no experience in the doctrinal fight for the Air Force's future. Arnold never attended the Air Corps Tactical School, and LeMay only received the abbreviated course just before the war. Arnold focused on the livelihood of the Air Force as a whole, and LeMay concentrated on victory; neither spent much time on the broader academic issues. For Arnold and LeMay the need to validate prewar theory did not tint their decision making; winning the war mattered. Some historians, like Conrad Crane, focus on the disparate circumstances of the Pacific as the breeding ground for destruction gone wild. He focuses on a belief in Arnold's preoccupation with success bringing an independent air service and the lack of oversight by theater commanders like MacArthur and Nimitz allowing LeMay to shape bombing policy by "military necessity." This necessity then enabled a justification for area attacks "as ending the war quickly, saving American lives, demonstrating a true victory through airpower, and securing a strong position to bargain for postwar status as an independent service."[1]

Herman Wolk follows part of Crane's logic and is sure that "in Arnold's mind, the performance of the B-29s in the Pacific was linked directly to the future creation of an independent air force," so one may see establishment of an independent Air Force in 1947 as proof of Arnold's ulterior motives all along.[2] But that victory came from the combined efforts of airmen around the world during and after the war more than the specific actions of the B-29 crews. It did not hurt, though, that the rain of fire over Japan culminated in surrender without the U.S. invasion and gave tangible proof of the value of airpower and its wielding by airmen independent of ground commanders. On the whole, membership on the winning team in World War II paid dividends of its own, and it was only natural that at every step of the way Arnold, the 20th AF, and the rest of Air Force team did their utmost to achieve victory both on and off the battlefield. The efforts over Japan offered a unique opportunity to showcase the abilities of the air arm, and Arnold, ever active on all matters related to his command (he did work himself into multiple heart attacks during the war), took full advantage of the publicity opportunity, just as he and his successors did with the atomic bomb in the post-war years. In the end they got what they wanted, an independent Air Force, and the means to get there blend together on the pages of history, the product of a whole team effort, not solely the result of one campaign in the Pacific.

In reality the justification for U.S. action aligns itself much more closely with Kenneth Werrell's more focused belief that "LeMay's tactics had but one goal: to inflict the maximum damage on the enemy with minimum casualties on the American side. Earlier tactics had failed on both counts. To be sure of success, he needed information on Japanese targets, but intelligence was sparse, in comparison with the bombing campaign against Germany."[3] Postwar considerations aside, Arnold, Norstad, LeMay, and every man in the 20th AF did what needed to be done to bring the war to a close as soon as possible. The ultimate goal of destroying Japan's ability to make war never changed. That Japan possessed no bottlenecks and its targets lay dispersed and hidden throughout its cities forced the hand of the U.S. leadership. The possibility long considered became a reality, and firebombing commenced. When the results came out well beyond that of precision bombing, and with few drawbacks for the attacking forces, no compelling military argument existed to not continue and expand the campaign. Regardless of the crudeness of the operations, against Japan firebombing achieved the goal of strategic bombardment by destroying its industrial base.

• • •

Robert McNamara in the documentary *Fog of War* asked whether the bombing campaign he helped orchestrate as part of the statistical control unit of the 21st BC was proportional to the situation of the war. This question offers a good gauge of the ethical validity of the actions in the context of the total war occurring in the Pacific at the time. McNamara declined to answer his own question, but others did. European philosopher A. C. Grayling specifically refers to the area bombing as "not proportional." He explains how whole industry presented a legitimate target, but by moving down the slippery slope to including workers as targets, and by physical proximity their families and neighbors too, the viability of the American actions dissolved. "This was the point at which moral trespass occurred, because it is where disproportion enters," Grayling writes. "It is sometimes said that we make virtues of our necessities; in this case we allowed what we mistakenly supposed was a necessity to make our vices." He views the collateral damage to the areas around the targets as avoidable if greater care or humanity took the place of general destruction. Grayling's argument suffers from a reliance on the perceived omniscience of current military operations, where precision bombs hit precision targets and wars end in days instead of years. Crane picks up on Grayling's argument and tries to look at the situation from the standpoint of the decision makers at the time, finding that "concerns for humanity could not override the desire for efficiency." Desire in this instance is better replaced with need, as the Air Force and military in general needed to effect years' worth of destruction on Japan in the course of months before an invasion. It was not so much a desire for efficiency as a need to do what had taken two and a half years in Europe in only a year against Japan. In that sense efficiency easily overrode concerns for a group of people seen as all sharing in responsibility for the execution of war and production of war materials.[4]

Yet on the surface Grayling appears right. Destroying cities in a war goes beyond what is necessary to win. But unlike wars before or since, the all-encompassing nature of World War II and privations caused by its continuation opened the door to all means necessary that would end the war. Historian Richard Frank concludes in his book *Downfall* that any calculation of the morality behind U.S. actions against Japan must look past the losses from bombing, the A-bombs, or the projected losses on both sides in the event of an invasion and that "any moral assessment of how the Pacific did and could have ended must consider the fate of [these] Asian noncombatants and the POWs." Stopping the war as soon as possible saved not only American and Japanese lives but also the lives of over 100,000 noncombatant Asians caught in the grip of Japanese occupation or control. Thus the loss of proportionally smaller numbers of Japanese civilians and their personal possessions fails to outweigh the cost in lives wrought by the war itself.[5]

The question of proportion also raises the issue of morality. It seems almost foolish to attempt a justification or condemnation of an act of war when war exhibits man's greatest inhumanity to man. Despite this, the effort to judge the actions of others out of context continues. Grayling writes in his sensationalist condemnation of area bombing, *Among the Dead Cities*: "If area bombing is a moral crime, then the bombings in the last six months of the war in both the European and Japanese theaters of war have what lawyers call an aggravated character—and intensified moral questionability, partly because victory was no longer genuinely doubtful." His argument hinges on the impending end of the war in 1945 and the overkill perpetrated on the Germans and Japanese. This emphasis on hindsight as evidence in the condemnation of Allied leaders implies not only that they knew of the ensured near-term demise of the Axis powers but that those same Axis nations admitted it as well. The ample scholarship of recent years on Japan's decision-making process shows that despite the dramatic battlefield reversals since Midway, only in the last couple of months of the conflict did the politically impotent people realize their position or the military dictatorship even entertain the idea of peace, much less defeat. Condemning actions based on what the Allies presumably assumed and the Axis did not believe makes this argument for the immorality of the area bombing of Japan null and void. The U.S. commanders in the Pacific applied the maximum available pressure to the Japanese to bring about the end of the war as soon as possible. If these same leaders believed so fervently in the impending collapse of the Japanese, why did they continue to plan and arm for an invasion? Historian Thomas Searle notes that postwar chronologies and memoirs have led to several erroneous conclusions by historians: "One is that the primary goal of USAAF incendiary bombing of Japan (like British incendiary bombing of Germany) was to 'demoralize the urban population.' In fact, Japanese industry was the primary target of the area raids, as it was for precision raids." Likewise, he points out, "Another mistaken view is that the leaders of the USAAF did not fully accept the fact that they were killing large numbers of civilians." This is in error, he says, because "civilian casualties were one of the explicit objectives of area incendiary bombing approved by both the USAAF and the Joint Chiefs of Staff." He is correct, though it is more accurate to say that U.S. leaders condoned but did not encourage killing of civilians, as the workers' deaths and loss of their homes hurt the industry and supported the overall goal of eliminating the Japanese ability to fight. Even after dropping of the atomic bombs, efforts continued to bomb Japanese conventionally and prepare for an invasion of the Japanese homelands. Every action taken by the Americans sought to end the war as quickly as possible and held no pretense about when that end would occur.[6]

Realizing the potential for the American people to view the Air Force's actions as cruel and indiscriminate, the Air Force made an effort to better sell their actions to the American people and the world when it insisted from the outbreak of hostilities that their efforts would not be expended on civilians alone. In Europe, when first asked to join the British in night area attacks, the Americans refused. Later, after D-Day and with the war drawing to a bloody conclusion, the British again pressed for American participation in the area bombing of German cities as part of Operations Thunderclap and Hurricane. Arnold "rebuked the British for their plan; 'I will not condone attacks on purely civilian objectives.'" But this time the American leadership proved powerless to resist participating. When Americans did join the British bombing efforts, commanders like Gen. Carl Spaatz emphasized the military nature of the targets they hit, despite the discrepancy.[7] The same held true in the Pacific. The initial attacks centered on the six cities with the largest industrial output. The follow-up target areas provided by the JTG also directed their destruction toward the concentrations of industrial targets in the immediate area. All of these areas came with copious amounts of evidence describing their importance to Japanese war output. Only when the campaign spread to all of Japan's cities did the ambiguity creep in, but mainly because the facts about Japanese industrial location and dispersal remained scarce. Striking the smaller cities obviated this information void by seeking to destroy any and all production capability or support in the areas. The leaders knew the massive consequences of their actions, both the bad and the good; the good outweighed the bad.

Historians of air operations in World War II like to lump British and U.S. incendiary tactics together, as if they came from a single strategy. The motives are drastically different, though, making the Americans' actions more palatable if not justifiable. The British resorted to incendiary attacks out of retaliation for their own suffering under German bombing and as a form of aerial justice more than anything. While the difficult logistics of daylight precision bombing contributed to the movement to night area attacks, the British sought retribution for the indiscriminate attacks on British cities by German bombers. This payment in kind drove their willingness to torch brick-and-mortar German cities. The Americans, in contrast, settled on area incendiary attacks on Japan because the wooden cities amplified the effects on their distributed economic structure. Even while burning down Japan the AF did its best to avoid participating in Europe in the kind of indiscriminate raids the British conducted.

The one aspect that does not emerge in the discussion of motives for the American actions is racism. The fury and shock of the war, especially in the Pacific, stirred up emotions among the American people based both on the actions and the ethnic background of the enemy. It is fair to say that the disdain for the Axis powers fed off a racial element, but the assertion that military decisions, especially strategic-bombing decisions, found a footing in this hatred is unfounded. The individual airman or rifleman may have acted in combat with a hatred for the enemy, but at the top of the command structure the personal feeling gave way to strategic concerns. Unfortunately, many historians and philosophers have not been able to separate the personal and professional aspects of the decision making in the war. Michael Sherry, in his leading work on airpower, sees past the rhetoric on the home front and in the media to characterize the actions of LeMay and others as "other nations were bad because they were enemies, not the other way around. Their job was to win a war." No great ulterior motive drove people's actions as they prosecuted the war. Still, the revisionist historians look for deeper psychological reasons for actions taken during the war and take facts out of context to make the decisions of the United States and its allies into crimes with aggravated character. At the personal level the desire for revenge and disregard for the lives of the enemy played a major role in keeping up the intensity of the fighting both on the battlefield and the home front. In *War without Mercy: Race and*

Power in the Pacific War, John Dower reminds the reader that "it is easy to forget the visceral emotions and sheer race hate that gripped virtually all participants in the war. . . . Race hate fed atrocities, and atrocities in turn fanned the fires of race hate." The ferocity of the war kept the furor alive but did not guide the decisions made at the highest levels. Japan's fate was sealed by its vulnerability to fire, not a personal dislike of the Japanese people by Arnold, LeMay, or anyone else. The stories of Japanese atrocities and the brutal nature of war in the Pacific desensitized the participants to the violence and allowed them to make sober decisions without undue hardship. After reading Arnold's war diaries, historian Ronald Schaffer concluded: "The atrocities in the Philippines . . . together with other evidence of Japanese brutality," made it clear that "the Japanese military forces had crossed a line between moral and immoral behavior [and] justified to Gen. Arnold the kind of warfare his air forces conducted." To Shaffer the decision did not come as a response to the enemy's actions, but was eased in its acceptance by the belief that the Japanese deserved no better. Crane echoes similar sentiments regarding the entire bombing force: "It was much easier to hate the enemy in the Pacific theater. Racism played a part as did the sneak attack on Pearl Harbor and reports of Japanese atrocities. . . . Airmen, however, again reflected the attitudes of society."[8] But despite these conclusions no concrete evidence supports the belief that the decisions made by the Air Force were based on racism or malfeasance.

Still, historians press on in the false belief that some greater malfeasance drove the Air Force to burn down the cities of Japan. Crane goes on to call terror a "formal objective" of the raids, while Grayling refers to the missions as a "concerted smashing . . . [of] its people and its cultural heritage," as "an attempt at annihilation" attributable to "racism towards and anger against the Japanese." But no compelling evidence is provided that backs up these claims. Even Sherry eventually surrenders to this belief in racism as a motive: "The ultimate fury of American aerial devastation came against Japan not because it was more fanatical, but because it was relatively weaker. . . . It was the relative ease of attacking Japan by air that tempted Americans into the fullest use of airpower. As an image, Japan's fanaticism was real enough in the minds of many Americans. But it served mainly

197

to justify a course of bombing rooted in strategic circumstances and the emotional need for vengeance." A dehumanization of the Japanese as a people made actions against them acceptable in this time of war. Again, though, these feelings bolstered the courage of the average fighting man but did not guide the broad strategic or tactical decisions of the war.[9]

Neither LeMay nor Arnold nor the president nor the Joint Chiefs of Staff gave any indication that they hated the Japanese and let their personal feelings guide their actions. This holds true for all of the major commanders in World War II. Even Patton, who famously railed against the Huns and wanted to murder them, respected them as a people and a nation: his job, however, required their utter defeat. After the war LeMay acknowledged that had they lost the war he and the other American leaders would have been tried as war criminals, hardly the admission of a man who did not acknowledge the value of human life or the humanity of the enemy. The actions taken by American commanders in World War II reflect a desire to end the war victoriously, not to annihilate an enemy people.

Ultimately, Japan burned because it could, and the Air Force needed it to. In a piece of controversial irony, the tactic so derided ultimately played a major role in winning the war. The efforts of the 20th AF and the brave B-29 crews tore Japan down so far that the war ended without invasion. Like the assertions made about Operation Linebacker II in Vietnam, such a simple statement leaves out many factors and generates much debate, but no one may deny that the enemy surrendered without American troops on the ground and with its cities smoldering ruins.

NOTES

Abbreviations

AFHRC   Air Force Historical Research Center, Maxwell Air Force Base, Alabama
COA   Committee of Operations Analysts
JTG   Joint Target Group
USSBS   United States Strategic Bombing Survey

Introduction

1. Kerr, *Flames over Tokyo*, 337–38.

2. The Air Force suffered through various name changes until it finally won its independence in 1947, most notably the Army Air Corps (AAC) before World War II and the Army Air Force (AAF) during World War II. Even AAF was further refined to United States Army Air Force (USAAF) in some contexts. For simplicity the generic term "Air Force" is used here except where specific to the context of the document.

3. Hansell, *Strategic Air War against Germany and Japan*, 79.

4. Doolittle to Spaatz, January 30, 1945, quoted in Schaffer, *Wings of Judgment*, 96–97.

1. The Origins of Destruction

1. Schaffer, *Wings of Judgment*, 21, 23.

2. Clodfelter, "Molding Airpower Convictions," 96–98.

3. Greer, *Development of Air Doctrine*, 48–49, 57; Finney, *History of the Air Corps Tactical School*, 64; Faber, "Interwar US Army Aviation," 211.

4. Finney, *History of the Air Corps Tactical School*, 66–68.

5. Greer, *Development of Air Doctrine*, 51, 111–12, 115.

6. Hansell quoted in Faber, "Interwar US Army Aviation," 219. Emphasis in the source.

7. Hansell, *Strategic Air War against Germany and Japan*, 13.

8. Hansell, *Strategic Air War against Germany and Japan*, 7, 10. Emphasis in the source.

9. Hansell, *Strategic Air War against Germany and Japan*, 13.

10. Faber, "Interwar US Army Aviation," 218.

11. Hansell, *Strategic Air War against Japan*, 3.

12. "Historical Analysis: Joint Doctrine Air Campaign Course" (lecture, April 30, 1996), http://www.au.af.mil/au/awc/awcgate/readings/awpd-1-jfacc/awpdproc .htm, 39, 48–49.

13. Schaffer, *Wings of Judgment*, 33; "Historical Analysis Joint Doctrine," 52.

14. The range issue from the Philippines to Japan did not stop some in the Air Force at the time, in the event a war started, from contemplating retaliatory attacks against Japan using planes from the Philippines. Like most prewar plans for the Pacific, this one became obsolete within the first few weeks of December 1941.

15. All aircraft performance numbers, unless otherwise noted, are derived from Gunston, *Illustrated Encyclopedia of Combat Aircraft*; and Gunston, *American Warplanes*. They represent ideal numbers but provide useful comparison.

16. Vander Meulen, *Building the B-29*, 86, 96.

17. Hansell, *Strategic Air War against Japan*, 39; Phillips, *Rain of Fire*, 19–20; 33rd Statistical Squadron, "XXI BC Graphic Summary of Operations, May 1, 1945," AFHRC, 762.3011, roll 9750.

2. The Makings of a Mission

1. Kantor and LeMay, *Mission with LeMay*, 238–39.

2. Werrell, *Archie, Flak, AAA, and SAM*, 53.

3. Werrell, *Archie, Flak, AAA, and SAM*, 53.

4. Werrell, *Archie, Flak, AAA, and SAM*, 53; War Department Military Intelligence Division, "Preliminary Report on the Japanese Air Defense System," October 18, 1944, AFHRC 170.227-4, roll 3449, 1, 74.

5. Crabtree, *On Air Defense*, 87–99.

6. "XXI BC Graphic Summary of Operations, May 1, 1945," AFHRC, 762.3011, roll 9750. Claims of enemy aircraft destroyed are often greatly exaggerated owing to the stresses of combat and double counting.

7. Operational Analysis Section XX BC, "Combat Performance of the Remote Control Turrets of B-29 Aircraft," February 10, 1945, AFHRC 761.01, roll 25762, 1.

8. USSBS, 63:10.

9. Sakaida and Takaki, *B-29 Hunters of the JAAF*, 26.

10. USSBS, 63:10.

11. USSBS, 63:34.

12. USSBS, 62:55.

13. Headquarters 7th Air Force, *Intelligence Summary No. 12, Vol. 2*, April 21, 1945, AFHRC 740.607, roll 9531.

14. Sakaida and Takaki, *B-29 Hunters of the JAAF*, 14–16.

15. Sakaida and Takaki, *B-29 Hunters of the JAAF*, 29, 88.

16. Sakaida and Takaki, *B-29 Hunters of the JAAF*, 119; USSBS, 63:29.

17. Giangreco, *Hell to Pay*, 88; USSBS, 62:25.

18. 1st Lt. Otto P. Pflanze Jr., "Appendix IV: The Weather Service in the Pacific Ocean Areas" (Baltimore: AAF Historical Office Overseas Organizational History Branch, 1946), AFHRC 702.01, roll 8917, 25.

19. Pflanze, "Appendix IV," 24.

20. CG BOMCOM 21 to DEPCOMAF 20, February 12, 1945, "High Level Wind Velocities Over Japan 1 Dec 1944 to 6 Feb 1945," AFHRC 762.7411, roll 9768.

21. Harahan and Kohn, USAF Warrior Studies, 54-55.

22. McFarland, America's Pursuit of Precision Bombing, 222; Sherman, "The Secret Weapon," 82. CEP is a measure of bombing accuracy that reflects the distance from the center of the target in which 50 percent of the bombs will hit. A CEP of 164 feet means that half of the bombs dropped would land within 164 feet of the target center. CEP is a convenient way to account for many bombs being dropped with some hitting the target and some missing by a wide margin. In World War II the measurement reflected the accuracy of the planes and bombsight much more than the "dumb bombs" of the time. Today it is used as a measurement for specific types of ordnance.

23. Harahan and Kohn, USAF Warrior Studies, 59-60.

24. Hansell, Strategic Air War against Japan, 32-33.

25. McFarland, America's Pursuit of Precision Bombing, 182.

26. HQ XXI Bomber Command Operations Analysis Section, "Gross Errors in Bombing" January 16, 1945, AFHRC 702.161, roll 8924.

3. Planning Japan's Demise

1. Doolittle, I Could Never Be So Lucky Again, 247; Sherry, Rise of American Air Power, 31, 102, 124.

2. Kerr, Flames over Tokyo, 41; USSBS, 53:78.

3. Kerr, Flames over Tokyo, 29, 31.

4. Kerr, Flames over Tokyo, 32.

5. USSBS, 53:78.

6. An appliance fire is one that requires a piece of mechanized firefighting equipment (an appliance) to extinguish.

7. USSBS, 10:8; USSBS, 15:49, 54.

8. Toland, The Rising Sun, 670; Jansen, The Making of Modern Japan, 644.

9. USSBS, 53:3; www.nycgo.com.

10. USSBS, 15:54, 57, 61.

11. A-2 Far East Target Section, "Japanese Incendiary Attack Data," October 1943, AFHRC 142.621, roll 2721, 10-11. The copy obtained from AFHRC (roll 2721) is incomplete and confusing. While most of the pages are there, some are missing from the digital copy (including the cover). Closer examination shows this to be the October 1943 report. Also, the page numbers restart in each section, accounting for the sudden jumping and restarting of the numbering. Any historian wishing to read this document should obtain a microfilm version of it from the AFHRC, not the digitized version.

12. Far East Target Section, "Japanese Incendiary Attack Data," 6.

13. Kerr, *Flames over Tokyo*, 49, 51, 54; USSBS, 90:146, 175, 192.

14. Craven and Cate, *Army Air Forces*, 2:354.

15. COA to Gen. H. H. Arnold, November 11, 1943, "Report of Committee of Operations Analysts on Economic Objectives in the Far East," AFHRC 118.04-9A, roll 2389, 4. Hereafter cited as COA report on Japan, 1943.

16. USSBS, 54:13.

17. COA report on Japan, 1943, 1.

18. COA report on Japan, 1943, 1–2.

19. COA report on Japan, 1943, 2.

20. COA report on Japan, 1943, 3.

21. COA report on Japan, 1943, 3.

22. COA report on Japan, 1943, 4.

23. COA report on Japan, 1943, 6; USSBS, 37:21.

24. COA report on Japan, 1943, 7, 26.

25. COA report on Japan, 1943, 26.

26. COA report on Japan, 1943, 8, 32.

27. Kerr, *Flames over Tokyo*, 46; Sherry, *Rise of American Air Power*, 171.

28. Col. Guido Perera to Assistant Chief of Air Staff, Plans, February 6, 1944, "Economic Effects Which Might be Achieved by VLR Operations from Chengtu and Saipan in 1944–45," AFHRC 118.04-2, roll 2388.

29. Committee of Operations Analysts, "Vulnerability of Japanese Economic Objectives to Strategic Air Bombardment," February 6, 1944, AFHRC roll 28223.

30. Col. Guido Perera to Brig. Gen Haywood Hansell, May 9, 1944, "Targets for Divider," AFHRC 118.04-2, roll 2388.

31. Hansell, *Strategic Air War against Japan*, 48.

32. AC/AS, Intelligence, Analysis Division, "Estimation of Force Required to Neutralize a Selected List of Japanese Targets," May 15, 1944, AFHRC 118.04D-2, roll 2390.

33. Col. Guido Perera to Col. Richard Lindsay, June 8, 1944, "Attack on Japanese Strategic Targets," AFHRC 118.04-2, roll 2388, 1.

34. Perera to Lindsay, "Attack on Japanese Strategic Targets," 2.

35. Perera to Lindsay, "Attack on Japanese Strategic Targets," 6.

36. Office of Strategic Services Research and Analysis Branch, "Japanese Small-Scale Factories in Relation to Air Bombardment," June 30, 1944, AFHRC 118.04-2, roll 2388.

37. "Japanese Small-Scale Factories in Relation to Air Bombardment."

38. USSBS, 59:7.

39. LeMay and Yenne, *Superfortress*, 86.

40. Fowler Hamilton to Col. Guido Perera, August 29, 1944, AFHRC 118.04-2, roll 2388.

41. Col. Guido Perera to Col. Richard Lindsay, August 29, 1944, "Status of Studies on Incendiary Attack on Japanese Urban Industrial Areas," AFHRC 118.04-2, roll 2388.

42. COA, "Economic Effects of Successful Area Attacks on Six Japanese Cities," September 4, 1944, AFHRC 702.01, roll 8917.

43. Minutes of COA meeting, September 10, 1944, AFHRC 118.042-2, roll 2393.

44. Minutes of COA meeting, September 10, 1944.

45. Minutes of COA meeting, September 10, 1944.

46. Minutes of COA meeting, September 10, 1944.

47. Minutes of COA meeting, September 13, 1944, AFHRC 118.042-2, roll 2393.

48. Minutes of COA meeting, September 13, 1944.

49. Minutes of COA meeting, September 13, 1944.

50. Minutes of COA meeting, September 13, 1944.

51. Minutes of COA meeting, September 14, 1944, AFHRC 118.042-2, roll 2393, 20, 35–36.

52. USSBS, 50:22, 30–31. Emphasis added.

53. USSBS, 40:5–6.

54. Minutes of COA meeting, September 27, 1944, AFHRC 118.042-2, roll 2393, 39–41.

55. Minutes of COA meeting, September 27, 1944, 41; USSBS, 42:70–71.

56. Minutes of COA meeting, September 27, 1944, 73.

57. Minutes of COA meeting, September 27, 1944, 70.

58. Minutes of COA meeting, September 27, 1944, 71.

59. Minutes of COA meeting, September 28, 1944, AFHRC 118.042-2, roll 2393, 12.

60. Minutes of COA meeting, September 28, 1944, 13, 22.

61. Sherry, *Rise of American Air Power*, 230, 234.

62. COA, "Revised Report of the Committee of Operations Analysts on Economic Targets in the Far East," October 10, 1944, AFHRC 118.04-9A, roll 2389. Kamikazes were not yet a threat. They would not appear until the end of the month at the Battle of Leyte Gulf.

63. COA to Gen. H. H. Arnold, October 10, 1944, "Revised Report of the Committee of Operations Analysts on Economic Targets in the Far East," AFHRC 118.04-9A, roll 2389, 1.

64. COA to Arnold, October 10, 1944, "Revised Report," 2–3.

65. COA to Arnold, October 10, 1944, "Revised Report," 5.

66. COA to Arnold, October 10, 1944, "Revised Report," 50.

67. Sherry, *Rise of American Air Power*, 221.

68. JTG, "Part I—Principles for Selection of Air Targets," April 16, 1945, AFHRC 142.660, roll 2727, 2. While dated April 1945, this document, like many of the JTG's documents, likely received constant update, and the copy retrieved from the archives is from later in the war. The principle remain the same, even if some of the specific analysis later in the document would have received revision as operations progressed.

69. JTG, "JTG Estimate No. 1: Strategic Air Employment Suitable to the Current Strategy of the Japanese Air War," December 23, 1944, AFHRC 142.660, roll 2727.

70. JTG, "JTG Estimate No. 1," 5.

71. JTG, "Japanese Aircraft Industry General Analysis," January 6, 1945, AFHRC 142.6606, roll 2733.

72. JTG, "Japanese Aircraft Industry General Analysis," 1, 5.

73. JTG, "Japanese Urban Areas General Analysis," February 26, 1945, AFHRC 142.6606, roll 2735, 3, 19.

74. JTG, "Japanese Urban Areas General Analysis," 6.

75. JTG, "Japanese Urban Areas General Analysis," 6–7.

76. JTG, "Japanese Urban Areas General Analysis," 11–12.

77. JTG, "Japanese Urban Areas General Analysis," 14.

78. JTG, "Japanese Urban Areas General Analysis," 14.

79. JTG, "Japanese Urban Areas General Analysis," 15.

80. JTG, "Japanese Urban Areas General Analysis," 25–26.

4. Hansell's 21st Bomber Command

1. The base on Guam still exists and still supports U.S. Air Force long-range bombing operations. Today it is known as Anderson Air Force Base.

2. Craven and Cate, *Army Air Forces*, 5:111, 113.

3. Memo from Brig. Gen. Lauris Norstad to Brig. Gen Haywood Hansell, November 11, 1944, quoted in Craven and Cate, *Army Air Forces*, 5:554; Hansell, *Strategic Air War against Germany and Japan*, 177–78.

4. Norstad quoted in Sherry, *Rise of American Air Power*, 222.

5. Gen. H. H. Arnold to Henry Stimson, January 13, 1945, AFHRC 145.81, roll 2794.

6. Norstad and Hansell quoted in Kerr, *Flames over Tokyo*, 117–18. Times are local, so the results on the Hankow raid on December 18 (China time) came to Washington late on December 17 or early on December 18, allowing Norstad to act on them on December 18 (Washington time). Hansell, *The Strategic Air War against Germany and Japan*, 217.

7. Hansell, *Strategic Air War against Japan*, 28.

8. Lt. Gen. Millard Harmon for Brig. Gen Haywood Hansell to Gen. H. H. Arnold, November 25, 1944, "San Antonio Two," AFHRC 760.1621, roll 9683.

9. COMAF 20 to COMGENBOMCOM 21, January 3, 1945, "Failures of Airborne A/C to Bomb Primary Targets," AFHRC 762.01, roll 9738.

10. Wolk, *Cataclysm*, 127. The period of Arnold's recovery is a bit of a mystery. Sources disagree about the amount and frequency of his contact with his subordinates who took his place in Washington, notably Norstad with the 20th AF and Eaker and Giles running the Air Force as a whole. The one point that is not disputed is how ingrained his philosophy was with his subordinates. Arnold picked individuals who knew his intentions and dedicated themselves to carrying them out. In a credit to his command structure, his absence from Washington was hardly an issue.

11. COMAF 20 to COMGENBOMCOM 21, January 16, 1945, "Priority of Attack by XXI Bomber Command," AFHRC 760.1621, roll 9683.

12. Memo from Brig. Gen Haywood Hansell to Gen. H. H. Arnold, January 14, 1945, quoted in Craven and Cate, *Army Air Forces*, 5:567.

13. Craven and Cate, *Army Air Forces*, 5:568; Hansell, *Strategic Air War against Germany and Japan*, 211–12.

14. Hansell, *Strategic Air War against Japan*, 49; USSBS, 15:126.

15. Searle, "'It Made a Lot of Sense,'" 126.

16. Kerr, *Flames over Tokyo*, 137–38. Kerr quotes the report and draws the conclusion, based on the language of the unsigned document, that it was written by a flight surgeon.

17. COMGENBOMCOM 21 to COMGEN AF 20, January 20, 1945, "Info on Incendiary Damage," AFHRC 702.162–59, roll 8938; COMAF 20 to COMGENBOMCOM 21, January 23, 1945, "Importance of Japanese Target," AFHRC 760.1621, roll 9683.

18. Maj. Gen. Curtis LeMay to Gen. H. H. Arnold, February 4, 1945, "Analysis of Radar Bombing and Navigation," AFHRC 762.01, roll 9738.

19. Craven and Cate, *Army Air Forces*, 5:539, 545, using data from 33rd SCU, "A Statistical Summary of Its Operations against Japan."

20. BOMCOM 21 to DEPCOMAF 20 (PAO), February 8, 1945, "Planning VLR Ammunition Requirements REURTEL-ECON 5070," AFHRC 702.162-59, roll 8938.

21. Kerr, *Flames over Tokyo*, 134; Sherry, *Rise of American Air Power*, 266.

22. Craven and Cate, *Army Air Forces*, 5:539–40; McNamara in *Fog of War*, DVD.

23. Craven and Cate, *Army Air Forces*, 5:572; Kantor and LeMay, *Mission with LeMay*, 343.

24. COMAF 20 to BOMCOM 20, BOMCOM 21, and DEPCOMAF 20 POA, February 19, 1945, "Target Directive," AFHRC 702.161, roll 8924.

25. Craven and Cate, *Army Air Forces*, 5:573; Harahan and Kohn, USAF *Warrior Studies*, 60–61.

5. Losses Per Unit of Target Destruction

1. Kantor and LeMay, *Mission with LeMay*, 345; "XXI BC Graphic Summary of Operations, May 1, 1945," AFHRC, 762.3011, roll 9750. The book from May was used because it included data from after the March strikes for comparison. There is no reason to believe that the data for previous months changed in this cumulative report.

2. 33rd Statistical Control Unit, "XXIST BC Command Book," February 1945, AFHRC 762.01, roll 9738; Kantor and LeMay, *Mission with LeMay*, 351 (emphasis in the source).

3. McFarland, *America's Pursuit of Precision Bombing*, 174.

4. 33rd Statistical Control Unit, "Statistical Summary of Aircraft and Crew Losses," February 18, 1945, AFHRC 762.01, roll 9738; Kantor and LeMay, *Mission with LeMay*, 308.

5. Locations immune to bombardment would be in caves, which the Japanese often used as dispersal sites. BOMCOM 21 to COMAF 20, February 11, 1945, "Apparent Effort of Japanese to Disperse Aircraft Industry," AFHRC 760.1621, roll 9683;

COMAF 20 to COMGENBOMCON 21, February 11, 1945, "Apparent Effort of Japanese to Disperse Aircraft Industry," AFHRC 760.1621, roll 9683.

6. Harahan and Kohn, USAF Warrior Studies, 60–62; Sherry, Rise of American Air Power, 284–85.

7. Kantor and LeMay, Mission with LeMay, 347.

8. Kantor and LeMay, Mission with LeMay, 347–48, 355.

9. Each major city and target received a code name that incremented every time the planes went to that target. The code name for the Tokyo area was Meetinghouse. Meetinghouse 1 was the moderately successful area attack of February 24; the May 9–10 mission was Meetinghouse 2.

10. Frank, Downfall, 16–18. Casualty figures for the Tokyo mission vary depending on source and factors such as accounting for bodies that were washed out to sea, assumptions about persons who had fled the city before or after the attack, and the large problem of identifying the bodies. Estimates range from Frank's quote of at least 79,466 "by actual—and minimum—count" to 85,793 in both the USSBS report and Craven and Cate, all the way over 100,000 per more informal assumption. Today, according to Frank, an estimate of at least 100,000 is accepted, though he puts it in perspective when he points out that it took at least twenty days to clear all of the remains. Frank, Downfall, 16–18; USSBS, 90:67; Craven and Cate, Army Air Forces, 5:617.

11. "Daily Intelligence Summary," March 12, 1945, AFHRC 142.0321-4, roll 2648. This summary appeared two days after the mission and reflects the understanding of the intelligence community in the Marianas at that time.

12. Kerr, Flames over Tokyo, 173; Craven and Cate, Army Air Forces, 5:616–17.

13. Kantor and LeMay, Mission with LeMay, 353.

14. Maj. E. B. Gates, "Daily Intelligence Summary," March 12 and 13, 1945, AFHRC 142.0321-4, roll 2648.

15. Maj. Gen. Curtis LeMay to 73rd, 313rd, and 314th BWS, March 14, 1945, "Tentative Plan for Immediate Future Operations," AFHRC 702.01, roll 8917.

16. "Daily Intelligence Report," March 23, 1945, AFHRC 142.0321-4, roll 2648; Maj. Gen. Curtis LeMay to All Staff Sections, March 19, 1945, "Messages of Congratulations," AFHRC 762.01, roll 9738.

17. "Air Intelligence Report Vol. 1, No. 3," March 22, 1945, AFHRC 762.549, roll 9766, 3–4.

18. Headquarters XXI Bomber Command, "Phase Analysis Incendiary Operations," no date, AFHRC 762.549, roll 9766, 4.

19. LORAN, a system of radio transmitters allowing users to triangulate their position, survived into the twenty-first century assisting mariners. It was rendered obsolete by GPS.

20. "Phase Analysis Incendiary Operations," 15, 18.

21. "Phase Analysis Incendiary Operations," 39–41.

22. "Phase Analysis Incendiary Operations," 25–28.

23. "Phase Analysis Incendiary Operations," 30–32.

24. "Phase Analysis Incendiary Operations," 42–44.

25. Statistical Control Office, Twentieth Air Force, to Brig. Gen. Lauris Norstad, April 4, 1945, "Statistical Summary of March Operations of the Twentieth Air Force," AFHRC 145.81, roll 2794.

26. Norstad to LeMay, April 20, 1945, and Norstad, memo, April 10, 1945, "Recommended Intensification of Attack on Japan Immediately Following V-E Day," quoted in Wolk, *Cataclysm*, 131–32.

27. COMAF 20 to COMGENBOMCOM 21, March 19, 1945, "Bombing Emperor's Palace," AFHRC 702.161, roll 8924.

28. Sherry, *Rise of American Air Power*, 289. Norstad was speaking to reporters at the time.

29. COMAF 20 to COMGENBOMCOM 21, March 28, 1945, "Target Selection," ARHRC 702.161, roll 8924; Craven and Cate, *Army Air Forces*, 5:624–25.

6. Down the Path of Destruction

1. USSBS, 95:2–3.

2. USSBS, 94:2, 41.

3. USSBS, 94:227.

4. USSBS, 96:8; USSBS, 91: 62, 71.

5. Maj. H. P. Hesler, HQ 21 BC Office of Ordnance Officer, to Deputy Chief of Staff for Supply and Maintenance, January 17, 1945, "Summary of Ordnance Section Activities," AFHRC 702.01, roll 8917. For example, on Saipan as of January 1, 1945, the bomb dumps contained 2,181 2,000-pound and 3,382 1,000-pound bombs, and also held 43,945 500-pound bombs. The planned receipts over the next months paralleled these numbers.

6. USSBS, 95:3, 192.

7. USSBS, 15:2–3.

8. USSBS, 37:5; USSBS, 46:1, 6.

9. USSBS, 55:36; USSBS, 16:75; USSBS, 22:21; USSBS, 21:42; USSBS, 19:5, 23.

10. USSBS, 43:12.

11. USSBS, 66:17; USSBS, 54:42–43.

12. USSBS, 16:136, 141; USSBS, 17:116.

13. 21st BC A-2 Section (Intelligence), "Recommended Bombing Altitudes and Flak Evasion," April 1945, AFHRC 702.161, roll 8924.

14. The 21st BC accomplished destruction of the Nakajima New Ota Plant in one mission on February 10. Bombing from 27,000 feet they placed 10 percent of their bombs in the compact target area. Most of the buildings received damage and seventy-four Frank fighters received damage or destruction. JTG, "Japanese Aircraft Industry General Analysis," April 6, 1945, AFHRC 142.6606, roll 2733, 1.

15. JTG, "Japanese Aircraft Industry General Analysis," 2.

16. JTG, "Japanese Urban Areas General Analysis: Annex II Urban Area Attacks against Selected Industrial Concentrations," April 28, 1945, AFHRC 142.6606, roll 2735, 1.

17. JTG, "Japanese Urban Areas General Analysis," 1.

18. JTG, "Japanese Urban Areas General Analysis," 2.

19. Norstad quoted in Schaffer, *Wings of Judgment*, 138.

20. Craven and Cate, *Army Air Forces*, 5:636; "Daily Intelligence Summary," April 18, 1945, and April 16, 1945, AFHRC 142.0321-4, roll 2648.

21. Craven and Cate, *Army Air Forces*, 5:636; Sherry, *Rise of American Air Power*, 300; Kantor and LeMay, *Mission with LeMay*, 373 (emphasis in the source).

22. Hesler, "Summary of Ordnance Section Activities."

23. Kantor and LeMay, *Mission with LeMay*, 369.

24. Diary of the Chief of Staff of the 33rd Statistical Control Unit, March 17, 1945, AFHRC 762.01, roll 9738.

25. Captain James H. Hubbell, "Appendix VI Logistical Support: Ammunition Supply for the XXI Bomber Command," AAF Historical Office Overseas Organizational History Branch USASTAF Section, January 1946, AFHRC 702.01, roll 8917, 11.

26. Hubbell, "Appendix VI Logistical Support," 17.

27. Sherry, *Rise of American Air Power*, 283.

28. Hubbell, "Appendix VI Logistical Support," 22.

29. Hubbell, "Appendix VI Logistical Support," 18.

30. Col. H. A. R. Robertson, Director of Operations, to Lt. Gen. Giles, June 5, 1945, "Incendiary Bomb Stock on Hand for XXI Bomber Command," AFHRC 702.01, roll 8917.

31. Maj. Gen. Junius W. Jones to Deputy Commander, 20th AF, Pacific Ocean Areas, July 5, 1945, "Preliminary Report on Stock Levels of Bombs for XXI Bomber Command," AFHRC 702.01, roll 8917.

32. Maj. Gen. Curtis LeMay to Maj. Gen. Lawrence Kuter, July 10, 1945, "TAI Preliminary Report on Stock Levels of Bombs for XXI Bomber Command," AFHRC 702.01, roll 8917.

7. Death Throes

1. DEPCOMAF 20 POA to COMGENBOMCOM 21, May 11, 1945, "Statement of Policy," AFHRC 760.1621, roll 9683.

2. Memo for Assistant Chief of Air Staff, Intelligence, "Japanese Situation—Week Ending 5 April 1945," attached to daily intelligence summary for April 5, 1945, AFHRC 142.0321-4, roll 2648; COMGENBOMCOM 21 to COMAF 20, April 15, 1945, "Enemy Fighter Reaction Mission No. [illegible]," AFHRC 702.162-64, roll 8939.

3. Col. J. D. Garcia, HQ XXI BC A-2, to D C/s, Operations, June 6, 1945, "Additional Urban Industrial Area Targets," AFHRC 702.01, roll 8917; JTG, "Japanese Urban Areas General Analysis: Annex II Urban Area Attacks against Selected Industrial Concentrations," April 28, 1945, AFHRC 142.6606, roll 2735.

4. Col. Baskin R. Lawrence Jr., Acting Chief, Evaluation Section of the JTG, to JTG, January 20, 1945, "Reduction of Bomb Wastage through Reducing the Size of the Attacking Formation," AFHRC 142.660, roll 2727.

5. COMAF 20 to COMGENBOMCOM 21, June 9, 1945, "Target Directive," AFHRC 760.1621, roll 9683.

6. COMGENBOMCOM XXI to AAFPOA (ADMIN), ATTN: CHEMICAL OFFICER, April 18, 1945, AFHRC 702.162A, roll 8968.

7. Kerr, *Flames over Tokyo*, 262.

8. JTG, "Japanese Urban Areas General Analysis: I. Current Developments," ca. June 15, 1945 (not marked), AFHRC 142.660, roll 2727, 1, 7–8.

9. JTG, "Japanese Urban Area General Analysis," 1, 3.

10. Commanding General XXI BC to Maj. Gen. Lawrence Kuter, June 22, 1945, no title available, AFHRC 142.660, roll 2727.

11. Commanding General XXI BC to Kuter, June 22, 1945.

12. Commanding General XXI BC to Kuter, June 22, 1945; JTG, "Annex I Weapon Recommendations," June 8, 1945, AFHRC 142.6606, roll 2735, 1, 4.

13. USSBS, Office of the Chairman, *European Summary Report*, 33, 30, 12.

14. Schaffer, *Wings of Judgment*, 183–84.

15. USSBS, 54:1.

16. USSBS, 11:12; USSBS, 54:85; USSBS, 55:20; USSBS, 45:4; USSBS, 11:170–71.

17. USSBS, 54:9–10; USSBS, 21:25; Giangreco, *Hell to Pay*, 69, 164.

18. Hansell, always the proponent of precision targets, points out that despite its lack of popularity among other planning groups, the Strategic Air Intelligence Section pushed oil targets. Hansell, *Strategic Air War against Germany and Japan*, 238.

19. USSBS, 51:121.

20. USSBS, 51:65–66; USSBS, 52:68; USSBS, 64:109; USSBS, 51:7.

21. USSBS, report 55; USSBS, 56:26–27.

22. USSBS, 15:28–30; USSBS, 55:29; USSBS, 16:201–2; USSBS, 17:69–70, 155, 171.

23. USSBS, 15:30–31; USSBS, 55:30; USSBS, 56:27.

24. USSBS, 16:111–12; USSBS, 20:29.

25. USSBS, 40:28.

26. USSBS, 16:111–12, 161.

27. USSBS, 17:14; USSBS, 21:5.

28. USSBS, 49:49–51, 64.

29. USSBS, 16:311 and 324.

30. USSBS, 44:3; USSBS, 46:2.

31. USSBS, 11:4, 164.

32. Frank, *Downfall*, 350–51. Frank notes that the American caloric intake at the time amounted to 3,400 calories a day.

33. USSBS, 18:57; USSBS, 42:92.

34. USSBS, 15:26; USSBS, 24:9.

35. USSBS, 42:87–88; USSBS, 15:26.

36. COMGENBOMCOM 21 to CG 58 BW CG 73 BW CG 313 BW CG 314 BW, June 16, 1945, "Warning Order," AFHRC 702.162-73, roll 8941.

37. Craven and Cate, *Army Air Forces*, 5:656.

38. Schaffer, *Wings of Judgment*, 140.

39. Harahan and Kohn, USAF *Warrior Studies*, 65–66.

8. Interpreting the Campaign

1. Crane, *Bombs, Cities, and Civilians*, 7, 35, 124, 161.

2. Wolk, *Cataclysm*, 109.

3. Werrell, *Blankets of Fire*, 157.

4. Grayling, *Among the Dead Cities*, 233, 258; and Crane, *Bombs, Cities, and Civilians*, 133.

5. Frank, *Downfall*, 163. After the initial loss of some 100,000 people in the March 9–10 Tokyo mission, the human losses dropped off significantly in subsequent raids. As the word spread of the destruction the Japanese people started evacuating vulnerable areas or at least were better prepared to effect an escape when the flames reached their city.

6. Grayling, *Among the Dead Cities*, 78–79; Searle, "'It Made a Lot of Sense,'" 114–15.

7. Crane, *Bombs, Cities, and Civilians*, 109, 112.

8. Sherry, *Rise of American Air Power*, 180; Dower, *War without Mercy*, 11; Schaffer, *Wings of Judgment*, 154; Crane, *Bombs, Cities, and Civilians*, 59.

9. Crane, *Bombs, Cities, and Civilians*, 134; Grayling, *Among the Dead Cities*, 168–69; Sherry, *Rise of American Air Power*, 246.

BIBLIOGRAPHY

United States Strategic Bombing Survey Reports

CIVILIAN DEFENSE DIVISION

4 *Field Report Covering Air-Raid Protection and Allied Subjects, Tokyo, Japan.* Washington DC: GPO, 1947.
5 *Field Report Covering Air-Raid Protection and Allied Subjects in Nagasaki, Japan.* Washington DC: GPO, 1947.
6 *Field Report Covering Air-Raid Protection and Allied Subjects in Kyoto, Japan.* Washington DC: GPO, 1947.
7 *Field Report Covering Air-Raid Protection and Allied Subjects in Kobe, Japan.* Washington DC: GPO, 1947.
8 *Field Report Covering Air-Raid Protection and Allied Subjects in Osaka, Japan.* Washington DC: GPO, 1947.
9 *Civilian Defense Report No. I: Hiroshima, Japan Field Report.* Washington DC: GPO, 1945.
10 *Summary Report Covering Air-Raid Protection and Allied Subjects in Japan.* Washington DC: GPO, 1946.
11 *Final Report Covering Air-Raid Protection and Allied Subjects in Japan.* Washington DC: GPO, 1947.

MORALE DIVISION

14 *The Effects of Strategic Bombing on Japanese Morale.* Washington DC: GPO, 1947.

AIRCRAFT DIVISION

15 *The Japanese Aircraft Industry.* Washington DC: GPO, 1947.
16 *Mitsubishi Heavy Industries, Ltd (Mitsubishi Jukogyo KK) Corporation Report No. I (Airframes and Engine).* Washington DC: GPO, 1947.
17 *Nakajima Aircraft Co., Ltd. (Nakajima Hikoki KK) Corporation Report No. II (Airframes and Engine).* Washington DC: GPO, 1947.
18 *Kawanishi Aircraft Co. (Kawanishi Kokuko Kabushiki Kaisha) Corporation Report No. III (Airframes).* Washington DC: GPO, 1947.

19 *Kawasaki Aircraft Industries Co., Inc. (Kawasaki Kokuki Kogyo Kabushiki Kaisha)*. Washington DC: GPO, 1947.

20 *Aichi Aircraft Co. (Aichi Kokuki KK) Corporation Report No. V (Airframes and Engines)*. Washington DC: GPO, 1947.

21 *Sumitomo Metal Industries, Propeller Division (Sumitomo Kinzoku Kogyo KK, Puropera Seizosho) Corporation Report No. VI (Propellers)*. Washington DC: GPO, 1946.

22 *Hitachi Aircraft Co. (Hitachi Kokuki KK) Corporation Report No. VII (Airframes and Engines)*. Washington DC: GPO, 1947.

23 *Japan International Air Industries, Ltd. (Nippon Kokusai Koku Kogyo KK) Corporation Report No. VIII (Airframes)*. Washington DC: GPO, 1945 (sic).

24 *Japan Musical Instrument Manufacturing Go. (Nippon Gakki Seizo KK) Corporation Report No. IX (Propellers)*. Washington DC: GPO, 1946.

25 *Tachikawa Aircraft Co. (Tachikawa Hikoki KK) Corporation Report No. X (Airframes)*. Washington DC: GPO, 1947.

26 *Fuji Airplane Co. (Fuji Hikoki KK) Corporation Report No. XI (Airframes)*. Washington DC: GPO, 1946.

27 *Showa Airplane Co. (Showa Hikoki Kogyo KK) Corporation Report No. XII (Airframes)*. Washington DC: GPO, 1946.

28 *Ishikawajima Aircraft Industries Co., Ltd. (Ishikawajima Koku Kogyo Kabushiki Kaisha) Corporation Report No. XIII (Engines)*. Washington DC: GPO, 1946.

29 *Nippon Airplane Co. (Nippon Hikoki KK) Corporation Report No. XIV (Airframes)*. Washington DC: GPO, 1946.

30 *Kyushu Airplane Co. (Kyushu Hikoki KK) Corporation Report No. XV (Airframes)*. Washington DC: GPO, 1947.

31 *Shoda Engineering Co. (Shoda Seisakujo) Corporation Report No. XVI (Components)*. Washington DC: GPO, 1946.

32 *Mitaka Aircraft Industries (Mitaka Koku Kogyo Kabushiki Kaisha) Corporation Report No. XVII (Components)*. Washington DC: GPO, 1947.

33 *Nissan Automobile Co. (Nissan Jidosha KK) Corporation Report No. XVIII (Engines)*. Washington DC: GPO, 1946.

34 *Army Air Arsenal and Navy Air Depots Corporation Report No. XIX (Airframes and Engines)*. Washington DC: GPO, 1947.

35 *Underground Production of Japanese Aircraft (Report No. XX)*. Washington DC: GPO, 1947.

BASIC MATERIALS DIVISION

36 *Coals and Metals in Japan's War Economy*. Washington DC: GPO, 1947.

CAPITAL GOODS, EQUIPMENT, AND CONSTRUCTION DIVISION

37 *The Japanese Construction Industry*. Washington DC: GPO, 1946.

38 *Japanese Electrical Equipment*. Washington DC: GPO, n.d.

39 *The Japanese Machine Building Industry*. Washington DC: GPO, 1946.

BIBLIOGRAPHY

ELECTRIC POWER DIVISION

40 *The Electric Power Industry of Japan.* Washington DC: GPO, 1946.
41 *The Electric Power Industry of Japan (Plant reports).* Washington DC: GPO, 1947.

MANPOWER, FOOD, AND CIVILIAN SUPPLIES DIVISION

42 *The Japanese Wartime Standard of Living and Utilization of Manpower.* Washington DC: GPO, 1947.

MILITARY SUPPLIES DIVISION

43 *Japanese War Production Industries.* Washington DC: GPO, 1946.
44 *Japanese Naval Ordnance.* Washington DC: GPO, 1946.
45 *Japanese Army Ordnance.* Washington DC: GPO, 1946.
46 *Japanese Naval Shipbuilding.* Washington DC: GPO, 1946.
47 *Japanese Motor Vehicle Industry.* Washington DC: GPO, 1946.
48 *Japanese Merchant Shipbuilding.* Washington DC: GPO, 1947.

OIL AND CHEMICAL DIVISION

49 *Chemicals in Japan's War.* Washington DC: GPO, 1946.
50 *Chemicals in Japan's War, appendix to the report of the Oil and Chemical Division.* Washington DC: GPO, 1946.
51 *Oil in Japan's War.* Washington DC: GPO, 1946.
52 *Oil in Japan's War, appendix to the report of the Oil and Chemical Division.* Washington DC: GPO, 1946.

OVERALL ECONOMIC EFFECTS DIVISION

53 *The Effects of Strategic Bombing on Japan's War Economy, appendixes A, B, and C.* Washington DC: GPO, 1946.

TRANSPORTATION DIVISION

54 *The War against Japanese Transportation, 1941–45.* Washington DC: GPO, 1947.

URBAN AREAS DIVISION

55 *Effects of Air Attack on Japanese Urban Economy, Summary Report.* Washington DC: GPO, 1947.
56 *Effects of Air Attack on Urban Complex Tokyo-Kawasaki-Yokohama.* Washington DC: GPO, 1947.
57 *Effects of Air Attack on the City of Nagoya.* Washington DC: GPO, 1947.
58 *Effects of Air Attack on Osaka-Kobe-Kyoto.* Washington DC: GPO, 1947.
59 *Effects of Air Attack on the City of Nagasaki.* Washington DC: GPO, 1947.

MILITARY ANALYSIS DIVISION

62 *Japanese Air Power.* Washington DC: GPO, 1946.
63 *Japanese Air Weapons and Tactics.* Washington DC: GPO, 1947.

64 *The Effect of Air Action on Japanese Ground Army Logistics.* Washington DC: GPO, 1947.

65 *Employment of Forces under the Southwest Pacific Command.* Washington DC: GPO, 1947.

66 *The Strategic Air Operation of Very Heavy Bombardment in the War against Japan (20th Air Force).* Washington DC: GPO, 1946.

71a *Air Campaigns of the Pacific War.* Washington DC: GPO, 1947.

NAVAL ANALYSIS DIVISION

72 *Interrogations of Japanese Officials, vols. I and II.* Washington DC: GPO, n.d.

PHYSICAL DAMAGE DIVISION

90 *Effects of Incendiary Bomb Attacks on Japan (a Report on Eight Cities).* Washington DC: GPO, 1947.

91 *The Effects of the Ten-Thousand-Pound Bomb on Japanese Targets (a Report on Nine Incidents).* Washington DC: GPO, 1947.

94 *The Effects of the Four-Thousand-Pound Bomb on Japanese Targets (a Report on Five Incidents).* Washington DC: GPO, 1947.

95 *Effects of Two-Thousand-, One-Thousand-, and Five-Hundred-Pound Bombs on Japanese Targets (a Report on Eight Incidents).* Washington DC: GPO, 1947.

96 *A Report on Physical Damage in Japan (Summary Report).* Washington DC: GPO, 1947.

G-2 (INTELLIGENCE) DIVISION

97 *Japanese Military and Naval Intelligence Division, Japanese Intelligence Section, G-2.* Washington DC: GPO, 1946.

98 *Evaluation of Photographic Intelligence in the Japanese Homeland. Part I: Comprehensive Report.* Washington DC: GPO, 1946.

99 *Evaluation of Photographic Intelligence in the Japanese Homeland. Part II: Airfields.* Washington DC: GPO, 1946.

100 *Evaluation of Photographic Intelligence in the Japanese Homeland. Part III: Computed Bomb Plotting.* Washington DC: GPO, 1946.

101 *Evaluation of Photographic Intelligence in the Japanese Homeland. Part IV: Urban Area Analysis.* Washington DC: GPO, 1946.

102 *Evaluation of Photographic Intelligence in the Japanese Homeland. Part V: Camouflage, Concealment, and Deception.* Washington DC: GPO, 1946.

103 *Evaluation of Photographic Intelligence in the Japanese Homeland. Part VI: Shipping.* Washington DC: GPO, 1946.

104 *Evaluation of Photographic Intelligence in the Japanese Homeland. Part VII: Electronics.* Washington DC: GPO, 1946.

105 *Evaluation of Photographic Intelligence in the Japanese Homeland. Part VIII: Beach Intelligence.* Washington DC: GPO, 1946.

106 *Evaluation of Photographic Intelligence in the Japanese Homeland. Part IX: Coast and Anti-aircraft Artillery.* Washington DC: GPO, 1946.